The Authors:

An award winning travel writer, Pam Hobbs has contributed to leading magazines and newspapers in both Canada and America for more than twenty years. Her *Adventure Guide to Canada* (Hunter Publishing/MPC, 1991) is a collection of her travel articles on Canada previously published in Canada's national newspaper *The Globe and Mail*, and illustrated by her husband Michael Algar. She is a member of the Society of American Travel Writers' Canadian chapter.

Michael Algar, an accountant whose career has included senior positions in business and government, has for many years spent much of his spare time travelling and writing. His articles and photographs on shipping, sport aviation and travel have appeared in many major Canadian magazines and newspapers.

The authors live in Mississauga, Ontario, from where they travel extensively.

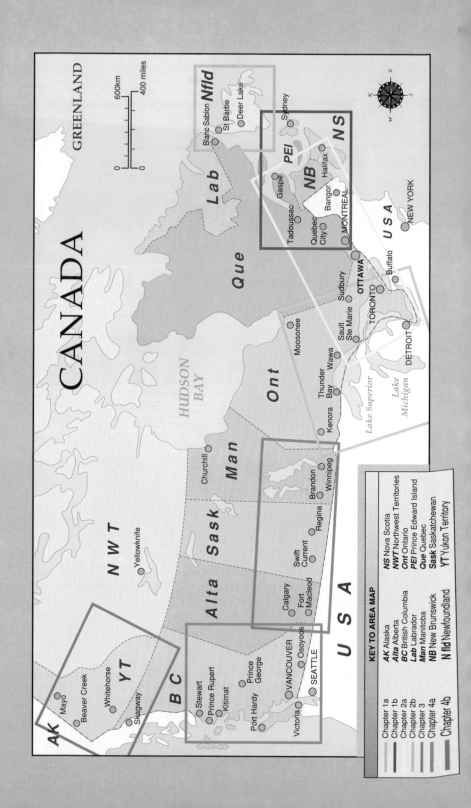

CANADA

GREENLAND

HUDSON BAY

Lake Superior

Lake Michigan

AK
Mayo
Beaver Creek
Whitehorse
Skagway
YT

BC
Stewart
Prince Rupert
Kitimat
Prince George
Port Hardy
VANCOUVER
Victoria
Osoyoos
SEATTLE

NWT
Yellowknife

Alta
Calgary
Fort Macleod

Sask
Swift Current
Regina

Man
Churchill
Brandon
Winnipeg

Ont
Kenora
Thunder Bay
Wawa
Moosonee
Sault Ste Marie
Sudbury
OTTAWA
TORONTO
DETROIT
Buffalo

Que
Lab

Nfld
Blanc Sablon
St Barbe
Deer Lake
Sydney

Gaspe
Tadoussac
Quebec City
MONTREAL
Bangor
Halifax
PEI
NB
NS

USA
NEW YORK

USA

600km
400 miles
0

N
E
W
S

VISITOR'S GUIDE
CANADA

Pam Hobbs & Michael Algar

MPC

HUNTER

Published by:
Moorland Publishing Co Ltd,
Moor Farm Road West, Ashbourne, Derbyshire DE6 1HD, England

Published in the USA by:
Hunter Publishing Inc, 300 Raritan Center Parkway, CN 94, Edison, NJ 08818

ISBN 0 86190 382 X

MPC Production Team:
Editorial & design: John Robey
Cartography: Alastair Morrison

British Library Cataloguing in Publication Data:
A catalogue record for this book is available from the British Library.

Colour origination by: Sele & Color, Bergamo, Italy

Printed in Hong Kong by: Wing King Tong Co Ltd

Front cover: Lake Louise, Alberta (*Michael Algar*)
Rear cover: Indian dancer at Banff National Park (*Alberta Tourism*)
Title page: dog mushing in the Yukon (*Yukon Government*)

Illustrations have been supplied as follows: Alberta Tourism: pages 191,
211; Calgary Stampede page 170; C. P. Hotels: page 207; New Brunswick
Tourism: pages 19 (left), 66; Nova Scotia Tourism: page 39 (lower); Prince
Edward Island Government/J. Sylvester: pages 19 (right), 31, 35; Quebec
Government: pages 38 (top), 115, 122, 124; Saskatchewan Government:
page 162; D. Weedon/M. Macri: page 158; Yukon Government: pages 227,
230, 234.
All other illustrations were supplied by Michael Algar.

For Hayley and Sam. May they see it all.

CONTENTS

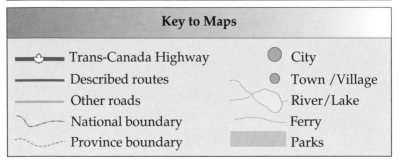

Key to Symbols Used in Text Margin and on Maps

Recommended walks

Garden

Fort

Other place of interest

Winter sports

Nature reserve/Animal interest

Church

Building of interest

Archaeological site

Museum/Art Gallery

Beautiful view/Scenery, Natural phenomenon

Parkland

Key to Maps

Trans-Canada Highway

Described routes

Other roads

National boundary

Province boundary

City

Town /Village

River/Lake

Ferry

Parks

How To Use This Guide

This MPC Visitor's Guide has been designed to be as easy to use as possible. Each chapter covers one or more itineraries and gives all the background information to help you enjoy your visit. MPC's distinctive margin symbols, the important places printed in bold, and a comprehensive index enable the reader to find the most interesting places to visit with ease.

At the end of each chapter an Additional Information section gives specific details such as accommodation, addresses and places to visit, making this guide a complete sightseeing companion.

At the back of the guide the Fact File, arranged in alphabetical order, gives practical information and useful tips to help you plan your holiday — before you go and while you are there.

The maps of each region show the main towns, villages, roads and places of interest, but are not designed as route maps and motorists should always use a good recommended road atlas.

INTRODUCTION

As part of a 1992 survey adults in fifteen countries were asked how they perceived Canada. The general consensus was that it is a land of trees, wide open spaces and extremely long cold winters. Most travellers from overseas have similar views, embellished by images of red-coated mounties, black bears, Rocky Mountains, and the Niagara Falls. In truth there is all this and considerably more, as you will realize when you start planning your visit.

Considering the country's size and diversity this can be daunting, so for travel purposes it has been broken it into manageable chunks. Spread over ten million square kilometres (3.8 million square miles) of land and fresh water, Canada is the second largest country in the world — exceeded only by Russia. Bounded by the Atlantic, Arctic and Pacific Oceans on the east, north and west respectively, Canada occupies most of the northerly part of North America. From eastern Newfoundland to where the Yukon Territory borders the State of Alaska in the west is a distance of 5,520km (3,400 miles). Travelling north to south, from Ellesmere Island in the Arctic to Lake Erie on the US border, is 4,630km (2,900 miles).

The country is divided into ten provinces and two territories and, as travellers soon discover, each retains its own character and cultures. Canada's population is approximately 27 million, most of whom live in a band roughly 160km (100 miles) wide above the United States border. Close to 16 per cent of Canadians were born in another country. Most recent immigrants have settled in the prosperous industrial and agricultural regions of southern Ontario, and along the valleys and coast of British Columbia. Here, entire communities reflect the cultures of nations contributing to the great Canadian mosaic. Interestingly, 61 per cent of Canadians list their mother tongue as English, 24 per cent as French and 0.05 per cent as an aboriginal language.

Politically, Canada is a federal state in which the provinces have a great deal of autonomy over internal affairs. In recent years, powerful forces in Quebec have demanded even more powers so that the province could eventually, through what is described as 'sovereignty association', become only loosely connected with the rest of the country. Or, it could become totally independent.

Currently Canadians outside Quebec tend to prefer a strong central government, although such sentiment may be less pronounced in the West. Aboriginal peoples continue to argue for the right to self government.

In recent years attempts have been made to develop a national constitution which reconciles the less extreme views of Canada's future. A failed national referendum of October 1992 brought an end to the latest of these, and the search for political concensus acceptable to the diverse population continues. In the meantime disagreements are entirely peaceful, and internal politics have little effect on visitors.

Itineraries

In spite of Canada's size, many visitors embark on a once-in-a-lifetime trip that takes them from coast to coast. Most allow four to six weeks to travel the Trans-Canada Highway from St John's, Newfoundland, to Victoria in British Columbia. Some then tackle the northerly route from Vancouver to the Yukon by road or ferries.

In this guide seven tours are described, each taking between six and thirty-three days. These are circular itineraries, starting at major entry points from the United States, Europe, Australia and the Orient. Provincial boundaries are largely ignored so as to follow national transportation routes. They are written in such a way that part of a tour can easily be omitted or may be extend with side trips.

The itineraries in this book include the major cities, towns and recreational areas. Smaller centres and landmarks of special interest are included, and acceptable accommodation is available in every region covered.

By European standards Canadian distances are enormous, but visitors who have invested heavily in time and airfares will want to see as much as they can. For this reason particular attention is paid to driving distances, ensuring that itinerary outlines are realistic. Longer stays are suggested in certain national parks where a rest may be called for.

Beautiful though they are, the Northwest Territories are not included because they are not readily accessible by motorists. However an address is given where you can obtain tourist information should you consider an escorted tour of the territories.

Alternatives to Car Travel and Highway Hotels

National and provincial parks provide wonderful havens for weary travellers. Some have luxury resorts, others are limited to self-catering cottages and campgrounds. Although styles and rents vary, park accommodation is inevitably clean and comfortable, with a rustic character that adds greatly to the environmental theme.

Some visitors arrive with backpacks and hiking boots, ready for the great outdoors. They are not disappointed as it is a commodity that Canada has plenty of.

More hardy explorers paddle canoes along ancient waterways, portaging their craft as Indians, traders and voyageurs did long before them. Moreover, they do not have to go far from major cities to reach such wilderness routes. Just three hours north of Toronto for example, in Algonquin Provincial Park, you can hire all your gear and take off for a week or a month. If that sounds too rugged, you can sample the wilderness through all-day excursions on foot or by canoe, returning at night to a resort.

Cycling is increasingly popular, for gentle jaunts around flat Prince Edward Island, or more strenuous mountain tours and long-distance safaris beneath a wide prairie sky.

In this country of innumerable lakes and waterways, houseboats offer a diversion from highway driving. With a floating home you can travel the canal systems, potter about in traditional 'cottage country', and even hunt for Ogopogo in Lake Okanagan.

Travelling families and compatible friends may find that rental of a motorhome (usually known as a recreational vehicle or RV) is a practical alternative to the car/motel. Affordable and enjoyable, these self-contained units enable you to get a little closer to nature.

Via Rail, the national passenger service, has revamped its long-distance trains with a new interior decor, dining cars, showers and dome-roofed coaches. It takes three and a half days to journey from Toronto to Vancouver by rail. Often tourists stop along the way, lodging at the great railway hotels and resorts as did early twentieth-century vacationers on adventure tours from Europe.

Geography

Canada's terrain is a wonderful kaleidoscope, shaken to present a different view for every province. During a series of Ice Ages, almost all of its land was covered with sheets of compressed snow some two miles deep. Retreating glaciers smoothed the rock, leaving huge gouges that filled to form countless lakes and bogs.

In the Maritime provinces, the northern reaches of the Appalachian mountain chain have been eroded by ice and oceans to form gently rounded highlands, wild seascapes with towering cliffs and pretty inlets.

In some parts of the country sediments collected on prehistoric lake bottoms remained undisturbed by subsequent glaciation, and now provide basins of rich agricultural soil. In consequence, farming regions such as the Annapolis and Saint John valleys, and Prince Edward Island, are as productive as they are picturesque.

The Canadian Shield is an immense semi-circular plateau of ancient granite rocks covering half of Canada. Sweeping from the Arctic north of Labrador and Quebec in the east, it continues around the Hudson Bay shores of Ontario and Manitoba, and then back up to the Arctic islands of the Northwest Territories. Heavily forested in places, it is also rich in

Explore the grandeur of Canada's national parks in the comfort of a motorhome — Banff National Park, Alberta

The spectacular scenery of Lake Duffy in British Columbia

minerals and a major source of hydro-electric power. Although access to regional wilderness can be difficult, the Canadian Shield's starkly beautiful scenery has attracted some of our most eminent artists, while southern areas are developed for recreation. South of this Shield, the temperate agricultural and industrial lowlands of Ontario and Quebec are the most populous segments of Canada.

West of the Canadian Shield and stretching to the Rocky Mountains, a belt of flat plain sweeps down from the Arctic to include much of the Prairie provinces: Alberta, Saskatchewan and Manitoba. The warmer southern regions of these provinces are ideal for farming. They also yield much of the nation's petroleum products, as well as coal and potash. For visitors the Prairies offer unsung vacation opportunities at ranches and farms, where horseback safaris are organized with overnights under canvas or in ranch accommodation.

From the eastern foothills of the Rocky Mountains to the Pacific coast's offshore islands, some of Canada's most diverse landscapes take in parts of Alberta and the Yukon and all of British Columbia. Here a series of mountain ranges run north to south, rising majestically from rich river valleys and reflecting in turquoise lakes. In the south you will drive through prosperous orchards, verdant rain forests and deserts where cactii flourish by the highway in the shadow of snow-traced mountains.

Tourists can have it all: isolated islands steeped in native lore, brash new cities, glaciers, alpine meadows, wilderness preserves, pristine lakes and rivers, and hot springs in use long before the Europeans came this way. Beaches can be deserted even in mid-summer and fishing villages unchanged in a hundred years. Routes of gold prospectors, fur traders, voyageurs and courageous pioneers are intact. Riding trails, railway lines and waterways lead beyond regions served by roads.

History

Exactly when the first people made their crossing from Asia to North America is in some dispute. Scientists agree that the earliest widespread occupation of this continent began about 12,000 years ago although there is some evidence of settlements before that time. Migrants are thought to have travelled down the western side of the continent, then branched out north and east as the Ice Age glaciers retreated.

It is believed that when the first Europeans arrived about a thousand years ago, aboriginal inhabitants numbered two or three hundred thousand. They had already evolved into language and cultural groups as diverse as the peoples of Europe.

Aboriginal nations living comfortably in the Pacific coast's benign climate developed a civilization with a strong artistic tradition. Between the Rocky Mountains and the Great Lakes the nomadic Plains Indians' culture was based on extended family groups which hunted buffalo and smaller animals. Northern forest hunters occupying the boreal forest lands between Alaska and the Labrador coast were nomadic hunters, using lances, bows and arrows, traps and snares. In the sparsely occupied Arctic region, Inuit hunters lived in skin shelters in summer and igloos in winter. Occupying southerly lands east of the Great Lakes, hunters and gatherers often became farmers who built their homes in fortified villages.

Now, across the country you can visit Indian villages, museums and exhibitions which tell their story well. Some of the finest are on the west coast where groups of totem poles stand in silent eloquence, while museums throughout Canada devote whole floors to the way of life of Canada's original inhabitants.

Legends may recall European adventurers who came here before them, but it was tenth-century Vikings who left sound evidence of a settlement on Newfoundland's northern tip. At L'Anse aux Meadows their community has been reconstructed on site, enhanced by displays of domestic articles retrieved from the original village.

The fifteenth century was an era of discovery. Just five years after Christopher Columbus reached America John Cabot, searching for a short route to the East on behalf of the king of England, arrived at Cape Breton Island on the craggy shore of Nova Scotia. Within a few years, British, French, Portugese and Basque fishermen were exploiting the rich cod fishing banks off Nova Scotia and Newfoundland.

The next milestone in Canada's history came in 1534, a time when the Spanish were colonizing the Caribbean and Latin America. Jacques Cartier received a charter from France's king to search for gold and a route to the East. In all he made three voyages to the Gulf of St Lawrence, travelling as far as the present-day Montreal and Quebec, but his discoveries led to no permanent settlement.

Fish and whales gave sixteenth-century Europeans good cause to visit Canada during summer months. They would spend brief periods on shore processing their catch, then return home at summer's end. England's Sir Humphrey Gilbert claimed part of Newfoundland for his Queen in 1583 and some small colonies were founded there.

Fishermen had little reason to suffer through Canadian winters, but by the turn of the century fur traders did. In the late 1500s European hat makers developed a new style of durable, waterproof hat made from beaver pelts. Such headgear became so fashionable that in 1602 Henry IV of France chartered a fur trading company. The following year its agent Samuel de Champlain sailed on his first voyage of exploration. He created the colony of Port Royal in Nova Scotia's Annapolis Valley in 1605, and three years later moved his headquarters to what we now know as Quebec City. There he befriended Algonquin and Huron Indians who controlled access to fur trading in the west. He joined the Algonquins for a raid on the Iroquois, even lending them musketeers to speed up the job. Understandably, this earned him the everlasting enmity of the Iroquois.

Champlain began a series of explorations along the Ottawa Valley, into Georgian Bay, around Lake Ontario, and south of the Saint Lawrence

River. His routes were followed by traders and missionaries, who for a time focused their energies on Huronia, north of present-day Toronto. But along with Christianity the Jesuits, and traders who followed, spread European diseases which ravaged the Huron population. Weakened, and few in number, the Hurons eventually fled with the handful of 'black robes' (as the Jesuits were known), who had been spared capture and torture by marauding Iroquois.

Despite apathy in Versailles, Montreal was founded in 1642 and Champlain's successors pressed on through to the centre of the continent. When Louis XIV came to the throne he renewed France's interest in this struggling colony of 3,000 Europeans. His ministers not only dispatched an army to subdue the Iroqouis but also actively stimulated immigration and trade.

At that time, although Britain's colonies in New England continued to grow, her Canadian interest had flagged since 1610 when Henry Hudson discovered the northern bay which bears his name. This situation emphatically changed as demand for beaver hats rose to dizzying heights. In 1670 Charles II chartered the Hudson's Bay Company, giving it rights to govern the huge land mass draining into the bay that would be known in future as Rupert's Land. Within this territory, the company set up trading posts to obtain beaver pelts from the Indians. Several of these have been recreated or restored today, giving visitors a peek into this fascinating period of Canada's past.

The long struggle over North America between Britain and France started with the War of the League of Augsburg (1689-97). Its outcome basically confirmed the territorial status quo, demonstrating that the French and British colonists' future was in the hands of Europe's monarchs. When the War of Spanish Succession ended in 1713 with the Treaty of Utrecht, New France lost Acadia (part of Nova Scotia) along with all claims to Hudson Bay and Newfoundland, but she retained Île Royale (Nova Scotia's Cape Breton) and Île St Jean (Prince Edward Island) while her mainland possessions stretched south of the Hudson Bay watershed from Labrador to the Mississippi, and down to the Gulf of Mexico.

France's loss of Acadia left her Gulf of St Lawrence colonies so vulnerable to attack that she built the massive fortress of Louisbourg on Île Royale. Britain responded with construction of the Citadel at Halifax, and also sent settlers to this new capital of Nova Scotia. Now both fortresses are popular with visitors, especially Louisbourg which introduces them to a day in the life of New France during the mid-1700s.

Around this time the European population of New France was 80,000, while that of Britain's English- speaking colonies in America numbered some two million. Even so the perceived threat in Nova Scotia represented by the 10,000 French-speaking Acadians was unhappily resolved in 1755 by forcibly transporting them to other colonies. Today, in the rich farmlands of Nova Scotia's Annapolis Valley, tribute is paid to those Acadians expelled from their homes. Some relocated on the shores of Northern New

Brunswick where a recreated village at Caraquet illustrates how they survived. To this day succeeding generations have retained French as their first language.

In 1756 France sent reinforcements under the Marquis de Montcalm, who had fought a number of successful actions in Upper New York. Two years later, British troops led by Generals Amherst and Wolfe smashed Louisbourg. Wolfe met Montcalm in battle at Quebec City and when it concluded with a British victory, both generals lay mortally wounded. Now in Battlefield Park a monument pays tribute to their valour, while ground markers trace events of the decisive battle.

Under the 1763 Treaty of Paris, France lost all of North America except for Louisiana (which was sold to the United States in 1803) and the tiny islands of St Pierre and Miquelon. Britain created the French-speaking colony of Quebec out of a rectangle of land around the St Lawrence River. Île St Jean was later renamed Prince Edward Island. Île Royale became Cape Breton Island and later merged into the colony of Nova Scotia.

Eighteenth-century explorers and fur traders continued to push west across the continent. In the 1730s-40s the La Vérendrye family reached the Saskatchewan and Missouri Rivers. By the 1750s Antony Henday of the Hudson's Bay Company was into the foothills of the Rocky Mountains. That great explorer James Cook sailed across the Pacific and arrived on the North American coast in 1778. Fourteen years later, George Vancouver came to look at it in greater detail. A year after that, the North West Company's Alexander Mackenzie travelled overland from Lake Athabasca to Bella Coola on the Pacific Ocean, a journey to extend the fur trade across the continent. More explorers followed. Simon Fraser descended the river which bears his name in 1808, and in 1811 David Thompson followed the Columbia River from its source to the ocean.

The arrival of Europeans dramatically changed the lives of Canada's native peoples. Prairie hunters caught wild horses and acquired guns to pursue the buffalo upon which they depended, and soon the vast herds disappeared. Everywhere the natives' land was developed by immigrants, and these nomadic peoples were confined to reservations. (Only now are they receiving compensation for loss of lands.)

At the end of the American Revolution (1775-83) British North America was forced to relinquish regions to the west and south of the Great Lakes to the United States of America. This caused families loyal to the British crown to emigrate from the former thirteen colonies into Quebec and Nova Scotia. Their demands for greater autonomy led to the establishment of New Brunswick. Quebec was divided into Lower and Upper Canada, but later restructured into a single Province of Canada with east and west divisions.

The War of 1812, an extension of the Napoleonic wars, broke out between Britain and the United States. Although invasions and battles in eastern Canada were numerous, the most permanent outcome was creation of the 49th parallel as the western frontier between Canada and the

United States. The early ninteenth-century brought continued expansion, stimulated by immigration from Europe and the United States. Fur trading posts in Rupert's Land, that huge Hudson's Bay Company fiefdom in the country's core, became permanent settlements. The largest of these was at Red River around the present-day city of Winnipeg, which has been a destination for immigrants since 1812.

Enormous political and economic pressures were brought to bear on British North America by the American Civil War (1861-5) and its aftermath. Although communication improved with the development of steamships and railways, the eastern colonies remained scattered and separated. Meantime, at the other end of the country the two colonies of Vancouver Island and British Columbia were stimulated economically by discovery of gold along the Fraser River — the first of many important mineral discoveries.

A movement towards union of the Atlantic provinces also attracted the Province of Canada, and in 1867 the British North America Act brought the Dominion of Canada into being. Next, in 1870, the Hudson's Bay Company charter was terminated. This resulted in Rupert's Land and the grasslands to the south becoming the Northwest Territories of the Dominion. Soon after, the North West Mounted Police was formed as a symbol of sovereignty over the territories. British Columbia joined Canada in 1871, in return for the promise of a trans-continental railway.

Completion of that railway in 1885 changed the face of Canada. Now immigrants from Europe and the United States could be transported to the interior and agricultural products and lumber sent by rail to ports on the east and west coasts. In 1905 the remaining prairie provinces of Alberta and Saskatchewan were formed from sections of the Northwest Territories.

The Yukon Territory was incorporated in 1898. Manitoba expanded to its present boundaries in 1912. Newfoundland, formerly a British colony, became Canada's tenth province in 1949. By the end of this century, the eastern section of the Northwest Territories will have been separated to form the new territory of Nunavut.

Some Other Important Dates in Canadian History
• Canada entered World War I in 1914 as part of the British Empire. Nearly 61,000 Canadians were killed during this war, most of them in Western Front battles such as the Somme, St Elio, Ypres and Vimy.

• In December 1917 a munitions ship explosion in Halifax harbour had the unhappy distinction of being the largest man-made disaster until Hiroshima.

• In 1931 the Statute of Westminster gave Canada complete autonomy. At Canada's insistence, Britain's parliament retained certain powers which were not completely relinquished until 1982.

• In 1939 Canada entered World War II as an independent state. Over one million Canadians contributed to the war effort, and 42,000 gave their lives. Financed largely through the American Lease-Lend plan, Canada expanded its industrial base to provide enormous quantities of supplies and equipment for the Allied cause. This economic growth carried over into the post-war era to push Canada into the ranks of the world's leading industrial states.

• In 1959 the jointly owned and operated United States/Canada St Lawrence Seaway was opened, permitting ocean-going ships access to the Great Lakes ports in both countries.

• In 1962 the Trans-Canada Highway from St John's Newfoundland in the east to Victoria, BC on the west coast was completed.

Cultural Pot-Pourri

Because of the diversity of its people, the terrain and even climate, each province has fairs and festivals relevant to regional cultures. (Provincial tourist offices provide dates and venues.) On the east coast even the smallest communities celebrate their sea harvests. In the Highlands of Cape Breton, Canada's only Gaelic College hosts highland dancing, bagpipe and fiddling festivities. Acadian culture is celebrated in New Brunswick; winter carnivals in Quebec City and Ottawa. Ottawa also holds a Spring Festival when its millions of tulips grown from Dutch bulbs are in bloom. In Toronto Caribana is North America's greatest Caribbean parade, and this city's ten days 'Caravan' celebrates ethnic populations with food and entertainment in pavilions of many nations.

Pow-wows and festivals of aboriginal citizens in authentic costumes are always a big hit with visitors. Two of the largest gatherings of North American nations are on Ontario's Manitoulin Island and in Banff National Park, Alberta.

Communities in the western provinces stage rodeos, the best known being the Calgary Stampede and Exhibition held each July.

History is kept alive across the country in authentic recreations of early forts and missions, and superb museums funded usually by provincial governments. While there are far too many to list here, the following are definitely worth a detour.

The Royal British Columbia Museum in Victoria has one of the finest exhibits relating to Pacific Coast native peoples. In Barkerville you can taste the excitement of the gold rush era. Alberta's Fort Edmonton Park traces the history of Edmonton from its beginning as a Hudson's Bay Company post. This province's Tyrrell Museum of Palaeontology contains all kinds of dinosaur skeletons built from bones unearthed in the neighbouring Alberta Badlands. Head-Smashed-In Buffalo Jump in the Albertan prairies is a world heritage site reconstructing an ancient buffalo hunting ground.

Saskatchewan has its Western Development Museums recounting different aspects of life in the Prairies. The fur trade is vividly described in Winnipeg's Museum of Man and Nature, and on the outskirts of this city

Lower Fort Garry is North America's only remaining stone fort and trading post of that era. Every summer, on the northern shores of Lake Superior, Old Fort William is the scene of a Great Rendezvous with voyageurs from Quebec coming to exchange trade goods for furs brought in from northern outposts. Central Ontario has the stunning recreation of Ste-Marie Among the Hurons, the seventeenth-century Jesuit Mission destroyed by its builders.

In southeast Ontario, on the banks of the St Lawrence River, Upper Canada Village is an impressive recreated community portraying the day-to-day lives of European settlers who came here in the 1800s. Quebec City has its Citadel and Battlefield Park on the Heights of Abraham, New Brunswick its Acadian Village and a Loyalist Historic Settlement at Kings Landing near Fredericton. One of the most interesting recreations is the Fortress of Louisbourg, the eighteenth-century maritime stronghold in Nova Scotia.

Prince Edward Island's Green Gables may not be of true historic consequence, but its visitors outnumber those at some more traditional landmarks. And, finally, where it all began, L'Anse aux Meadows on the northerly tip of Newfoundland is the Viking settlement rebuilt now on the basis of archeological evidence. As living museums, these sites pump new blood through the veins of Canada's past, with multi-media introductions, costumed guides and animators, and often restaurants serving meals prepared as they would have been in the represented period.

The Arts and Architecture

Thanks largely to dedicated fund-raisers and generous culturally-minded citizens, Canada is rich in the visual and performing arts. Its symphony orchestras and ballet companies are internationally acclaimed, and when it comes to theatre, Toronto — as its politicians so often tell us — is truly world class. Summer theatre in resort areas is usually of high calibre. Museums and art galleries, both large and small, can be outstanding.

If visitors remember Canada for its architecture, it is likely for the imposing buildings of the early 1900s, especially those with steep copper roofs weathered to a distinctive shade of green. They are the federal and provincial parliament buildings and old city halls, lofty railway stations, ponderous hotels and resorts built by railway barons to resemble European châteaux.

Imaginative, futuristic architecture is usually seen in buildings designed for expositions, theatres, museums and galleries. Weather plays its part in city layouts. First-time visitors to Montreal and Toronto are intrigued by the extent of building underground. It is possible to spend days, or even months below ground impervious to biting winter winds or the steamy days of August.

Shopping

Canada has climate-controlled shopping malls, so large they can be confusing. Biggest of these is West Edmonton Mall, which at 44ha (109 acres) has all the razamataz of an indoor amusement park. A midway, ice skating rink, wave pool, cinema, themed streets and hundreds of shops are just some of its attractions.

Far more interesting are country-style stores stocked with indigenous crafts and produce. Items to look for on the west coast include native carvings in wood and soapstone, and Cowichan sweaters which are warm as well as waterproof. Country fairs produce colourful handmade quilts, some of the finest created by Mennonite women in southwestern Ontario. In Quebec's St-Jean-Port-Joli you will see intricate wood carvings; in the Gaspé wooden *bateaux* are offered from roadside stands. And do not forget the maple syrup, to pour on your pancakes when you are back home.

Sports

Canadians learn to skate on ice usually before they reach school age, and if there is not a municipal rink nearby suburban fathers spend many a frigid evening flooding their back yards so junior can get some ice time. Visitors to Canada between October and May will want to catch one of the national ice hockey league games, although tickets can be hard to come by. Depending on play-off dates, hockey and baseball seasons can overlap. Some baseball fans of the 1992 World champion Toronto Blue Jays are so keen that they get a headstart on summer by watching the team at Spring training in Florida.

Over the past decade or two pollution has taken its toll on fish in Canada's lakes and rivers, and overfishing has drastically reduced commercial fish stock in the Atlantic. Even so this is considered one of the best countries in the world for sport fishing. Regional tourist offices supply pamphlets listing the rules: where to get a licence, the seasons for different species, and where you can hire the necessary gear. Fly-in fishing can be a new and exciting experience for overseas visitors. And even amateurs will enjoy a half or full day excursion with a guide who will supply all necessary gear and cook a shore lunch using part of your catch.

Golf, tennis, trail riding, hiking, swimming, boating, skiing and most other outdoors sports and activities are pursued across Canada, the only complaint by participants being that surrounding scenery is so beautiful that it is distracting.

Wildlife

Even in these times of shameful destruction of the world's wildlife and their habitats, Canada has enough to warrant organized and independent viewing. Most exciting probably are the polar bears in Hudson Bay. Churchill in northern Manitoba is acknowledged as the polar bear capital of the world. Reached by air or rail from Winnipeg, its bears come into town in September and October on their way south to their winter habitat. Summer travellers to Churchill will not be disappointed either, since they are treated to a mosaic of arctic flowers as well as beluga whales in the bay.

Western outfitters arrange safaris into the mountains to photograph grizzly bears, cougars, and other 'big game.'

Whale watching has become a big draw for tourists in British Columbia's Pacific Rim National Park, where sea-lions and grey whales cavort offshore. In the Saguenay River of Northern Quebec, cruise boats on week long itineraries include a day with the whales. Meantime, off New Brunswick's Grand Manan Island, an Ocean Search programme will put you in a small inflatable craft a few feet from the right whales.

In Canada experience living history —
Kings Landing Historical Settlement in
New Brunswick

... or sample some of its interesting
and varied cuisine

Remember those cuddly white baby seals with doleful eyes who used to be bludgeoned to death on ice-packs off the east coast? Well, nowadays tourists are taken by helicopter onto the ice for the close-up photograph of a lifetime.

Seabird sanctuaries are always enjoyable excursions for visitors to the Atlantic provinces. Puffin colonies on Newfoundland's Avalon Peninsula and a variety of seabird species at Cape St Mary's are easily visited. On Bonaventure Island, reached by boat from Percé on Quebec's Gaspé Peninsula, you can actually walk right up to the cliff top where gannets return to the very same ledge they vacated the winter before. Grand Manan is also known for its 300 bird species, as well as seascapes that cause some visiting artists to become permanent residents.

One of the places most frequented by bird watchers is tiny Point Pelee National Park, a sliver of land pointing into Lake Erie which is on the flight path for migrating birds. In September hundreds of thousands of Monarch butterflies are an incredible sight, as they gather at Canada's most southerly spot before taking off to winter in Mexico.

National and provincial parks have large populations of deer, black bears, moose and elk. Algonquin Provincial Park, north of Toronto is one of the few places in the world where you can still hear the timber wolves howl.

Suggested Itineraries

This book is divided into four chapters, representing Canada's major regions. Although each itinerary is divided into daily sections, the time scale does not have to be rigidy adhered to. Instead it should be regarded as an indication of the time taken to cover the route and of the places worth visiting in the area. Some visitors may want to spend more time walking or looking round museums for instance, while others might prefer just to travel from place to place and look at the main sights. Use these itineraries as a guideline and plan your visit so as to see the places that interest you most.

The four **Atlantic Provinces** are included in a single 33-day itinerary covering approximately 6,000km (or nearly 4,000 miles) which starts at Montreal. Arriving by air from overseas, you could just as easily begin your tour in St John's (Newfoundland), or Halifax (Nova Scotia). Coming from the United States, you would probably start off at the Maine/New Brunswick border.

This Atlantic Canada tour takes in all the major cities and towns and regional points of interest. Time can be saved by reserving sections such as Newfoundland or Prince Edward Island for another visit. Also suggested are excursions from Halifax, or a side trip from Prince Edward Island to Quebec's Magdalen Islands if you have an extra few days.

The second chapter, **Central Canada**, contains two itineraries. First is a 21-day, 3,900km (2,400 mile) circular tour that originates in Toronto or

Montreal and covers the more populated regions of Quebec and eastern Ontario. This takes in some of Canada's largest cities, special places of interest and recreational areas. Excursions from major centres are also suggested.

The second circular itinerary takes eight days and covers 3,900km (2,400 miles). This link between the central provinces and the Prairies is frequently part of a trip from Ontario to the Rocky Mountains or the Pacific coast. In spite of the long distances to be driven, it is a very worthwhile journey in itself, especially for outdoors enthusiasts. A side trip by train to James Bay, an inlet of the Arctic Ocean, has even been included.

Chapter Three covers the **Prairie Provinces** in a 3,500km (2,200 mile) circular itinerary over eighteen days. Again there are suggested side trips, including one to the shores of Hudson Bay. The tour originates in Winnipeg, or alternatively Calgary or Edmonton, taking in the prairies as far as the foothills of the Rocky Mountains.

The fourth and final chapter covers **Western Canada** and includes the mountainous section of Alberta and parts of British Columbia and the Yukon Territory. The first itinerary is structured as an extension of the Prairie Provinces chapter, originating in Calgary or Edmonton, but it could just as well start in Vancouver. Covering a distance of 2,500km (1,500 miles) it takes fourteen days, more if extended by excursions from Vancouver and Victoria.

In this chapter, the second itinerary takes eight days and covers 2,250km (1,400 miles) in addition to a fifteen-hour ferry-boat ride. This circular trip takes you up the British Columbia coast, then into the interior of the province before returning to Vancouver. The third trip is to the Yukon Territory by air, sea or road, in six days, with 1,350km (840 miles) of driving once you arrive.

We have included campgrounds suitable for RVs among our suggestions for overnight accommodation. Many commercial campgrounds do not permit tents, but most national, provincial and municipal parks do.

We have not included admission charges for places of interest. Most are government operated which means costs are fairly modest. Families with children are usually admitted for the price of two adults.

Seniors (60 or 65 years old and over) can expect discounts on public transportation, admissions and some accommodation. Occasionally this concession is limited to residents.

1
THE ATLANTIC PROVINCES

Montreal is chosen as the starting point for a circular tour of Canada's four Atlantic provinces, although the city itself is described in another chapter. This is the most logical entry point for overseas visitors arriving by air. By road it is 540km (336 miles) east of Toronto, and 50km (31 miles) north of the US border. This tour could also begin at other points along the way: Halifax, Nova Scotia, which is the arrival point for some overseas flights, or St Stephen in New Brunswick where road traffic arrives from America and from Canada west of Montreal. Although these Atlantic provinces are well served by air, visitors often choose the ferries between Maine and Nova Scotia, and from the mainland to Prince Edward Island or Newfoundland, simply for the pleasurable experience.

This 33-day tour can be reduced to three weeks by eliminating the Newfoundland and Labrador portion. A few more days could be shaved off by leaving Prince Edward Island or the Fundy coast and Fredericton for a future visit. Although it is a great pity to miss these places, it is preferable to shorten your trip rather than fit it all into a shorter time.

Atlantic Canada comprises four provinces: Newfoundland and Labrador, and Canada's three smallest provinces: New Brunswick, Nova Scotia and Prince Edward Island, collectively known as The Maritimes.

The region has a long indented coastline, no part of the land being more than 160km (100 miles) from the sea. Most is much closer, causing the entire area to be dominated by the ocean's moods and contrasts. On the one side a turbulent Atlantic can send huge waves crashing against tall cliffs, or as surf onto wide beaches of fine silvery sand. On the other, the Gulf of St Lawrence's more sheltered waters are calm enough and warm enough for sea bathing by even the most timid. The Bay of Fundy's enormous tides bring constant shifts in seascapes. These plankton-rich waters attract numerous fish species and marine mammals, including a variety of whales. Leisure fishermen acknowledge the river trout and salmon, and game fishing offshore, to be unrivalled.

The regional landscape is hilly, especially in New Brunswick and on Cape Breton Island. Newfoundland has its own northwestern mountain range. Elsewhere broad valleys and plains are devoted to agriculture, and the traveller is never far from the huge coniferous forests that provide the basis for an intensive lumber industry.

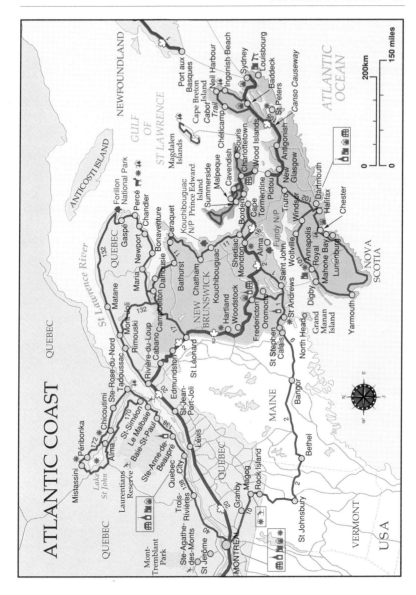

Sensational sea and landscapes have resulted in the creation of national and provincial parks with leisure facilities for everyone who enjoys the outdoors. But wilderness does not necessarily mean roughing it. These environmental preserves have become grand settings for luxury resorts and hotels, cottages equipped for self catering and serviced campsites. Also for anyone seeking a total wilderness experience, since they can still pitch a tent off the beaten track and relish pristine scenery, far from civilization yet within the safety of a government-operated park.

Visitors coming to Atlantic Canada by road will arrive in **New Brunswick**, largest and most westerly of the three maritime provinces, bounded by the sea on three sides and by Quebec and Maine to the west. For good reason New Brunswick is described as the 'picture province'. Driving through it you will encounter constantly changing vistas that include forests stretching to the horizon, rich agricultural farmlands of the Saint John River Valley and 2,250km (1,400 miles) of coastline.

In the late eighteenth century, following the American War of Independence, colonists loyal to the British crown founded New Brunswick. About 35 per cent of the population are French-speaking descendents of the Acadians — inhabitants of New France who were deported in 1755 and who returned after France relinquished most of her North American colonies. Completely bilingual, they are always pleased to talk with visitors about their heritage.

Physically connected to the rest of Canada by a narrow isthmus, **Nova Scotia** is almost entirely surrounded by sea. The coastline, particularly on Cape Breton Island, has some of the most beautiful scenery in all of Canada. Sailing enthusiasts enjoy the huge natural harbours such as Halifax and Sydney, and protected waters of the Bras d'Or Lakes. Picturesque fishing ports are perfect subjects for artists and photographers. Beaches, which range from wide golden strips groomed by Atlantic rollers to protected little bays, are all pleasure. The capital, Halifax, is one of the country's most attractive cities, very compact and easily explored on foot. With all this going for it visitors readily agree with local licence plates proclaiming Nova Scotia as Canada's Atlantic Playground.

This province has a unique heritage. Chartered as a colony by James I in 1621, and named by its founder Sir William Alexander after his Scottish homeland, 35 per cent of the populace today claims Scottish ancestry. Others trace their roots to the French-speaking Acadians, migrants from New England who arrived before and after the American Revolution, Germans and fellow immigrants from other parts of Europe. Early history is depicted in the sprawling British Citadel in Halifax, and its French rival at Louisbourg. Reminders of the times when Nova Scotian merchants sent a huge fleet of sailing ships off to the far corners of the world are in evidence in smaller harbours around the coast.

Prince Edward Island is the smallest and proportionately the most heavily populated of Canada's provinces. Micmac Indians were its first known inhabitants; they called it *Abegweit* which translates as 'cradle of the waves'. Many a visitor today will echo the sixteenth-century explorer Jacques Cartier's sentiments when he described the island he named Île St-Jean as 'the fairest land that may possibly be seen'. French settlement began in 1720, and these people were expelled when the British captured the island in 1758, later renaming it after a son of King George III. Canada's provincial politicians met here at Charlottetown to plan the 1867 Confederation. However it was not until five years later that Prince Edward Island joined the new Dominion of Canada.

About 40 per cent of Prince Edward Island is devoted to agriculture, its rich red soil splashed with bottle green leaves of potato crops in season. Depleted fish populations mean that commercial fishing is not what islanders would like it to be. Lobsters are very important though, and shell-fish cultivation is a growth industry. Tourism is taken very seriously by the islanders. In summer the pleasant climate, and warm inshore waters washing some 800km (500 miles) of silken beaches, combine with adorable little villages and friendly people to attract the same loyal tourists year after year.

Prince Edward Island National Park takes in a 40km (25 mile) section of the north shore blessed with some of the island's finest bathing beaches. Here holiday accommodation extends to beachfront campsites, hotels, motels, cottages, small inns and large resorts. Golf courses and tennis courts overlook the sea. Fishing charters give visitors an enjoyable few hours whether they bring home your dinner or not.

The island capital of Charlottetown beckons with a wide range of accommodation and good restaurants, excellent theatre, (including that all-time favourite *Anne of Green Gables*) and the past brought to life in restored historic areas. Across the island you will find plenty of 'down home' entertainment, of which your first choice should be a traditional lobster supper. Then, if you can stir yourself from the beach, you will want to take at least one of the three signposted scenic drives around different sections of the island.

The province of **Newfoundland and Labrador** became part of the Canadian confederation in 1949. Closer to Europe than any other part of North America, Newfoundland was the first of England's colonial possessions. From the time Sir Humphrey Gilbert claimed this 'new found land' in 1583, a few small settlements were established in spite of severe difficulties. French fishermen started communities on the west coast, where you will find some French-speaking villages still.

With its economy soundly based on the fisheries the capital of St John's grew slowly into a flourishing, if isolated, merchantile centre. Elsewhere, settlers lived in small 'outports', often giving them fanciful names like Heart's Content, Blow-me-Down, Squid Tickle and Come-by-Chance.

Centuries of isolation caused Newfoundlanders to develop their own customs, and a unique accent with a rich variety of unusual words and idioms. They have a distinctive sense of humour, and a charm that captivates every visitor. Given half a chance they will show you a 'toime' — meaning a good time. When you leave they'll wave you off with a cheery 'and don't be a stranger now'.

Fishing remains an important industry, despite great difficulties caused by a temporary ban on commercial cod fishing. Lumbering, mining and offshore petroleum resources are also very important. More recently the provincial government has aggressively developed tourism. This is long overdue in view of the scenic grandeur, natural resources and deep sense of hospitality ingrained in Newfoundlanders.

The province has few if any down-market tourist attractions. Only St John's has large city-type hotels and amenities. The small hotels and motels are comfortable, the B & Bs a real delight. Local cuisine, much of it based on codfish, is tasty and robust.

Two large national parks and many provincial parks ensure enjoyment of Newfoundland's rugged beauty. Hunting and fishing opportunities abound. Seabird colonies in the Avalon Peninsula attract wildlife watchers. The climate is relatively warm in summer, but rain and sea fogs can be a nuisance. For the best weather you should visit Newfoundland between mid-July and mid-September. Even then you may see icebergs floating off shore.

Montreal to Edmunston (680km/423 miles, 1 day)

This tour of the Atlantic provinces is based on the premise that visitors will have toured the cities of Quebec's St Lawrence River valley on previous trips, or plan to do so later. Therefore this first part of the route takes you 680km (423 miles) without stopping anywhere for more than an hour or so, between Montreal and Edmundston, New Brunswick, via the Trans-Canada Highway.

Guests at Montreal hotels will find it easiest to leave the city by crossing the Champlain Bridge, then taking Rte 30 north until it joins Rte 20, the Trans-Canada Highway. Driving through the city from the west, follow the Trans-Canada Highway, Rte 40, until it joins Autoroute Decarie (Rte 15), and then cross the Champlain Bridge.

There is not much to detain the tourist in the 250km of highway between Montreal and **Lévis**, on the St Lawrence's south shore opposite Quebec City. Further on, about 100km (62 miles) east of Lévis, **St-Jean-Port-Joli** dates from 1721. This village is Quebec's prime centre for wood-carvers whose *habitant* figures are in gift-shops across the country. Other artisans produce carved miniature boats, pottery, paintings and woven goods. An enjoyable coffee stop, the area has a number craft workshops, small museums and restaurants.

A further 100km (60 miles) is the small city of **Rivière-du-Loup**. This one-time railroad town has a paper-mill you will likely smell before you see it. Otherwise it is largely dependent on service industries. In the centre of town is a rather spectacular waterfall. A seasonal ferry service links the city with **St-Simeon** on the Charlevoix Coast of the St Lawrence, and in autumn boat tours operate from here to see the whales off the mouth of the Saguenay River.

From Rivière-du-Loup, the Trans-Canada Highway (now Rte 185) turns inland. In the 110km (68 miles) to the New Brunswick border the road passes through lumbering and farming communities, including St-Louis-du-Ha!-Ha! and Cabano. A Government of Quebec tourist information centre indicates the approaching border with New Brunswick.

At the border, where the Trans-Canada Highway becomes NB Rte 2 it is a good idea to stop at the New Brunswick Tourist Information Centre for maps, brochures and general advice on tourism.

Jutting into Maine, this area was the source of 60 years of border negotiations between Canada and the United States during the nineteenth century. Impatient of their treatment as pawns, residents founded their own mythical Republic of Madawaska with **Edmundston** as its capital. Nowadays, the tradition continues as the focus of community activities.

Edmundston is an important pulp and paper centre lying at the junction of the Madawaska and Saint John Rivers. It was first settled in 1790 by Acadians who left the Fredericton area when Loyalists arrived following the American Revolution. They were joined by French-speaking families from Quebec, and later by English-speaking settlers. The city has an upbeat, largely francophone, ambience. Hand-loomed fabrics and wood-carving are regional craft specialities.

A rural scene in the Acadian Historic Village

Local events include the Foire Brayonne which honours the Republic in early August. October brings the Festival de la Gastronomie, featuring local cuisine. The Madawaska Museum on the Trans-Canada Highway records local history; Notre Dame des Sept Doleurs church contains a museum and woodcarvings by the renowned New Brunswick artist Claude Rousel. At St-Jacques, north of Edmundston, Les Jardins de la Republic Provincial Park has a cultural and recreation centre, with heated pool and an automobile museum. Also a full service campground. There are a number of restaurants in town, and we have listed two of the motels.

Edmundston to Caraquet (300km/186 miles, 1 day)

This drive takes you down the Saint John River Valley to **St-Léonard**, then leaves the valley to cross the Restigouche Uplands in the northeast corner of New Brunswick to Chaleur Bay.

The return journey will include the Fredericton area of the lower Saint John valley, but with more time available you might want to make a diversion into the valley before continuing. To do so follow the Trans-Canada Highway down the broad valley, past pretty tree-lined villages and towns. **Hartland** is site of a much-photographed covered bridge, which at 391m (1,282ft) is the longest structure of its kind in the world.

Returning to the scheduled itinerary, take Rte 17 from St-Leonard to **St-Quentin**, a centre of an area renowned for its salmon fishing and the extensive forests of birch, ash, pine and maple which make it such a photographer's pleasure in Fall. It is also the gateway to the Carleton Provincial Park, a wilderness reserve offering a variety of camping, canoeing, hiking and other outdoor activities, as well as some spectacular vistas.

Rte 17 continues on passing through rolling hills and rapid streams flowing into the Restigouche and Matapedia Rivers, teeming with salmon. At **Tide Head**, the Matapedia River forms an estuary which flows into Chaleur Bay. Tide Head is a major centre for growing fiddleheads, the edible fern tips that taste a little like asparagus, and are a unique Canadian delicacy. Interesting views appear from high over the estuary as the road (now Rte 11) approaches **Campbellton** (population 9,000). Dispossessed Acadians settled here in 1757, followed by an influx of Scots who were responsible for the name. Keen fishermen may well want to stay awhile. Accommodation is perfectly acceptable and outfitters will equip you for salmon fishing. From Campbellton, either follow the coast road (Rte 134) which passes through interesting little towns such as **Dalhousie,** or the faster Rte 11 direct to **Bathurst**. This town has a number of hotels/motels and restaurants where travellers may prefer to overnight after visiting Caraquet, since accommodation there is somewhat limited.

Rte 11 continues along the coast through a series of Acadian fishing communities until it reaches the **Acadian Historic Village**, one of Canada's finest living museums, a working community built to demonstrate how the Acadian people lived here between 1780 and 1890. The ancient system of sluices and dikes, used by the Acadians to reclaim fertile farmlands from the sea, have been restored to working condition. Village 'residents', both children and adults, go about their chores, following many of the crafts and occupations necessary for survival in this once-isolated community. The village restaurant serves typical Acadian dishes of the period. (Their poutine rapee, a boiled ball of potato flour stuffed with pork and smothered with molasses, sounds awful but it is really delicious). A small motel and another restaurant are located close-by.

Beyond the village is **Caraquet**, with accommodation and an ocean-side provincial park for campers. Founded in 1750, Caraquet is regarded as the cultural capital of Acadia, and is also home to one of the largest fishing fleets in New Brunswick. Naturally, there is a number of restaurants serving sea-food Acadienne. 15 August is the national Acadian holiday, its festivities climaxed by the ceremonial Blessing of the Fleet.

Caraquet to Kouchibouguac National Park and Moncton (320km/200 miles, 2 days)

The first part of this drive takes you 170km (106 miles) to Kouchibouguac National Park. Leaving Caraquet, continue on Rte 11, passing through a number of fishing communities to **Chatham**, a lumber town and site of a large Canadian armed forces base. From there the road runs inland to Kouchibouguac, a small community at the park entrance.

Kouchibouguac National Park is one of New Brunswick's hidden treasures in that vacationers tend to head for its better known sister park at Fundy. Kouchibouguac's appeal lies in its 25km (15 miles) of broad sand beaches trimming surprisingly warm water. A variety of bird-life is attracted to the beaches, lagoons and salt marshes and seals are often sighted on the more remote shores. Kellys Beach amenities include changing rooms, showers, lifeguards and a snackbar. Away from this hub you can relax on the sand relatively undisturbed. Kouchibouguac has 25km (15 miles) of cycling trails, escorted walks, interpretive programmes and a restaurant where lobster is the house speciality. Campers have a choice of primitive or fully-serviced sites and although motel accommodation is available at the park entrance, Kouchibouguac is included only as a brief respite from driving.

The alternative to an overnight at Kouchibouguac is to continue on to **Moncton**, a further 150 km. As far as **Shediac** the coastal road passes through a number of villages and skirts some delightful beaches, while Rte 11 is a short distance inland. At Shediac join the Trans-Canada Highway (Rte 2) west to Moncton.

Moncton is chosen as an overnight stop because it is a major transportation centre offering plenty of good accommodation, of which two examples are listed, less than an hour's drive from the ferry terminal to Prince Edward Island. At Moncton on a bend in the Petitcodiac River, the high Fundy tides produce a bore which is most noticable when tides are highest. The town is also known for its Magnetic Hill where an optical illusion gives the impression that cars are coasting uphill.

Birthplace of a Nation

The 'cradle' or 'birthplace' of Canada is a title given to Charlottetown because it was here in September 1864 that a group who became known as Fathers of Confederation met for the first time, with a view to uniting the provinces. Initially, representatives of the three Maritime Provinces had agreed to meet. Then the Province of Canada (to become Ontario and Quebec) asked to join them, and when the conference finally got underway twenty-three delegates were assembled.

Now a slide show in the city's handsomely restored Province House recalls those events. Several of the offices are furnished as they were in the 1860s, including the room where the original meetings took place.

During subsequent conferences in Quebec and London (England) courtship of the provinces evolved into marriage, and in 1867 Canada was born. One hundred years later that event was commemorated by construction of Charlottetown's Confederation Centre. Opened by Queen Elizabeth II, it houses theatres, an excellent art gallery, a library, restaurant, provincial archives and spacious exhibit areas. 1 July is Canada Day, celebrated on Ottawa's Parliament Hill, in the grounds of provincial legislative buildings and in homes across the country.

Province House, Charlottetown, where the Dominion of Canada was formed

Campers will find several overnight options at Shediac, including Parlee Beach Provincial Park which has a terrific beach. Claiming to be the 'Lobster Capital of the World', Shediac has a lobster festival in July. Restaurants feature lobster and other superfresh seafoods. Motel accommodation in town is not the greatest.

Moncton to Prince Edward Island (130km/81 miles, 4 days)

Leaving Moncton or Shediac, follow Rtes 15 and 16 to Marine Atlantic's

Prince Edward Island ferry terminal at **Cape Tormentine**, 90km (56 miles) from Moncton. Boarding is on a first-come first-served basis. In summer, it is well to get here early because queues lengthen during the day.

Arriving at the ferry terminus at **Borden** on Prince Edward Island, you will find a large, efficient tourist bureau where literature and maps are available and the staff ready to assist in selecting accommodation. The choice of hotels and resorts, farms, small inns and B & B lodgings on the island is so wide that no specific recommendations are made, beyond one large hotel and two charming inns in Charlottetown. Sites are usually well maintained in privately operated campgrounds as well as national and provincial parks. Be warned though that this is one of Eastern Canada's favourite tourist destinations, and it is a wise traveller who reserves at least the first night's lodging in advance.

Prince Edward Island is by far the smallest of Canada's provinces, 224km (139 miles) long and between 4km and 60km (2.5 and 37 miles) wide, so it is easy to explore all parts of the island. First-time visitors will probably want to head for Charlottetown, 56km (35 miles) east of Borden via the Trans-Canada Highway, or Prince Edward Island National Park, 25km (15 miles) north of Charlottetown. Both destinations can serve as a base for day trips.

Charlottetown, founded in 1768, was named after King George III's queen. Walking tours of the restored historic area, known as Old Char-

*Japanese tourists are
especially attracted to
the farmhouse at
Cavendish featured in*
Anne of Green Gables

Anne of Green Gables

Cavendish is a mecca for Japanese tourists who flock to see the home of their favourite storybook character: *Anne of Green Gables*. Even the waitress in a neighbourhood café speaks Japanese, and so does the gift shop's young clerk.

At Cavendish — Avalon in the Anne books — the nineteenth-century green and white farmhouse is everything fans want it to be. It is even furnished according to author Lucy Maud Montgomery's description. Raised by her grandparents who ran the local post office, Lucy Maud visited this home of her cousins as a child. In the grounds you will see the Haunted Wood, Babbling Brook and Lover's Lane familiar to her readers. The author's birthplace in nearby New London is open to the public. Her body is buried in Cavendish cemetery. There are conducted walking tours.

Although she wrote hundreds of short stories and poems, more novels and seven sequels to *Anne of Green Gables* (first published in Boston in 1908) none received such world acclaim as that original story about the red-haired spirited orphan 'Anne with an "e" '. The subject of movies and a television series, and translated into many languages, it has been a hit musical in Charlottetown's Confederation Centre every summer since 1967. Be prepared for summer crowds at Green Gables. Arrive early in the day and you can definitely capture a sense of the storybook characters who lived here in the mind of their creator. Shuffle through behind mid-afternoon tour groups and it is just another nice period home.

lotte Town, recall an era when this was a colonial seaport. Its importance in Canadian history is as the site of the 1864 conference which led to the formation of the Dominion of Canada three years later. Province House, venue of those meetings, houses the provincial legislature and is also a national historic site. You will likely hear more about the talented Harris brothers in your island travels. Many of Charlottetown's churches and public buildings, and some of the island's grand old homes were designed by William Harris. His brother Robert was an artist whose most famous commission was the *Fathers of Confederation* showing all the signatories at Charlottetown. Nearby, the Confederation Centre of the Arts provides some cool, quiet time after a few days of sun, sand and sea. Stage productions here are thoroughly professional, the best loved being a musical based on Lucy Maud Montgomery's *Anne of Green Gables*.

Charlottetown (population 16,000) has direct airline connections with Halifax and Moncton. It has a number of good hotels as well as motor inns belonging to major chains. Visitors may well be charmed by the city's small inns and B & B lodgings. Restaurants will happily schedule dinner reservations to accommodate theatregoers.

♣   **Prince Edward Island National Park** is one of Canada's most visited parks. Only 26 sq km (10 sq miles) in area, it stretches along 40km (25 miles) of the island's northern coastline, with broad sand beaches edging a comfortably warm ocean, an area of sand dunes and salt marshes and habitat to some 210 species of birds. Park accommodation ranges from resort hotels to sea-side cottages, many of which are rented to perennial visitors for a week, a fortnight or even the whole summer. The park has three excellent campgrounds suitable for RVs and trailers.

Supervised beaches, hiking trails, golf, tennis and lawn bowling facili- ties are all well used. At little harbours such as **Covehead**, charter boats will take you fishing for cod, mackerel and tuna. (If you do not choose to catch your own, you can buy fresh fish here to cook at your campsite, or ready cooked for eating on the dock.) Close to the park, enchanting villages offer visitor accommodation in cottages and inns as well as B & Bs and private campgrounds. Restaurants are as casual or as elegant as you want them to be, with menus relying heavily on fresh seafood and local produce. The most visited spot in the park is **Cavendish** for the farm- house immortalized by Lucy Maud Montgomery's *Anne of Green Gables*.

Whether you stay in the National Park, in Charlottetown, or elsewhere in one of the farm communities, you will enjoy touring. To make this easy the island is divided into three scenic routes, each of which can easily be accomplished in a day.

Perhaps most popular is the Blue Heron Drive, named after one of the island's bird species. This circular route takes in the centre of the island, incorporating north shore villages bordering the park, as well as Charlottetown and a portion of the south coast. On this route **Victoria** is a particularly pretty coastal village, home of one of the island's summer stock theatres. At Stanley Bridge, a short diversion will take you to **St Ann's** where members of the parish church are said to have originated the island's famous lobster suppers as a fund-raising activity. Now the church basement has a fully licenced restaurant serving fixed-price meals of mussels, lobster, salad and dessert (or selections from a full a la carte menu), along with home-spun entertainment. Other communities soon caught on to lobster suppers as money-makers, and you will now see them advertised all over the island.

Lady Slipper Drive, named after the province's floral emblem, em-braces Prince County at the west end of the island. The information centre at **Wilmot**, just outside **Summerside** on the south coast, previews the drive's attractions with audio-visual presentations, artifacts and photo-murals. Summerside (population 8,000) is the island's second big urban centre. Its fortunes have fluctuated, firstly as a shipbuilding port, then centre of wildly profitable fox fur production, and finally as a military base which recently closed. It remains an agricultural centre and port from which potatoes are shipped world-wide. Boom times are reflected in the churches and solid wood-frame houses lining the tree-shaded streets, some of which now offer B & B in summer. A recreated pioneer village at **Mont-Carmel** is representative of Acadian settlement in the area from the

The Silver Foxes of Summerside

Nineteenth-century adventurers who made their fortunes in beaver pelts are legendary, but Prince Edward Island's silver fox pelts fetched $100 each in London at a time when a beaver skin brought in only $2.50.

It began in the late 1800s when a farmer named Charles Dalton noted that litters of red foxes occasionally included a silver cub. His attempts to breed the silver beauties failed, until he replicated the fox's natural habitat and then he found himself with a perfect breeding pair. He shared his secret with a fishing buddy and four neighbours, each of whom was sworn to secrecy. Such was their success that by 1900 one of the group's fox skins sold for $1,807 when local eggs cost 8¢ a dozen and a farmhand earned $7 a week.

Eventually one of the six broke the pact by selling a fox to his nephew, who in turn sold two pairs for $5,000 each. Soon islanders were mortgaging everything for a share in a breeding fox. But it was not to last. World War II brought shipping problems, and soon after fox furs lost their popularity.

Now in Summerside you will see some very grand houses from that period. Luxurious beyond their time, many had electric wiring although it was several decades before electricity came to the island. One such house is now the International Fox Hall of Fame, where you can learn more about the farmers and their secret that made them wealthy beyond all dreams. Another is a gracious inn. As for Charles Dalton, the farmer who started it all, he became Sir Charles, and Lieutenant Governor of Prince Edward Island.

One of the grand houses built by the rich silver-fox farmers at Summerside

early nineteenth century. Consisting of a church, school house, smithy and general store, it is staffed by costumed guides. The road skirts **Malpeque Bay**, a large body of water which almost cuts the island in half, and is famous as the source of ten million cultivated oysters shipped annually to all parts of North America. On its shores **Green Park Provincial Park** has a museum and interpretive centre telling about the island's ship-building history, founded by migrants from Devonshire in England.

The King's Byway Drive, a circular tour of Kings County, follows the coastal road around the island's eastern side. A comprehensive information centre at **Poole's Corner** describes the area's cultural history in great detail. **Souris** is a nice little town and terminus for the ferry to the Magdalen Islands (see page 36). Named after a plague of mice which literally ate early French settlers out of house and home, Souris provided a setting for Elmer Harris' play *Johnny Belinda*. Those interested in the island's fishing heritage should visit Basin Head Fisheries Museum. In any case, the nearby dunes and bathing beach are very appealing. Disused cannery docks and a connecting bridge provide great fun for local youngsters, who like to leap from them into the deep water. There are other attractive little communities on this drive, including **Montague** and **Murray River**. Also, closer to Charlottetown, **Orwell Corner Historic Village** is a recreated nineteenth-century cross-roads hamlet.

Following a stay in Prince Edward Island, the itinerary of the Atlantic Provinces continues eastward. Therefore the departure point from the island is the **Wood Islands** ferry terminal, 60km (37 miles) east of

Take home a memory of a visit to the fishing villages on Prince Edward Island

Charlottetown via the Trans-Canada Highway, which is also a segment of the King's Byway. While waiting for the ferry drop by the Nova Scotia information centre for brochures about that province.

• *Excursion to the Magdalen Islands*
A diversion to Quebec's Magdalen Islands is included at this point because Souris on Prince Edward Island is the car ferry terminus. (The Magdalens also have air links with Quebec City, Montreal and other mainland centres, as well as a weekly freighter service with limited passenger accommodation from Montreal.)

The Magdalen Islands, or Îles-de-la-Madeleine, are beyond doubt one of Canada's best kept vacation secrets. The 100km (60 mile) long hook-shaped archipelago consists of sixteen islands and rocks. A road has been built over the sandspits connecting six of the inhabited islands. The seventh, Entrée Island, is reached by ferry. The greatest attraction is the 300km (190 miles) of gorgeous sandy beaches, under the protection of red and grey sandstone cliffs sculpted by wind and sea.

These islands were first discovered by Jacques Cartier in 1534, and in 1597 were site of the first battle fought between England and France in North America. Most of today's 15,000 Madelinots are descendents of Acadians who were uprooted from their homes, or of people who arrived later from Quebec — along with the occasional shipwrecked mariner. The small steadfastly English-speaking community on Entrée Island stems largely from Scots who migrated to the New World after the eighteenth-century Highland Clearances.

Fishing for lobsters, scallops, cod, mackerel and halibut, along with canning, accounts for 45 per cent of the islands' economy. Some fishermen operate deep-sea fishing charters. Visitors also enjoy swimming, windsurfing, hiking, and horseback riding. But mostly it is the wild and remote seascapes, the Frenchness and laid back way of life that brings city people here to totally unwind.

Some of the Magdalens' excellent restaurants are owned by experts from Montreal and Quebec City who have chosen to escape those crowded cities. Artists and crafts people are attracted by the colours and natural materials available on these islands. Car, motorcycle and moped rentals are available at Cap-aux-Meules, the islands' capital. There is also a 24-hour taxi service. A few moderate-size hotels and inns are scattered across the islands, as are cottages, B & Bs and campgrounds. Since the islands' population can triple in summer advance reservations are essential. For a complete list of accommodation and campgrounds, write to Tourisme Quebec or the islands' own tourist authority.

Prince Edward Island to Baddeck, Nova Scotia, and the Cabot Trail (510km/320 miles, 2 days)

This drive will take you 210km (130 miles) from the ferry terminal at **Pictou**, NS, to Baddeck in the centre of Cape Breton Island. Follow the

Trans-Canada Highway (Hwy 106) to **New Glasgow** until the Trans-Canada becomes Hwy 104, then turn east. Because New Glasgow (population 10,000) is a local transportation centre, there is a number of motels close to the highway. More accommodation and a provincial tourism information centre are located at **Antigonish**. Along with many other place names in the area, Antigonish is derived from a Micmac Indian word, in this case meaning 'where branches are torn off'. Originally settled by soldiers in 1785, this was a centre for exporting lumber to Britain during the Napoleonic Wars. Its dominant culture remains Scottish to the extent that highland games are featured here each July. Buildings to the north of the highway house Francis Xavier University, founded in 1853 to educate Roman Catholic Highlanders.

The highway crosses Canso Causeway joining **Cape Breton Island** to the mainland. This island, probably sighted by John Cabot in 1497 and claimed for France by Jacques Cartier in 1534, was named Île Royale as part of New France until 1763 when it became part of British Nova Scotia. Some Acadians returned here after the deportations of 1755, and Loyalists arrived following the American Revolution, but most of the island's population is descended from the waves of Scottish immigrants who settled here in the early nineteenth century.

A tourist information centre on the island-side of the causeway will advise on Cape Breton's many attractions and on accommodation. Check your fuel gauge here, because it is some distance before the next service station near **Baddeck**. A pretty little town, once a ship-building centre but largely a vacation spot now, Baddeck is busy in summer as tourists fill its resorts and motels, shops, campgrounds, a marina and several good restaurants. Its harbour gives access to the Bras d'Or Lakes, a favourite yachting centre. Sailing cruises are available, trout fishing is excellent, and the supervised beach on Kitson Island is served by a free ferry.

At Baddeck the Alexander Graham Bell Historic Site commemorates the prolific life of the inventor of, among other things, the telephone. Bell summered in Baddeck for 37 years and his home, Beinn Bhreagh, has recently been opened to tourists. The museum contains working models, artifacts and audio-visual presentations describing Bell's amazing span of interests, which included agriculture, genetics, medical science, aeronautics and marine engineering. In Baddeck, he was involved in the first aircraft flight in the British Commonwealth, as well as some of the world's first hydrofoil craft experiments.

Set aside a full day for the **Cabot Trail**, a 300km (186 mile) circular tour of northern Cape Breton Island, because this is one of the most impressive drives in North America. For most of the drive the road follows the coastline, passing through farming country and fishing villages and at times skirting rugged headlands as it climbs the 500m (1,500ft) capes. Part of the route is through **Cape Breton Highlands National Park**, a wildly beautiful region reminiscent of the Scottish Highlands. The road is safe and well-maintained, but drivers may feel more secure close against the

Seal pups on the Magdalen Islands

Cycling in Nova Scotia

The Well-Dressed Scarecrows of the Cabot Trail

One of the curiosities on the Cabot Trail are the scarecrows at St Joseph du Moine. Here are close to a hundred — men, women and children, smartly dressed as if gathered for a scarecrow convention or Sunday lunch in the country. All are the handiwork of Joe Delaney, who a few years back planted potatoes and corn, only to have birds steal the lot. 'Better get some scarecrows, Joe,' his neighbours advised. He agreed. That night he made two, dressed as a man and woman, and had them facing the highway, arms raised with a Canadian flag in each hand. Instead of scaring birds they attracted tourists who stopped for photographs. Several suggested the pair should have children. Joe obliged.

Now motorists are so keen on the scarecrows that they send outfits and masks to encourage creation of new characters. Witches, celebrities, cyclists, wood cutters, playing children, babies in prams; they are all here with attendant props. Every one is different. Since they are clean and well clothed Joe was asked if he brings them in at night. He scratched his head in puzzlement and said no, it had never occured to him they might be stolen from their roadside stand — in any case folks are honest round here, and Joe went back to work on a new bridal party.

Some of the scarecrows on the Cabot Trail on northern Cape Breton Island

hillside walls. For this reason, it is best to follow the trail in a clockwise direction and campers are well advised to leave trailers in a campground.

5km (3 miles) south from Baddeck on Hwy 105 is a sign marking the trail. At **Margaree Harbour** on the island's west coast, this trail becomes a coast road, passing through Acadian fishing communities until it reaches the national park gates north of **Cheticamp**. A park information centre offers an introductory slide show, as well as advice on the whereabouts of good beaches, hiking trails and wilderness camping. (More information is available at various lookouts over the coastline and highlands.) Mountain bikes and windsurfing boards are available for hire. The bookstore has a wide selection of volumes about the island and rents out audio cassettes which describe the park as you drive. Campers will enjoy Cheticamp for the fishing and nature trails and wooded sites designed to accommodate everything from tents to RVs.

Neil Harbour on the east coast is a pretty fishing village beside a sandy bay where you can buy lobsters straight from the traps. Further down, **Black Brook Cove** has a superb beach and is the beginning of one of the most magnificent stretches of coast road. **Broad Cove** campground, 11km (7 miles) north of Ingonish on the Cabot Trail offers ocean and fresh-water swimming, along with the park's more sophisticated services suitable for RVs. In all, this park has six campgrounds. Advance reservations are not accepted, space being allocated on a first-come first-served basis. There are some private campgrounds nearby. Introductory programmes are featured in an information centre at the park entrance.

Ingonish, together with Ingonish Beach, Ingonish Centre and Ingonish Harbour, is a resort area providing hotel accommodation, campgrounds, tennis, swimming, and deep sea and freshwater fishing, as well as winter skiing. Keltic Lodge here is a justifiably famous Canadian resort and its scenic championship golf course is one of the finest in Atlantic Canada.

Continuing south there is more striking scenery as the trail switchbacks along the Gaelic Coast to **St Ann's**. This town's Gaelic College, the only one of its kind in North America, is devoted to the Gaelic language and law, Highland culture and crafts, bagpipe playing and highland dancing. Visitors are welcome. Gaelic Mod competitions, held in the first full week of August, bring entrants and spectators from several other countries. Baddeck, the starting point of this circular drive, is a further 24km (15 miles) along the trail.

Baddeck to Port aux Basques, Newfoundland (60km/37 miles, 1 day)

This journey, along the Trans-Canada Highway (Hwy 105) from Baddeck to the ferry terminal at North Sydney, retraces the Cabot Trail as far as South Gut St Ann's before passing through more memorable scenery to cross the Bras d'Or Lakes' northern ocean inlet. Visitors wanting to stay on the mainland can pick up the circular tour on its return from Newfoundland and continue to Louisbourg. If your itinerary includes Newfoundland and Labrador you should board the ferry at North Sydney. (There are also flights from the mainland to Corner Brook, Deer Lake, Gander and St John's and car rentals are available at these airports.)

The tour of Newfoundland will take about 11 days, from the ferry terminal at Port aux Basques, up the west side of Newfoundland to the northernmost point, and then across to Labrador. Returning south, it rejoins the Trans-Canada Highway and crosses the island to St John's, returning to mainland Nova Scotia via Argentia.

Ferry schedules between Nova Scotia and Port aux Basques, Newfoundland, are fairly complex since they depend on the time of the year and day of the week. During summer there are four sailings on Sundays (two of which are at night), one on Tuesdays and Fridays and two or three on the other days. In practice, there may be a shortage of vehicle spaces on the more desirable daytime sailings. Passengers should reserve as far in advance as possible and make their selections from the sailings available.

While the ferry boats have a limited number of cabins, their large reclining 'dayniter' seats are plentiful and quite comfortable even on the night sailings. The ships have cafeteria-style restaurants, bars, plenty of live 'down east' entertainment, free movies and Newfoundland and Nova Scotia tourist information offices.

Since the voyage to Newfoundland takes five hours reserve accommodation for the night in Port aux Basques, Corner Brook or Deer Lake, depending on your scheduled arrival time. Motels are listed for each of these communities. For campers, Cheeseman Provincial Park, near Port aux Basques, has facilities suitable for tents and RVs.

Port aux Basques to Gros Morne National Park (310km/193 miles, 1 day)

This drive is from **Port aux Basques**, along the Trans-Canada Highway, to Deer Lake and then north on the Viking Trail to Gros Morne National Park. Leaving Port aux Basques via the Trans-Canada Highway, call in at the tourist information centre just north of town for maps, brochures and advice on accommodation or island attractions.

The highway passes **Corner Brook** (population 25,000), Newfoundland's second largest city and site of one of the world's largest pulp and paper mills. It is situated on the Humber River, named by James Cook who was Newfoundland's marine surveyor before going on to global explorations. A great salmon river, it combines with terrific scenery to give sport fishermen every reason for staying a day or two.

A further 50km (30 miles) along the Trans-Canada Highway at **Deer Lake** turn north onto Hwy 430, the Viking Trail, and drive the 30km (19 miles) through deep forest to **Wiltondale**, for the south gate to **Gros Morne National Park**. Long Range Mountains in the park were sculpted by Ice Age glaciers, cutting out deep fjords (called ponds in Newfoundland) and valleys. Dominating the landscape is Gros Morne Mountain, a huge rock which emerged molten from between the earth's surface plates and then toppled over. Elsewhere are bogs and sand dunes and 72km (45 miles) of varied coastline. The result is some of the most dramatic scenery in eastern Canada, now within the boundaries of the 1,800 sq km (700 sq mile) national park. Because its features uniquely illustrate movements of the earth's crust, the park is also designated a UNESCO World Heritage site. Naturalists will be interested to know this is the point where three

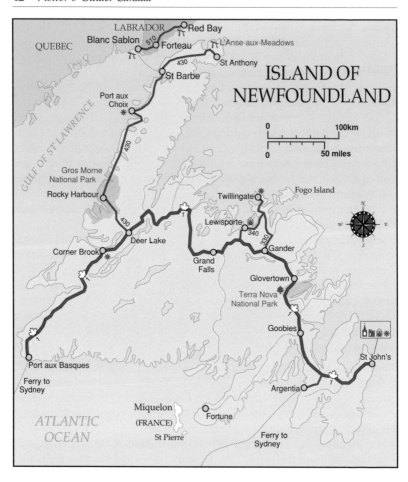

ecological zones meet: arctic alpine, boreal and temperate. More importantly, it is a wonderful place to hike, to fish for salmon and trout, and enjoy nature. The park has five campgrounds, two suitable for RVs.

An interpretive centre is located close to **Rocky Harbour**, a little fishing village with motel and cottage accommodation and a few other facilities. While in the park, be sure to visit **Lobster Cove Head** for the ocean views. Also try to allow time for the 4km (3 mile) hike into **Western Brook Pond**, for a memorable boat ride. Weather permitting, seal-watching cruises are available at **St Pauls** near the park's northern gate.

Gros Morne to St Anthony (370km/230 miles, 2days)

Leaving Gros Morne National Park continue on the Viking Trail (Rte 430) to L'Anse aux Meadows, through an area known locally as the French Coast for its numerous francophone fishing communities. On this stretch, the Long Range Mountains have moved inland so the vistas are less dramatic, but you are likely to see icebergs even in July and August. Soon they become commonplace: huge chunks broken off an Arctic glacier and melting into wondrous sculpted shapes, as they drift southwards like phantom ships into the warmer waters of the Gulf of St Lawrence.

A brief diversion to the interpretation centre at **Port aux Choix National**   ✳
Historic Park rewards with a presentation on the Archaic Amerindians who lived here approximately 5,000 years ago. The local economy depends on the shrimp fishery. Streams are rich in salmon, and trout pools yield record-size catches. When the road turns inland, it crosses a plain strewn with outcrops and glacial boulders to meet the coast at Pistolet Bay. At the junction with Rte 436, follow signs for about 30km (19 miles) to L'Anse aux Meadows.

The fishing village of **L'Anse aux Meadows** (from the French *méduses* meaning jellyfish) presents a picture postcard scene, but the main attraction is a national historic park on the site of the only authenticated Viking   ⺧
settlement in the New World. This is believed to have been Lief Ericson's colony following his landing with thirty-five men around 1,000AD. It became a base and winter camp from which they explored regions probably as far away as New Brunswick. The settlement had its own ship-repair facility, carpenter's shop, smithy and even the means to transform bog ore into iron. Ericson's brother, Thorvald was killed by natives, the *Skraelings* of the Sagas. And when a woman in Thorfinn Karlsefni's expedition gave birth here, her child was the first of European descent born in the New World.

The fishing harbour of L'Anse aux Meadows in Newfoundland

The Remarkable Dr Wilfred Grenfell

This extraordinary man is remembered in St Anthony, terminus of the Viking Trail and home base of the nineteenth-century pioneering doctor who left a comfortable home in England to practice medicine in Labrador and northern Newfoundland. By 1905 he had founded a hospital in St Anthony. Within a decade the International Grenfell Association operated four hospitals as well as six nursing stations along the Newfoundland/Labrador coast.

Travelling by dogsled to outlying areas, Grenfell was totally fearless. Now in his St Anthony home-cum-museum his heroics are stirringly recalled. One poignant story tells of the grief he experienced at having to kill some of his beloved dogs while stranded on an icepan. It happened when his sled, medical bag and even outer clothing were sucked into the freezing water, and he skinned three of the dogs to wrap himself in their furs. At night he formed a windbreak with the carcasses, pulling the remaining three dogs around him for added warmth. Next morning he awoke to the miracle of a small rowboat coming to his rescue.

Before he was through, Sir Wilfred started fishing co-operatives, schools and orphanages in these northern communities. His encouragement of local crafts spawned the manufacture of clothing from Grenfell cloth, produced to his specifications. Warm yet lightweight, it repels rain and snow, and is appreciated by explorers on major expeditions worldwide. You will find Grenfell cloth coats in stores throughout the Northern Peninsula, including one across from a statue of Dr Grenfell in St Anthony.

The park's replicated sod and stone houses and workshops give a fair idea of conditions a thousand years ago. An excellent interpretation centre contains archeological specimens; displays and audio-visual presentations explain how the Vikings may have lived in this settlement. In 1978, the park became the first entry in UNESCO's World Heritage list of cultural and natural sites.

In **St Anthony** Grenfell House is a museum commemorating the work of British-born Sir Wilfred Grenfell, a medical doctor who founded the Grenfell hospital missions to northern Newfoundland and Labrador. The museum illustrates not only Grenfell's work, but also the lives of the intrepid souls of the northern outports around the turn of this century. As the largest town in the area, St Anthony has suitable visitor accommodation. The area has a number of B & Bs, and the campground at Pistolet Provincial Park is suitable for RVs.

St Anthony to L'Anse au Clair, Labrador (140km/87 miles, 2 days)

This journey retraces the Viking Trail from St Anthony, 130km (80 miles) south to the Labrador Straits ferry terminal at **St Barbe**. A pleasant two-hour boat ride will take you past icebergs and whale sightings to **Blanc Sablon**, just inside the province of Quebec. The ferry service operates every day from May to December, with two and sometimes three sailings daily during July and August. Advance reservations are not accepted. Blanc Sablon is on Quebec time, 90 minutes behind Newfoundland.

From the ferry terminal drive along Rte 510 to **L'Anse au Clair**. This is a base for exploring the 80km (50 miles) of road along the Labrador Strait. The coastal terrain and fishing villages are similar to those on Newfoundland's Northern Peninsula. The main attraction is Red Bay, site of the world's whaling capital in the sixteenth century.

L'Anse au Clair, founded by the French in the early 1700s, is a fishing outport with some accommodation. **L'Anse au Loup**, **Capstan Island**, and **Forteau** are fishing communities whose ancestors came from Newfoundland in the nineteenth century to found permanent settlements. There is a campground in the provincial park with sites suitable for RVs beside the Pinware River, which is source of excellent salmon and trout fishing. **Red Bay** at the end of Rte 510 is the site of one of the earliest industrial complexes in the New World. Since 1976 archeologists have been uncovering remains of a Basque whaling station known to have operated here between about 1520 and 1585. In season its workforce of up to 1,000 men produced up to half a million gallons of enormously valuable whale oil. The shipwrecked galleon *San Juan*, found in Red Bay's harbour in near-perfect condition, was carefully examined before being returned to its watery grave. A modern visitor centre with audio-visual presentations, displays and artifacts is the base for conducted tours of the site.

L'Anse au Clair to Gander via Lewisporte and Twillingate (900km/560 miles, 3 days)

This flexible three-day itinerary allows for a late start on days when the first sailing of the return ferry from Labrador to Newfoundland is at mid-morning. From St Barbe's terminal retrace the Viking Trail 350km (217 miles) to **Deer Lake**, where you can overnight, or proceed another 210km (130 miles) along the Trans-Canada Highway to **Grand Falls**. Campers and RV travellers have a choice of Gros Morne National Park or a private campground at Birchy Lake, 80km (50 miles) east of Deer Lake on the Trans-Canada Highway.

Next day follow the Trans-Canada Highway east, but instead of continuing on to Gander, turn north to **Lewisporte** at Rte 340. This leisurely one-day, 170km (105 mile), diversion from the Trans-Canada Highway is for those interested in visiting more of the Newfoundland coast, its outports and particularly its particularly hospitable people.

Lewisporte is Marine Atlantic's terminal for services to communities in Northern Newfoundland and the Labrador coast, and also a centre for lobster fishing. Well worth a visit is the Museum Bye The Bay, (operated by the Women's Institute) for its wide range of local artifacts and photographs. The road continues over causeways linking one island to the next, past tiny villages of small clapboarded houses clinging to rocks beside bays and inlets. Wharves line the shore; fishing boats wait at anchor. You will encounter names like Birchy Bay, Chapel Island, Virgin Arm, Dildo Run, Herring Neck, Toogood Arm, and Hatchet Harbour, whose inhabitants are descendants of eighteenth-century migrants from England's West country. Some derive a living from farming and lumbering, but cod fishing has always been the mainstay. When the fishery was successful, this was the most prosperous part of Newfoundland. In consequence, wealthy merchants from Poole in England's Dorset built fine old houses in **Twillingate**. Here, in a former rectory a museum recalls the town's heyday when it was a major fishing and sealing port, had its own newspaper and even a cricket team.

If there is time continue to **Fogo Island** via Rte 335 from Boyd's Cove, then a ferry. First settled in the 1700s the community remained isolated until well into the twentieth century. Consequently locals have retained dialects and customs long forgotten in England. Fogo is probably derived from *fuego*, referring to the time when Portugese sailors saw the Beothuck Indians' campfires on the shore. The inlet called **Joe Batt's Arm** is named after a deserter from Captain James Cook's survey ship.

Route 330 takes you through lumber country back to **Gander**, on the Trans-Canada Highway. Because it is usually fog free, Gander was chosen by the British and Canadian governments in the 1930s as a Trans-Atlantic

Red Bay, Labrador

airways terminus. During World War II, it became one of the world's largest airports and a major air base. Until quite recently, many airlines used it as a refuelling stop. Now it is primarily a Canadian armed forces base and transportation and service centre for central Newfoundland.

Suitable hotel/motel accommodations and provincial parks with full service campgrounds are recommended for this brief itinerary. However, visitors who stay in outport B & Bs (listed by tourism authorities) will enjoy the bonus of meeting interesting locals, and learning more of the island's history and folklore first hand. If the Twillingate excursion appeals, then there are twenty similar scenic drives described in a free booklet available from tourism offices on various parts of the island.

Gander to Terra Nova National Park (80km/50 miles, 1 day)

It is only 80km (50 miles) from Gander to **Terra Nova National Park**, a 396 sq km (153 sq mile) preserve located on Bonavista Bay where the northern tip of the Appalachian Mountain chain was shaped by glacial activity. The park's geography is dominated by Newman Sound and Clode Sound, two very picturesque inlets. Lumbering and fishing began here in the late 1700s and today's explorers will come across the remains of communities

St John's harbour, Newfoundland

abandoned long ago. Information centres at **Newman Sound** and the south entrance tell visitors of the park's natural features, history and wildlife. Recreational facilities include swimming, boating, scuba diving, hiking and fishing. Twin Rivers has a challenging and scenic 9-hole golf course. At Newman Sound, professionally conducted boat tours include whale and bird watching, as well as a bit of cod jigging.

With only a group of cottages in the park and one small but pleasant motel close to the north entrance, travellers may choose to stay in Gander during their park visit. Newman Sound campground, 24km (15 miles) south of **Glovertown** on the Trans-Canada Highway, is suitable for RVs. Its facilities include a general store, restaurant, bike, boat and canoe rentals. Malady Head Campground at the north end of the park has a beach and nature trails. It caters for RVs and also has four primitive campgrounds.

Terra Nova National Park to St John's and Argentia (390km/242 miles, 3 days)

The 260km (162 mile) drive from Terra Nova National Park to St John's takes you past the small community of **Goobies** and the junction of Rte 210, which leads to the Burin Peninsula for a pleasant one-day circular excursion. **Fortune** near the end of the peninsula, is the ferry terminal for the French islands of **St-Pierre** and **Miquelon**. (These islands are also served by air from St John's, as well as Halifax and Sydney NS.)

St John's (population 82,000), the capital city of Newfoundland and Labrador, is an absolute gem. Modern convention spells the city's name this way to differentiate it from Saint John in New Brunswick. The name derives from John Cabot's arrival here on 14 June 1497, the feast day of St John the Baptist.

The harbour was already well known to European fishermen when Sir Humphrey Gilbert claimed the colony for England in 1583. For centuries, England and France warred for supremacy over Newfoundland. Final victory went to England in 1762 when St John's was recaptured after a brief French occupation. In 1823, it became the seat of government at the time Newfoundland received its first legislature.

By the 1870s, small manufacturing industries had been established, and by the turn of the century the city had become terminus for the now defunct trans-island railway which followed the same route as the present Trans-Canada Highway. St John's has been the site of many firsts. The first trans-Atlantic radio signal was received here from Britain in 1901. In 1919, pilots Alcock and Brown set off from St John's on the first successful non-stop trans-Atlantic flight.

The fisheries have sustained St John's throughout the centuries, and as they declined after World War I so did the city. World War II brought a return of the British Navy after 150 years, then came American bases and a construction boom. Confederation in 1949 resulted in welcome infusion of Canadian government funds. Close proximity to petroleum discover-

Newfoundland Cod

The first industry started by Europeans in Canada was cod fishing, when fifteenth-century fishermen came to work the Grand Banks. Now, with a two-year ban on commercial fishing of cod to replenish diminishing stocks, this way of life familiar to so many generations of Newfoundlanders is at a temporary halt.

Even so, cod continues to dominate the diet here on The Rock. Visitors are offered it in pies and stews, baked and broiled, and more often fried. Cod tongues, sliced and fried are as succulent as any scallop. Wash them down with screech (a local brew originating from dregs of rum casks drunk by sailors in the absence of anything better) and you will feel right at home.

If you are invited for a bit of cod jigging, you are not being asked to dance for your supper. It is a form of fishing with a line on a spool. Jerked like a puppet, it supposedly attracts the cod to a shiny 'jigger' at the end of the string. Expectations of a catch should not be high though. You may have to settle for an enjoyable boat ride, and salty chit-chat from your skipper.

ies on the Grand Banks has meant additional prosperity, but exploration is slowing in the face of rising costs and decreasing demand. With the virtual disappearance of cod stocks, the governments of Canada and Newfoundland are searching for new ways of stimulating the economy.

St John's long colourful history is recalled in the Newfoundland Museum with branches on Duckworth Street and the Murray Premises on Water Street. This has been the city's main commercial thoroughfare since the sixteenth century, and it is the oldest of its kind in North America. Preserved nineteenth-century buildings in the historic district attest to the past influence of merchants of English, Scottish and Irish ancestry. These days they represent more than history as many now house inviting shops, good restaurants and night spots featuring everything from jazz and rock to traditional Newfoundland folksongs.

In this area, noteworthy nineteenth-century buildings include the Georgian-style Commissariat House on King's Bridge Road, built to serve the garrison's Assistant Commissary General and now restored to period. The Colonial Building on Military Road was the first seat of the colonial government and then the province's legislature until it moved to the new Confederation Building overlooking the city. Also on Military Road is the Roman Catholic Basilica Cathedral of St John the Baptist, its twin towers visible all over the city. The Anglican Cathedral of St John the Baptist on Church Hill at Gower Street is now a National Historic Site, and possibly the finest example of ecclesiastical gothic architecture on the continent.

On the waterfront's Harbour Drive is an old trans-island railway passenger coach, now serving as a tourist information centre. Facing the harbour entrance, a park marks the spot where Sir Humphrey Gilbert came ashore to claim the land for England, and in doing so, founded the British Empire.

✳ Turning north to Duckworth Street and continuing east, you will come to Signal Hill Road. Signal Hill, overlooking the narrow harbour approach, gives superb views of the city, its harbour and the coastline. As a national historic park it commemorates a number of events. For one, in 1762 this was site of the last battle in North America between England and France. The Cabot Tower here commemorates Queen Victoria's Diamond Jubilee and the 400th anniversary of John Cabot's voyage to Newfoundland. In a small hospital close to the tower, in 1901 Guglielmo Marconi received the first radio signal from Poldhu in Cornwall. Then if you can be here at 3pm or 7pm on a Wednesday, Thursday, Saturday or Sunday between mid-July and late August you can witness the Signal Hill Tattoo, a re-enactment of military exercises performed in the ninetenth century by the Newfoundland Regiment.

✳ Close by Quidi Vidi Village has some of the oldest and most colourful houses on the continent. Also a restoration of the battery constructed by the French during their occupation in 1762, rebuilt and manned by the British until they withdrew from Newfoundland in 1870. Quidi Vidi Lake is the site of the St John's Regatta, which takes place on the first Wednesday in August. Held every year since 1826, it is considered to be North America's oldest sporting event.

Yet another national historic park is Cape Spear, reached from downtown St John's via Rte 11. It is site of Newfoundland's oldest lighthouse, situated on the most easterly point in North America. Parts of a gun ✳ battery built on the cape during World War II for the defence of St John's harbour are still in place.

St John's has direct air connections with a number of other Canadian cities and with London, England. The city has plenty of hotels and motels. Most prestigious is Canadian Pacific's Hotel Newfoundland, but there are also representatives of other chains and some independent hotels. Staff at the tourist information centre can suggest some first-rate B & Bs. The C. A. Pippy Park, a large municipal recreation area close to the city, has a full-service campground.

To avoid retracing the 905km (562 miles) of Trans-Canada Highway to Port aux Basques, a return to the mainland via Marine Atlantic's Argentia to North Sydney service is recommended. Sailings are at 9am on Wednesdays and Saturdays between early June and late October. In the opposite direction ferries operate on Tuesdays and Fridays, usually departing at 7am. The crossing takes between 12 and 14 hours. Advance reservations are essential and the sailing time should be confirmed the previous evening.

St John's to **Argentia** is 131km (81 miles) via the Trans-Canada Highway to Rte 100. As the ferry sails into Placentia Bay, it passes the point where British Prime Minister Winston Churchill and American President Roosevelt met aboard ship in 1941 to sign the Atlantic Charter.

North Sydney to Louisbourg and return (70km/43 miles, 1 day)

It will take the greater part of a day to do justice to Fortress Louisbourg, so those arriving in the evening from Newfoundland may choose to stay for two nights in the **Sydney** area, where there is ample visitor accommodation.

When the colony of Cape Breton Island was founded as a refuge for Loyalists escaping the American Revolution in 1784, Sydney was chosen as its capital. By the time the colony was rejoined to Nova Scotia after four turbulent decades, Sydney had only a few hundred inhabitants. Later, the demand for coal brought regional development. (These, the richest coalfields in eastern Canada, were first mined by soldiers from Louisbourg.) Discovery of iron ore in Newfoundland led to the building of a steel mill in 1899. Now, with that aging plant proving inefficient and demand for coal less predictable, this part of Cape Breton Island is economically

Costumed actors playing the part of French and Swiss soldiers at the restored Fortress Louisbourg

depressed. Still, with a population of 30,000, Sydney remains its principal city.

The Miners Museum in nearby **Glace Bay** features conducted tours of the Ocean Deeps Colliery. Feisty old miners conduct the tours, telling of child labour and hard work under appalling conditions. They recall relatives and friends who died here below the sea — bringing to mind a 1992 disaster at the province's Westray Mine where twenty-six men lost their lives. At Table Head on the outskirts of town, the Marconi National Historic Site commemorates the first west-to-east radio message with a scale model of the 1902 installation.

The modern town of **Louisbourg** is 34km (21 miles) from Sydney via Hwy 22. Established in 1713 because of its ice-free harbour and proximity to prolific fisheries, it was soon the site of an important French military base, now reconstructed in the national historic park. Fishing has remained a prime industry and coal mining in the area caused it to become a busy port. Today, tourism based on Fortress Louisbourg 3km (2 miles) away, is big business.

The fortress at Louisbourg has been a national historic site since 1928, but it was not until 1961 that Parks Canada began partial reconstruction based on extensive archeological research in France. As a result, roughly 20 percent of the eighteenth-century seaport and fortress, including many buildings and most of its fortifications, have been reconstructed. In the reception centre visitor introduction is by way of displays and films on Louisbourg past and present. From there a bus takes you to the townsite where a lot of walking is involved, and the sea-side site can be cool, so it is wise to dress appropriately.

Now one of Canada's finest living museums, Louisbourg was built following the Treaty of Utrecht (1713) which stripped France of her Newfoundland and Acadian colonies but permitted her to keep what is now part of Quebec, Cape Breton Island and Prince Edward Island. The French selected English Harbour, renamed Louisbourg, as the site of a stronghold to guard the Gulf of St Lawrence. It became a terribly expensive undertaking with a fortress designed by Vauban, the famous military engineer. There were naval facilities and workshops, a four-storey governor's residence, and a garrison of 1,400 troops. Within the thick, 3km-long (2 mile) walls, grew a substantial sea-port town which soon overflowed outside their limits. Cod-fish supplied the wealth, and by the 1740s Louisbourg had become a major port on the sea lanes between France, Canada, New England and the West Indies. In North America, its commerce was exceeded only by Boston and Philadelphia.

In 1745, Louisbourg was captured by the British navy and land forces from New England, but was restored to France by a peace treaty. After Britain recaptured it in 1758, the population was exiled to France and the fortifications were demolished.

The restored Fortress of Louisbourg is now populated by appropriately costumed bilingual animators acting the parts of known inhabitants in the year 1744, when the seaport fortress was at the height of its fortunes. There are governor, administrators, military officers and wealthy merchants, as well as innkeepers and their wives, fishermen, soldiers, maid-servants and many children playing games of the time. Stop and talk to them, for they love to tell you about day-to-day living in the fortress. (The actors' use of English is one of the few departures from authenticity permitted here.) There are conducted walking tours, while some buildings contain exhibits and video presentations. The restored taverns serve authentic French eighteenth-century meals at reasonable, but not period, prices.

Sydney to Halifax (440km/273 miles, 2 days)

The direct 440km (273 mile) route to Halifax retraces one already travelled until you reach New Glasgow, so you may opt for the slightly longer Rte 4 down the east side of the Bras-d'Or Lakes to the Canso Causeway. The most interesting community on this route is **St Peters**, initially called San Pedro by sixteenth-century Portugese fishermen, later St Pierre and finally Port Toulouse by the French at the time it supplied Louisbourg with wood. Loyalists who arrived in the 1780s gave St Peters its present name. The canal, dug initially in 1854 to connect interior lakes with the ocean, is now used largely by pleasure craft. The provincial park is a pleasant picnic spot and the Nicholas Denys museum celebrates life and times of the man who built the French outpost here in 1650.

From the causeway follow the Trans-Canada Highway to **Truro**, then Hwy 102 to Halifax. Truro was called Cobequid when it was a thriving Acadian community. After the Acadians' expulsion in 1755 they were replaced by immigrants from New England and the British Isles and it is now a prosperous farming centre with an agricultural college.

Halifax (population 115,000) was established in 1749 to counter the threat posed by France's Louisbourg and to exploit the fisheries off Nova Scotia's coast. Its citadel was constructed on a hill overlooking Chebucto Bay and 2,500 English settlers came to found Nova Scotia's new capital. A year later, the twin city of Dartmouth (population now of 63,000) was settled across the river. The ferry service between them (particularly enjoyable for the waterfront views) started two years later.

After 1763 when Britain attained supremacy over Canada, Halifax became the Atlantic headquarters for the army and navy. It also grew into a busy commercial centre, from which local shipowners sent their vessels all over the world. Halifax harbour was the gathering point for trans-Atlantic convoys during both World Wars. In December 1917, it was scene of a great disaster when a munitions ship exploded, killing 1,600 people and injuring 9,000 more.

Halifax is a small city, easily toured on foot with the help of a map from the tourism office. This you will find in Historic Properties, a national historic site consisting of eighteenth- and nineteenth-century harbourfont buildings. Once a place where pirates and privateers hid their loot, the cobbled streets are now busy with summer visitors to its bright little shops

and restaurants. This is where you can board Nova Scotia's famous
schooner *Bluenose II*, for a harbour cruise when she is in port. If she is away
from home, other boats do similar harbour tours.

Close by, the Maritime Museum of the Atlantic explains the region's
maritime history. The 1917 harbour explosion is only one of the disasters
recalled here. In an exhibit on the SS *Titanic* you will learn that the city sent
rescue parties to the sinking ship and some of the victims were buried
locally. Of Halifax's maritime personalities remembered, Enos Collins
(considered the wealthiest man in British North America in his time)
owned many of the waterfront buildings. His partner Samuel Cunard,
born here in 1789, started a fortnightly sailing to Liverpool with his
steamer *Britannia* and went on to create one of the world's largest shipping
companies.

The sailing schooner Bluenose II *in Halifax harbour, Nova Scotia*

The museum's upper level gives a good view of the harbour. Outside, two vintage ships may be boarded: the pioneer hydrographic ship *Acadia*, and the World War II corvette HMCS *Sackville* restored to her 1944 specifications.

Province House, between Hollis and Granville Streets to the north is recognized as one of the finest examples of Georgian architecture in North America. It has continued in use as seat of the provincial legislature since 1819 and is the oldest building of its kind in Canada. Guided tours are available daily in summer.

Two blocks north of Province House, Grand Parade has been the town square since the beginning. On one side is the City Hall and opposite it St Paul's Anglican Church, built in 1750 and now Canada's oldest Protestant church. Across from this church, the building housing the Five Fishermen Restaurant used to be an art school whose director was Anna Leonowens — also known as Anna of *Anna and the King of Siam*.

A walk up George Street brings you to the town clock, erected on the hill as a gift to the city by Prince Edward, the compulsively punctual son of King George III who was stationed here for six years from 1794. Beyond that is the Halifax Citadel National Park. The present star-shaped citadel dating from 1828 is the fourth built here since the original of 1749. A 50-minute multi-media presentation *Tides of History* is so stirring, it alone makes the visit worth-while. There are also guided tours and a series of exhibits tracing the fortress' evolution. The daily noon gun is a century-old tradition which reminds citizens of the citadel's purpose. In summer nineteenth-century military drills are performed by university students portraying 78th Highlanders and Royal Artillery gunners. In the canteen refreshments served to soldiers of the period are available.

Halifax is probably the best shopping centre on the Atlantic Provinces tour. In addition to several malls, the Historic Properties area has speciality and quality souvenir stores. Over in Spring Garden Road between St Mary's Basilica (at Barrington St) and the Public Gardens are the city's trendiest shops and restaurants. Try to finish up at the gardens. A haven for weary tourists, they include 6.5 ha (16 acres) of Victorian-style flower-beds and parklands, ponds, overfed ducks, a bandstand and velvety lawns to cushion tired feet.

Dartmouth, reached by two suspension bridges as well as the ferry, has organized walking tours. The Dartmouth Heritage Museum and the prefabricated Quaker whaler's house of 1785 are particularly interesting. About 7km (5 miles) outside town, the Black Cultural Centre contains exhibits on Nova Scotia's black population whose roots predate the ar- rival of the first black Loyalists.

Halifax's numerous hotels and motels include representatives of North America's major chains, plus some regionals and independents. The Chateau Halifax provides predictably good Canadian Pacific service, the Sheraton has memorable harbour views. This city has comfortable small inns and B & Bs, a university residence and a hostel. At Laurie Provincial

Via Rail

Although you cannot ride the rails from Newfoundland to British Columbia in one journey any more, there are services between Halifax, Quebec City, Montreal and Toronto — with stops in between. One of the world's great train adventures is Toronto to Vancouver, which takes three and a half days if you stay in the same train all the way.

Many travellers do this trip in one or two weeks, disembarking for several days at a time to enjoy the old railway hotels and resorts — as did adventurous vacationers at the turn of the century. The journey ventures into northern wildernesses not accessible by road, across great plains once filled with buffalo herds, through picture-postcard scenes of snow-capped mountains reflected in turquoise lakes, and finally farmlands leading to the coast.

Sleeping accommodation comes in various styles: double bedrooms with toilet and sink en suite, roomettes similarly equipped for singles, 'sections' which are bunk beds designed to convert to seats by day, and reclining daynighter seats. Meals on board are good, and the house-keeping efficient.

Since railway stations are usually located downtown, train travel is convenient whether you are on the three-hour run between Montreal and Quebec City, or settling in for a long-distance adventure. Sleeper reservations should be made well in advance of summer travel, especially on the ever popular Jasper to Vancouver section. Travel agents in Canada and abroad have details for independent travel as well as tour packages.

Park, 24km (15 miles) north of Dartmouth the campground has RV facilities.

Halifax/Dartmouth has direct airline connections with St John's, Quebec, Montreal and Toronto and cities beyond, as well as with London, England, and Amsterdam. Via Rail connects Halifax with Moncton, Saint John and Montreal and with US Amtrak services.

• *Excursion from Halifax (300km/185 miles, 2 days)*
In the interests of conserving time, this excursion is not included in the main itinerary, although it takes in several winsome seaside villages south of Halifax.

Head west from Halifax via Hwy 103 and turn off almost immediately at exit 2, then follow Rte 333 through several picturesque villages to **Peggy's Cove**. This hamlet of wooden cottages clinging to huge smooth rocks, brightly painted fishing boats and a well-placed lighthouse is the darling of Canada's landscape artists and calendar photographers. Regrettably, its fame has resulted in more summer visitors than it can comfortably handle.

Follow Rte 333 along the coast through more fishing communities to

Oak Island's Buried Treasure

Oak Island is a secretive place that refuses to give up the treasure thought to have been buried here this past 400 years. Island searches date back to 1796 when three young men found an old ship's block hanging from an oak tree that had apparently been used as a derrick. Beneath it was a depression in the soil, so naturally they began digging. Every 10ft to a depth of 90ft they found plank flooring, until at 96ft water rushed in and flooded the pit. Since that time more than a dozen expeditions have sought to overcome this water hazard. By now there are so many shafts nobody is sure which was the original.

Nothing of great value has been found in the so-called Money Pit, but scientific analysts confirm that bits and pieces brought up from it date to the sixteenth century. The mystery deepened in 1803 when a stone was unearthed at the 90ft level, with markings which translated to read: 'Forty feet below two million pounds are buried'. Experts estimate that using sixteenth-century tools the pit's rock-walled tunnels leading from the shore into the shaft, plus wooden platforms serving as hydraulic seals, would have taken approximately one hundred thousand man-hours to install. It is a real conundrum. Someone went to a lot of trouble to bury something, then secure it with a system to defy even modern technology. Why then would they be sloppy enough to leave above-ground evidence which could so easily have been removed? But perhaps they have the last laugh after all, as at several dollars a head for the island tour and with constant summer traffic, maybe the Money Pit deserves its name after all!

return to Hwy 103 and continue west to exit 8 which leads to **Chester**, located at the head of Mahone Bay with its 365 islands. A lovely little town, Chester was first settled by New England Loyalists in 1760 and now many of the historic wooden houses reflect this heritage. Regarded as one of the most scenic resorts in the country it has a golf course, summer theatre and bandstand concerts and is also a popular yachting centre. Small inns and restaurants, in town and in neighbouring communities, are welcoming.

Following Rte 3 as it turns south along the coast, you will see signs for a causeway to **Oak Island**, a private property thought to contain treasure ✳ possibly buried by Blackbeard, Captain Kidd or Henry Morgan.

Mahone Bay, the village at the head of the bay of that name, recalls the long, low pirate boats known as *mahonnes* which used to frequent the area. Founded by English, French and Swiss settlers in the mid-eighteenth century, this was once an important shipbuilding centre. Now it is a quiet little vacation and retirement village, known for its beautiful bay and the three churches grouped together in the centre.

Lunenburg (population 3,000), was originally founded by Acadians, but the British government brought in 1,500 'Foreign Protestant' settlers — German, Swiss and French Huguenot — in 1753 to counter the French

Roman Catholic presence in Nova Scotia. Even now the town's historic buildings, best seen by following the tourist bureau's walking tour, reflect a strong European influence. During the nineteenth century Lunenburg became Nova Scotia's major fishing centre, while its shipyards produced vessels to sail the world. Fishing and ship-building remain substantial industries. The schooner *Bluenose* featured on the Canadian dime was built here, as was *Bluenose II* and the replica of HMS *Bounty* used in the most recent film of the mutiny. No trip to Lunenburg would be complete without a visit to the Fisheries Museum of the Atlantic, and to the trawler *Cape Sable* and fishing schooner *Theresa E. Conner* moored at the museum wharf. A restaurant in the museum, serves super fresh seafood. **Blue Rocks**, 8km (5 miles) east of town on Rte 3 is a photogenic fishing village

Chester's attractive wooden houses reflect its New England heritage

that rivals Peggy's Cove for its beauty and is far less crowded. Campers have the best view in town from their sites (suitable for RVs) beside Lunenburg's tourist bureau which is located in the lighthouse on Blockhouse Hill. Two of the town's small inns are listed in the Additional Information. Restaurants feature seafood as well as regional German dishes. There is a dinner theatre, and lots of opportunities for golf, tennis and fishing. Lunenburg Folk Harbour Festival, held in early August, features folk music as well as competitions involving fish filleting, scallop shucking, dory racing and other traditional skills.

To return to Halifax, take Rte 324 north to Hwy 103 and turn east.

Halifax to Digby (240km/149 miles, 1 day)

This drive goes to Digby, with an overnight stay here for the ferry sailing to Saint John, NB, at 1pm. Unless you decide on the 5am sailing, there will be time to visit Yarmouth before boarding. If you dislike ferry crossings, return from Digby by driving 515km (320 miles) to Fundy National Park via **Amhurst** NS and rejoin the itinerary from there.

This route follows the Evangeline Trail, past historic sites that take you back to some of the early beginnings of present-day Canada. The French settled Port Royal on the Fundy shore in 1604. Their descendants became the Acadians who enclosed the shore-line, capturing rich marine sediment to build lush fields and meadows. When they were expelled, New England planters and British soldiers and settlers took over their properties, cleared more land and planted the orchards we see today.

Leave Halifax on Hwy 101 and after 65km (40 miles) is **Windsor** where the St Croix and Avon Rivers meet. Until the 1755 Deportations this was the large Acadian settlement of Pisiquid. At Fort Edward Blockhouse, now a museum, final arrangements were made for the Deportations. The oldest such structure in Canada, it remained in continuous use until after the War of 1812. Haliburton House, another museum, was home of Judge Thomas Chandler Haliburton; lawyer, politician, writer and finally British MP. His humourous and perceptive work *The Clockmaker*, along with others written around the character of Yankee salesman Sam Slick, tell much about Nova Scotia society in the first few decades of the nineteenth century.

Continuing along Hwy 101 for 30km (18 miles) you arrive at **Grand Pré**, a national historic site, once an Acadian village used by Henry Wadsworth Longfellow as setting for his narrative poem *Evangeline — a Tale of Acadie*. The poem describes a couple's separation during the Deportations and Evangeline's search throughout New England for her lover, only to find him at last close to death.

Evangeline is a fictional character, but as the church-museum's exhibits show, the story is based on historical fact. The peaceful French-speaking Roman Catholic Acadians, including some 2,200 in Grand Pré, were seen as a threat when they refused to swear allegiance to the British crown. And so, in 1755, they were literally taken from their homes and farms and deported in small groups to other British colonies and to parts of New France as far away as Louisiana (where their descendants became today's Cajuns). Many returned and founded new Acadian settlements in various parts of Atlantic Canada.

Another 115km (70 miles) on Hwy 101 brings you to **Annapolis Royal**, at one time focus of the English-French struggle for control of Acadia. The Annapolis Basin was discovered in 1604 by explorer Samuel de Champlain and Sieur de Monts, leader of a group of French settlers. The whole basin was called Port Royal, in honour of the French king. Blessed with a temperate climate and fertile soil, the area was developed immediately to become one of the first European settlements in the New World. Residents grew the first grain in North America, built the first mill and made the first converts to Christianity.

Port Royal National Historic Park, 8km (5 miles) west of Annapolis Royal, is a reconstruction of the first *Habitation*. Sited on the original foundation and constructed from the local materials that would have been used, the design is based upon original drawings and descriptions. With steep Norman roofs, tall chimneys, tiny windows and narrow entrance, it was as much fort as residence, but there was also time for relaxation. Here Champlain founded North America's first social club known as '*L'Ordre de Bon Temps*' and *Le Théâtre de Neptune* was the first theatrical presentation. Now that era is replicated by costumed guides, exhibits and a series of audio-visual presentations.

Raiders from the British colony of Virginia destroyed the *Habitation* in 1613 and built a fort at present-day Annapolis Royal in 1628. This site changed hands with the French often before being finally taken by the British and renamed Annapolis in honour of Queen Anne. It was capital of Nova Scotia until Halifax was founded and over time acquired the name Annapolis Royal. Fort Anne National Historic Park encloses the remains of the fortress. The officers' quarters have been restored to house a museum which chronicles Annapolis Royal's turbulent history.

While here visit the Annapolis Royal Historic Gardens, showing the evolution of gardens from the Acadian era, or the Annapolis Tidal Generating Station which harnesses the enormous Fundy tides to generate electricity.

It is 30km (19 miles) from Annapolis Royal to **Digby**. Named after the British admiral who conveyed Loyalists here in 1783, Digby became a centre for exporting lumber and fish products and now has one of the world's largest scallop fleets. There is ample overnight accommodation, including the well-known Pines Resort Hotel. Smith's Cove, a vacation centre close to the east side of town, has campgrounds with RV services.

As suggested earlier, you may like to continue on the Evangeline Trail to its finish at **Yarmouth**. Yarmouth was an Acadian community before being settled by New Englanders, later joined by Loyalist refugees from the American Revolution. In the nineteenth century it became one of Nova Scotia's major ship-building and ship-owning centres, second only to

Halifax in importance. The port is terminus of ferry services to Bar Harbor and Portland, both in Maine, USA.

Digby, NS, to Fundy National Park (140km/87 miles, 2 days)

This part of the tour provides a change of pace with overnight stops in one of eastern Canada's most popular national parks. Driving from the ferry terminal and through Saint John (which will be returned to shortly), join Rte 1 and drive east through **Sussex** to the junction with Rte 114.

Follow the signs to **Fundy National Park**, and continue to the eastern entrance where most of the facilities are located. **Alma**, just beyond this gate, once shipped lumber to Europe. Now it is a nice little village with some accommodation, stores and restaurants. The park has a motel and a large youth hostel, as well as self-catering chalets and six campgrounds — some suitable for RVs. Outstanding park facilities include beaches, a heated saltwater swimming pool, golf, tennis and lawn bowling.

The park's interpretation centre contains exhibits which explain the area's ecology and history. Lectures, films and slide shows, along with regional entertainment, are presented nightly in the natural amphitheatre. The 206sq km (80sq mile) park incorporates 13km (8 miles) of rugged coastline. The Bay of Fundy tides with a reach of up to 13m (43ft) provide great opportunities for beach-combing so long as you watch out for the incoming tide. Herring Cove, at the end of the park road, is a favourite for its views from the cliff top and for tidal pools teeming with life down below. Point Wolfe once had a thriving lumber mill. Now, its picturesque covered bridge and dam are good vantage points for watching beaver residents at work.

Inland the park's vistas change from one area to the next, with woodlands, meadows, lakes and abundant wildlife. Boating and trout fishing are popular. Naturalists conduct interesting walks, and there are also self-guided hiking trails of various lengths.

Fundy National Park to Fredericton (180km/112 miles, 1 day)

Leaving the park westwards along Rte 114, return to the Trans-Canada Highway (Rte 2) and turn west. There is now a 140km (87 mile) highway drive to Fredericton via **Sussex**, an important dairy-farming centre, and then along the lovely Saint John Valley.

Fredericton (population 44,700), New Brunswick's capital, is a very likable little city with tree-shaded streets, university and government buildings on the banks of the Saint John River. Natives and Acadians had settled the area in earlier times, but present-day Fredericton has its roots in Frederick's Town founded in 1783 as a 'haven for the King's friends' — namely Loyalists fleeing the aftermath of the American Revolution. These new arrivals soon demanded their own government, and in 1784 New Brunswick became a separate province incorporating much of mainland Nova Scotia. Fredericton was chosen in preference to Saint John for the capital because its position was safe from naval attack. It was designated as the British military headquarters and centre for education and culture. Christ Church Cathedral, consecrated in 1853, was the first cathedral built on British soil since the Norman conquest.

The British garrison left following Canada's Confederation and the arrival of Irish and Presbyterian immigrants altered the city's British and New England characteristics. Lumbering and agriculture brought a prosperity which is still evident in the large homes of 'lumber barons'. Some have been converted to comfortable B & B lodgings.

Best way to see this compact city is on foot, starting at the City Hall on Queen Street where you can pick up a car sticker for free parking. Built in 1876, it began as a community centre, combining city offices, magistrate's

Fundy National Park, New Brunswick

office and city jail, with an opera house on the second floor. Fully restored now, it still functions as city hall. A series of wall tapestries presents the city's history while a portrait of Prince Frederick, King George III's second son, reminds us after whom the city was named. Military past is represented by the Guard House on Carleton and Officers' Square on Queen Street. With band concerts and military displays in summer, its former officers' quarters house the York-Sunbury Historical Society Museum. This has exhibits reflecting local history, but perhaps the favourite item is a bullfrog that weighed something like 7lb (3.2kg) when adopted by a local fisherman, and was a whopping 42lb (19kg) when it finally died.

Along from the square is The Playhouse theatre and, diagonally opposite, the Beaverbrook Art Gallery. Both were donated by Lord Beaverbrook, who was born William Maxwell Aitken in Ontario but grew up to be a successful businessman in New Brunswick before moving to Britain. There he became a powerful newspaper proprietor and politician, and was raised to the peerage. The art gallery, sited in a pretty riverside park known as The Green, houses a world-renowned collection of paintings,

City Hall at Fredericton, the capital of New Brunswick

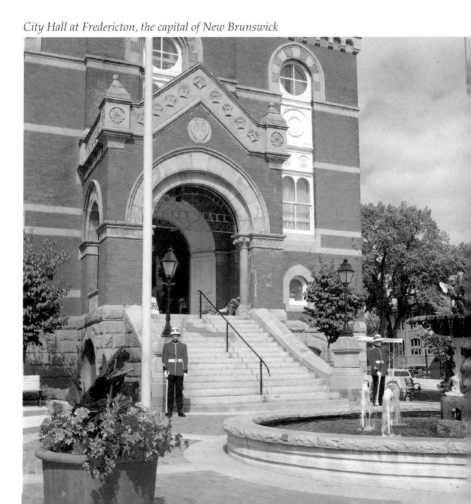

tapestries, furniture and sculpture. Of particular interest to overseas visitors is the large Cornelius Krieghoff collection which presents a colourful dimension to ninetenth-century Canadian history.

Opposite the art gallery, the Legislative Assembly Building was constructed in 1882, to replace the former Provincial Hall destroyed two years earlier. Its library contains a complete collection of Audubon's bird paintings and a 1783 copy of the *Domesday Book*. Joshua Reynolds' portraits of King George III and Queen Charlotte hang in the assembly chamber. Guided tours are available. Nearby on Church St, Christ Church Cathedral mentioned above is reputed to be one of the finest examples of decorated Gothic architecture on this continent. The nave is a replica of another in Norfolk, England. From the cathedral, University Avenue leads up the hill to the University of New Brunswick campus. The oldest provincial university in Canada, it was founded in 1785.

Try to allow half a day for **Kings Landing Historical Settlement**, a reconstruction of a typical early nineteenth-century Saint John River Valley village, 37km (23 miles) west of the city via the Trans-Canada Highway (Rte 2). In its reception centre, a wide variety of exhibits describe the role of Loyalists in area history. The peaceful riverside site has operating farms and gardens, grist and lumber mills as well as a store, forge, church and school. Costumed guides and attendants include local children who spend a week at a time here playing the roles of their pioneer counterparts. Kings Landing holds numerous fairs and festivals during the season, with many special childrens' events. Period meals are served in the King's Head Inn and there is also a cafeteria and snack bar.

As expected of a government centre and university city, Fredericton has good restaurants, hotels and motels, and excellent B & Bs. For campers, a commercial site is listed in the Additional Information as well as Mactaquac Provincial Park, located between the city and Kings Landing.

Fredericton to Saint John (100km/62 miles, 1 day)

The drive from Fredericton to Saint John via Rte 7 takes little more than an hour, but the longer Rte 102 along the Saint John River is more memorable. On this road **Oromocto**, a town with European roots as far back as the seventeenth century has been a military post since 1776. In the 1950s, when Canadian Forces established the nearby Gagetown base as the largest land training area in the British Commonwealth, the town's expansion followed a carefully detailed plan. The result has earned it the title 'Canada's Model Town'.

Saint John (population 77,000 and so spelled to differentiate it from St John's, Newfoundland) is New Brunswick's largest city. Samuel de Champlain who landed here in 1604 gave the river its name. The French settlement founded 30 years later was ceded to Britain following the Treaty of Utrecht in 1713, and the Acadian population was gradually replaced by colonists from New England. When 3,000 Loyalist settlers arrived on 18 May 1783, they literally founded the city overnight. In 1785 it became Canada's first incorporated city, the only one to be constituted by a Royal Charter.

Saint John quickly flourished in trade, manufacturing and shipbuilding to become a major centre for immigration, particularly from Ireland. The Great Fire of 1877 destroyed most of the city. This tragedy coincided with a decline in shipping and railway construction which brought competition from manufacturers in Central Canada. Recovery was gradual, spurred by development as a port for shipping western grain during winter when the St Lawrence and Great Lakes ports are frozen in. Now it has a pulp and paper industry and is an important transportation and shipbuilding centre. The city lays claim to many firsts, including North America's first police force, the first newspaper and bank in Canada. Inventions conceived here are as varied as kerosene and the tea-bag.

The waterfront and city centre have been attractively renovated with a pleasing blend of old buildings and modern facilities. Free conducted walking tours of the historic districts are available from the Saint John tourist bureau, located in Barbour's General Store, reconstructed to its early 1900s design, beside the Market Slip. The store is near Prince William Street, one of the few in Canada to be designated as a National Historic Streetscape. Market Square in this vicinity should be on your 'must-visit' list. So should King Street which leads to King Square, a park laid out in the design of a Union Jack and considered to be the city centre. Close by is the Loyalist Burial Ground, resting place for many of the city's founders. The City Market, established in the 1870s, is believed to be the oldest of its kind in Canada. A bright and lively place it has saucy vendors, at least one of whom appears regularly on television. Fresh produce is the very best nature can provide, with New Brunswick specialities such as fiddlehead greens and an edible sea vegetable called dulse. Seafood, pies, salads and more are served as take-away or to eat at tables provided, making this an excellent stop for an informal lunch.

The New Brunswick Museum, attractively situated in one of the city's leafy residential areas, is the province's treasure house, its contents creatively displayed for adults and children. Just out of town, the Reversing Falls are a natural phenomenon occuring with tide changes through the Saint John River gorge. They can be viewed from above at an interpretive centre beside the Reversing Falls Bridge, but the riverside park below will give you a better look at the seals and host of seabirds feasting on fish thrown up by the rushing waters. A kilometre (⅔ mile) east of the falls Carleton Martello Tower, a stone fortification from the War of 1812, is a National Historic Site affording fine views of the harbour.

On the other side of the city centre, the 870 ha (2,150 acre) Rockwood Park has a range of recreational facilities, including a zoo, swimming and boating, a golf course and a unique aquatic driving range. With walking and riding trails, formal gardens and a childrens' farm all reached by public transportation from downtown, this is a year-round playground for city dwellers. Campground sites here are suitable for RVs, their bonus

Kings Landing Historic Settlement in the Saint John River Valley, depicts daily life in an early nineteenth-century Loyalist village

being glorious views of the city and the Bay of Fundy beyond.

Saint John has motels belonging to national and regional chains as well as some independents and B & Bs. Three hotels in the central district are listed here. The Hilton, part of Market Square, hugs a harbour site. The Delta Brunswick is in the Brunswick Square complex on King Street. Smaller and less expensive, the beautifully restored Parkerhouse Inn is handily located close to King Square and Prince William Street.

Saint John to St Andrews (100km/62 miles, 1 day)

Rte 1 connects Saint John with St Andrews for a one-hour drive. Visitors with time available will enjoy an excursion for a day or two on **Grand Manan Island**, off the coast of Maine and reached by ferry from New

The decorative town clock at Saint John, New Brunswick

Brunswick's **Blacks Harbour**.

Forestry, fishing and gathering dulse (edible seaweed) are Grand Manan's main industries. In the last decade or so tourists have discovered the island's quiet beauty and natural assets. Binocular-hugging bird-watchers love to come here, as to date some 400 bird species have been recorded on this major eastern flyway for migatory birds. Whale-watching is extremely popular too, with organized tours in which viewers are taken in rubber craft from the mother boat to almost within touching distance of magnificent right whales. Deep sea fishing, hiking and camping are further options. The scenery has inspired artists and writers, so that some came here on vacation and stayed for ever. The Marathon Inn and other small inns, cottages and B & Bs comprise the only visitor accommodation, so it is well to reserve in advance. Anchorage Provincial Recreation Park has a pleasant campground with RV facilities. The ferry service operates up to six times daily during summer, less frequently on Sundays and at other times of the year. Reservations are not accepted. Sometimes there is a shortage of space for vehicles on the ferry. Accordingly you may want to leave your car on the mainland and walk the short distance to lodgings in North Head, or take a taxi to more remote points.

St Andrews (population 2,000 and also known as St-Andrews-by-the-Sea) was probably an Amerindian hunting camp before a group of New England settlers established themselves here in the 1760s. The arrival of Loyalists following the American Revolution is recalled in many of the pastel coloured clapboard houses they brought with them, and assembled on sites carefully laid out by army engineers. Until the 1850s when it went into economic decline, St Andrews' merchants traded with ports as far away as the West Indies.

The town was rediscovered around the end of the ninteenth century, when the railway brought wealthy summer residents from New England and central Canada. Among them was Sir William Van Horne, President of the Canadian Pacific Railway Co. The present Algonquin Hotel's predecessor was built in 1889 and helped establish the town as the summer resort it has remained ever since.

Notable historic sites include the Greenock Presbyterian Church, built in 1824 by Captain Christopher Scott to a design of delightful proportions. The carved oak tree with green foliage on its steeple recalls Captain Scott's birthplace in Greenock, Scotland. St Andrews Blockhouse National Historic Site alongside Centennial Park contains the wooden blockhouse, built as a defence during the War of 1812. Huntsman Marine Aquarium Museum explores the Bay of Fundy's marine life, with audio-visual presentations, displays and live exhibits, including harbour seals and a childrens' 'please touch' tank containing marine creatures. **Deer Island** and **Campobello Island** (once summer home of US President Franklin D. Roosevelt) are both accessible by a short, frequent ferry service.

Much of the town's appeal lies in its orderly tree-lined streets and harbour, in the many restaurants and craft and gift shops. St Andrews has a well-known golf course, as well as tennis and sailing facilities. Boats operating from the town wharf offer whale-watching and deep-sea fishing expeditions. The Sunbury Shores Arts and Nature Centre on Water St features exhibits and programs on the area's natural history and artistic community. Mostly though, you will want to wander at will past trim white houses with brass knockers and English-style gardens and smug-looking cats behind super-clean windows, relax on the deck of a waterfront restaurant or the porch of your hotel, or potter about the classy little gift shops.

In addition to motels and B & B's, St Andrews has good accommodation at the grand old Algonquin Hotel, and the Shiretown Inn (established in 1881). The Rossmount Inn is one of Canada's finest. Island View Campground has a picturesque location with sites suitable for RVs.

St Andrews to Montreal (850km/530 miles, 1-2 days)

More than half of this 850km (530 mile) journey from St Andrews to Montreal, via the United States, is along two-lane roads. Although it can be covered in one day, such hurrying does no justice to the lovely countryside. You may wish therefore to break the journey into two days, staying overnight in the United States. Non-Canadians will require a passport and visa to enter the United States.

St Stephen, 10km (6 miles) from St Andrews, is the border crossing town reached by a short international bridge from Calais, Maine. St Stephen was founded during the American Revolution, by a group of settlers intent upon establishing a lumber mill. The War of 1812 was not permitted to interfere with trade or friendship between locals and their 'enemies' across the St Croix River. In fact, they went so far as to lend the Americans some gunpowder for their 4 July celebrations. Today, the Ganong chocolate and candy shop and museum on Milltown Boulevard are the main attraction.

Leave Calais via State Rte 9 (check the fuel gauge because there are few service stations on the road) and proceed to Bangor. From there take Interstate 95 South (although the direction is westerly) to Newport, then join US Hwy 2 as far as St Johnsbury, Vermont.

This stretch of road takes you through foothills of the Longfellow Range and then the White Mountains. It is beautiful country, particularly when cloaked in autumnal foliage. Fishing, canoeing, hiking and whitewater rafting are popular in summer; alpine and nordic skiing in winter. There is some accommodation on Hwy 2, and in towns just off this route. For those who prefer to reserve ahead two motels are listed in the Additional Information, and the town of Bethel is suggested as being representative of small communities with attractively restored historic inns and B & Bs.

At St Johnsbury take Interstate 91 north to the Canadian border at Rock Island, where it becomes Quebec Rte 55, and continue north to Rte 10. Intersection 122 on this Autoroute is about 90 minutes from downtown Montreal. The area you drive through is described on pages 108-9.

Additional Information

Places to Visit

Baddeck, NS
Alexander Graham Bell Historic Site
Open: daily
☎ (902) 295-2069

Caraquet, NB
Acadian Historic Village
Rte 11, 10km west of Caraquet
Open: daily June to September
☎ (506) 727-3467

Charlottetown, PEI
Province House National Historic Site
University and Grafton Sts
Open: daily, July to September, closed
weekends rest of year
☎ (902) 566-7626

Dartmouth, NS
Dartmouth Heritage Museum
100 Wyse Rd
Open: daily in summer
☎ (902) 464-2300

Black Cultural Centre for Nova Scotia
Cherrybrook Rd, Westphal
☎ (902) 434-6223

Fredericton, NB
Beaverbrook Art Gallery
Open: daily
☎ (506) 458-8545

Kings Landing Historical Settlement
Prince William, off Rte 2 at Exit 259
Open: June to October ☎ (506) 363-5805

Halifax, NS
Maritime Museum of the Atlantic
Water and Prince Streets
Open: all year Monday to Saturday
☎ (902) 429-8210

Halifax Citadel National Park
Open: daily in summer
☎ (902) 426-5080

Glace Bay, NS
Marconi National Historic Site
Open: daily in summer

Miners Museum
Open: daily
☎ (902) 849-4522

L'Anse aux Meadows, Nfld
*L'Anse aux Meadows National Historic
Park*
Rte 436, 25km north of Rte 430
Open: daily mid-June to Labour Day,
park open all year
☎ (709) 623-2608

Louisbourg, NS
*Fortress of Louisbourg National Historic
Park*
3 km west of Louisbourg
Open: daily June to September, limited
services May and October
☎ (902) 733-2280

Lunenburg, NS
Fisheries Museum of the Atlantic
Open: mid-May to mid-October
☎ (902) 634-4794

Oak Island, NS
Oak Island Exploration Site
Open: mid-June to September

Port aux Choix, Nfld
Port aux Choix National Historic Park
Off Rte 430 at Port aux Choix
Open: daily mid-June to Labour Day
☎ (709) 623-2608

Red Bay, Labrador
Red Bay Basque Whaling Site
Open: Monday to Saturday mid-June to
September 30th
☎ (709) 920-2154

St Anthony, Nfld
Grenfell House
Near Curtis Hospital
Open: daily in summer
☎ (709) 454-3333

St Andrews, NB
*St Andrews Blockhouse National Historic
Site*
Open: daily June to mid-Sept
☎ (506) 529-4270

Huntsman Marine Aquarium Museum
Open: daily late-May to Oct
☎ (506) 529-4285

Saint John, NB
The New Brunswick Museum
277 Douglas Avenue
Open: daily in summer, closed Mondays
in winter
☎ (506) 658-1842

St John's, Nfld
Museum of Newfoundland
Open: daily
☎ (709) 576-5044

Signal Hill National Historic Park
Open: daily
☎ (709) 772-5367

Cape Spear National Historic Park
Open: daily mid-June to Labour Day
☎ (709) 772-5367

National, Provincial & Municipal Parks

New Brunswick
Anchorage Provincial Park
Grand Manan Island, off Rte 776
☎ (506) 662-3215

Caraquet Provincial Park
Rte 11
☎ (506) 727-3474

Fundy National Park
PO Box 40,
Alma, NB, E0A 1B0
☎ (506) 887-2000

Kouchibouguac National Park
Kouchibouguac, NB, E0A 2A0
Rte 11, 14 km east from Kouchibouguac
☎ (506) 876-2443

Mactaquac Provincial Park
Mactaquac,
16km west of Fredericton on Rte 2
☎ (506) 363-3011

Les Jardins de la Republic Provincial Park
8 km north of Edmundston
☎ (506) 735-4871

Parlee Beach Provincial Park
Hwy 133, east of Shediac
☎ (506) 532-1500

Rockwood (Municipal) Park, Saint John
North off Rte 1
☎ (506) 652-4050

Mount Carleton Provincial Park
40km from Saint-Quentin via Rte 180
☎ (506) 551-1377

Newfoundland & Labrador
Blue Ponds Provincial Park
28km south of Corner Brook on Trans-
Canada Hwy
☎ (709) 643-2541

John T Cheeseman Provincial Park
10km north of Port aux Basques on
Trans-Canada Hwy
☎ (709) 643-2541

Dildo Run Provincial Park
Rte 340, 2km from Virgin Arm, 15km
south of Twillingate
☎ (709) 535-6632

Jonathons Pond Provincial Park
Rte 330, 10km north of Gander
☎ (709) 535-6632

Gros Morne National Park
Rocky Harbour, Nfld A0K 4N0
☎ (709) 458-2417

Pinware River Provincial Park
Rte 510 40km north of L'Anse au Clair,
Labrador
☎ (709) 686-2088

C. A. Pippy Park, St John's
2km north off Trans-Canada Hwy
☎ (709) 737-3669

Pistolet Provincial Park
5km south of Raleigh on Rte 437
☎ (709) 686-2088

Terra Nova National Park
Glovertown, Nfld A0G 2L0
☎ (709) 533-2801

Nova Scotia
Cape Breton Highlands National Park
Ingonish Beach, NS, B0C 1L0
☎ (902) 285-2270

Laurie Provincial Park
Rte 2 10km north of Hwy 102, exit 5
☎ (902) 861-1623

*Lunenburg Tourist Bureau and
  Campground*
Blockhouse Hill Rd
☎ (902) 634-8100

Prince Edward Island
Prince Edward Island National Park
PO Box 487
Charlottetown, PEI, C1A 7L1
☎ (902) 672-2211

Green Park Provincial Park
Rte 12, 6km east of Tyne Valley
☎ (902) 831-2370

Accommodation

Annapolis Royal, NS
The Garrison House Inn
Junction Rtes 8 & 1
☎ (902) 532-5750

Dunromin Campsite and Trailer Court
2km east on Rte 1
☎ (902) 532-2808

Baddeck, NS
Inverary Inn Resort
Trans-Canada Hwy at exit 8
☎ (902) 295-2674

Silver Dart Lodge
Trans-Canada Hwy at exit 8
☎ (902) 295-2340

Baddeck-Cabot Trail KOA Kampground
8km west on Trans-Canada Hwy
☎ (902) 295-2288

Bras d'Or Lakes Campground
5km west on Trans-Canada Hwy
☎ (902) 295-2329

Bathurst, NB
Keddy's Motor Inn
80 Main Street
☎ (506) 564-6691

Journey's End Motel
1170 St Peter Ave
☎ (506) 547-8000
1-800-668-4200

Bethel & Farmington, ME, USA
The River View Motel
Hwy 2, 2 miles east of State Rte 26,
Bethel ME
☎ (207) 824-2808

Colonial Valley Motel
Hwy 2 at State Rte 4, Farmington ME
☎ (207) 778-3391

Birchy Lake, Nfld
Fort Birchy Park and Campground
Trans-Canada Hwy at Birchy Lake
☎ (709) 551-1318

Campbellton, NB
Destination Inn
157 Water Street
☎ (709) 753-5063
1-800-561-6399

Journey's End Motel
3 Sugarloaf Street West
☎ (506) 753-4121
1-800-668-4200

Caraquet, NB
Auberge de la Baie
Rte 11 at boul St-Pierre
☎ (506) 727-3485

Village Motel du Village
Rte 11,
south of Acadian Historic Village
☎ (506) 727-4447

Charlottetown, PEI
The Prince Edward
18 Queen St
☎ (902) 566-2222
1-800-441-1414

Dundee Arms Inn
200, Pownall St
☎ (902) 892-2496

Elmwood Heritage Inn
North River Road
☎ (902) 368-3310

Corner Brook, Nfld
Glynmill Inn
Valley Rd,
2km west of Trans-Canada Hwy
☎ (709) 634-5181

Holiday Inn
48 West Street,
2km west of Trans-Canada Hwy
☎ (709) 634-5381

Deer Lake, Nfld
Deer Lake Motel
On Trans-Canada Hwy
☎ (709) 635-2108

Driftwood Inn
3 Nicholsville Road
☎ (709) 635-5115

Digby, NS
The Pines Resort Hotel
Shore Road
☎ (902) 245-2511

Admiral Digby Inn
Shore Road
☎ (902) 245-2531

Fundy Spray Trailer Park
Smith's Cove
off Rte 1, 6km east of Digby
☎ (902) 245-4884

Edmundston, NB
Auberge Wandlyn Inn
3 km north on Trans-Canada Hwy
☎ (506) 735-5525

Journey's End Motel
5 Bateman Ave
(off Trans-Canada Hwy)
☎ (506) 739-8361
1-800-668-4200

Fredericton, NB
Sheraton Inn Fredericton
225 Woodstock Rd
☎ (506) 457-7000
1-800-325-3535

Journey's End Motel
255 Prospect St
☎ (506) 453-0800
1-800-668-4200

The Carriage House B & B
230 University Ave
☎ (506) 452-9924

Woolastock Wildlife Park and Campground
29 km west on Rte 2
☎ (506) 363-5410

Fundy National Park, NB
Caledonia Highlands Inn and Chalets
☎ (506) 887-2930

Fundy Park Chalets
☎ (506) 887-2808

Gander, Nfld
Fox Moth Motel
Trans-Canada Hwy
☎ (709) 256-3535

Clayton's Hotel Gander
Trans-Canada Hwy
☎ (709) 256-3931
1-800-563-2988

Grand Falls, Nfld
Mount Peyton Hotel
On Trans-Canada Hwy
☎ (709) 489-2251
1-800-563-4894

Halifax, NS
Chateau Halifax
Cogswell and Barrington Sts
☎ (902) 425-6700
1-800-441-1414

The Halifax Sheraton Hotel
1919 Upper Water Street
☎ (902) 421-1700
1-800-325-3535

Delta Barrington Hotel
1875 Barrington St
☎ (902) 429-7410
1-800-561-6111

Ingonish, NS
Keltic Lodge
2km from east gate park entrance
☎ (902) 285-2880

L'Anse au Clair, Labrador
Northern Lights Inn
L'Anse au Clair
☎ (709) 931-2332

Lunenburg, NS
Bluenose Lodge
10 Falkland St
☎ (902) 634-8851

Lunenburg Inn
26 Dufferin St
☎ (902) 634-3963

Magdalen Islands, Que
Hôtel Château Madelinot
Cape-aux-Meules,
☎ (418) 986-3695

Moncton, NB
Howard Johnson Motor Lodge
Exit 488A-B, Trans-Canada Hwy
☎ (505) 384-1050
1-800-654-2000

Nor-West Motel
Exit 488A, Trans-Canada Hwy
☎ (506) 384-1222
1-800-561-7904

North Head, Grand Manan Island, NB
Marathon Inn
North Head
☎ (506) 662-8144

North Sydney, NS
Clansman Motel
On Hwy 125 at exit 2 (close to ferry
terminal)
☎ (902) 794-7226

Arm of Gold Campground and Trailer Park
On Hwy 105 3km west of ferry terminal
☎ (902) 736-6516

Port aux Basques, Nfld
St Christopher's Hotel
1 km west of terminal on Caribou Rd
☎ (709) 695-7034

Rocky Harbour, Nfld
Oceanview Motel
Rocky Harbour
☎ (709) 458-2730

St Andrews, NB
The Algonquin
Adolphus St off Rte 127
☎ (506) 529-8823
1-800-441-1414

Shiretown Inn
Water St
☎ (506) 529-8877

Rossmount Inn
6km west on Rte 127
☎ (506) 529-3351

Island View Campground
6km west on Rte 127
☎ (506) 529-3787

St Anthony, Nfld
St Anthony Motel
St Anthony
☎ (709) 454-3200

Vinland Motel
St Anthony
☎ (709) 454-8843

Saint John, NB
Delta Brunswick
Brunswick Square,
King Street
☎ (506) 648-1981
1-800-268-1133

Hilton International Saint John
Market Square
☎ (506) 693-8484
1-800-445-6667

Parkerhouse Inn
71 Sydney Street
☎ (506) 652-5054

Rockwood Park (Campground)
☎ (506) 652-4050

St John's, Nfld
Hotel Newfoundland
Cavendish Square
☎ (709) 726-4980
1-800-441-1414

Best Western Traveller Inn
199 Kenmount Rd
(5 km west on Trans-Canada Hwy)
☎ (709) 722-5540
1-800-528-1234

Journey's End Hotel
2 Hill O'Chips
☎ (709) 754-7788
1-800-668-4200

Sydney, NS
Holiday Inn
On Hwy 4 3km east of Hwy 125 exit 6
☎ (902)539-6750
1-800-HOLIDAY

Wandlyn Inn
On Hwy 4, 4km east of Hwy 125 exit 6
☎ (902) 539-3700
1-800-561-0000

Terra Nova National Park, Nfld
Parkway Motel
Glovertown
Trans-Canada Hwy at north park entrance
☎ (709) 533-2222

Twillingate, Nfld
Anchor Inn Motel
Rte 340
Twillingate
☎ (709) 884-2776

Ferry Services

Prince Edward Island
Cape Tormentine, NB to Borden, PEI,
crossing time 45 mins
Summer sailings every 30 to 90 mins,
depending on time of day
☎ (902) 794-5700

Caribou, NS to Wood Islands PEI,
crossing time 75 mins
Frequency as above
☎ 1-800-565-0201

Grand Manan Island, NB
Blacks Harbour to North Head, Grand
Manan. Six sailings daily in summer,
crossing time two hours
☎ (506) 662-3724

Magdalen Islands
Souris, PEI to Cap-aux-Meules,
Magdalen Islands.
Two sailings daily in summer, (Tuesdays excepted) daily in shoulder seasons. No winter service. Advance
reservations *in both directions* are
strongly advised. (Also a weekly
passenger/freight service from Montreal)
☎ (418) 986-3278

Newfoundland
Between North Sydney, NS, and Port
aux Basques, year round, and Argentia
in summer
Fares for two persons and car: Port aux
Basque service, $95 plus $50-$100 for
private cabin if required. Argentia
service, $210 plus $110-$150 for cabin, or
$25 for 2 daynighter seats
☎ Mainland (902) 794-5700
   Port aux Basques (709) 695-7081
   Argentia (709) 227-2431

Labrador Straits
Between St Barbe, Nfld, and Blanc
Sablon, Que
(There is also a weekly passenger/
freight service between Blanc Sablon
and Rimouski and Sept Îles)
☎ (709) 722-4000

**Bay of Fundy (Nova Scotia, New
   Brunswick, Maine)**
Service between Digby and Saint John is
1pm daily, with two additional sailings
during summer. The daily service from
Saint John is at 10am, with additional
summer services. Crossing time is 2
hours 30 minutes.
Service between Yarmouth and Bar
Harbour is 4.30pm daily in summer, less
frequently at other times. Return sailing
from Bar Harbour is at 8am. Crossing
time is 6 hours.
☎ Digby NS (902) 245-2116
   Saint John NB (506) 636-4048
   Bar Harbor Me (207) 288-3395

Local Tourist Authority

Magdalen Islands, Que
Association touristique des Îles-de-la-
   Madeleine,
CP 1028,
Cap-aux-Meules, Que, GOB 1B0
☎ (418) 986-2245

2

CENTRAL CANADA

Central Canada comprises that huge segment between the Maritimes and the Prairies made up of Canada's two largest and most populous provinces, namely Ontario and Quebec. Sharing the St Lawrence River valley and the Canadian Shield, their scenery is often similarly endowed with great expanses of trees and lakes. They have the country's largest cities and a high proportion of its industries. But, with two very different language groups and cultures, they also have enormous differences.

Quebec stretches from the St Lawrence valley and the United States border in the south to the Hudson Strait in the far north; from the Atlantic waters of the Gulf of St Lawrence in the east to the Ontario border in the west. With a total area of about 1,540,000 square kilometres (600,000 square miles), Quebec is Canada's largest province, twice the size of Texas, three times that of France, seven times Great Britain. The tiny agricultural zone comprising the St Lawrence valley and lowlands, is home to most of the population.

A province in which 80 per cent of its people are French speaking, Quebec is a distinct society with its own unique culture. The walls of Quebec City enclose one enormous living memorial to the history of French culture in the Americas. Montreal is, after Paris, the world's second largest French-speaking city. A vibrant community that follows many modern European traditions, it also preserves historic links with the past.

These, along with other cities and towns provide visitors with constant reminders of New France, of Jacques Cartier's sixteenth-century explorations, of Samuel de Champlain and others who followed: explorers, soldiers, priests and traders, who constantly expanded the French influence. There are reminders too of long wars with the Indians and of two centuries of conflict between France and Britain.

Both to the north and south of the St Lawrence, the countryside is hilly, wooded and studded with countless rivers and lakes, making it ideal for summer vacationers. In winter skiing is superb. Resorts are usually open all year round. For outdoors enthusiasts, hunting and fishing here are at their best, while the provincial and national parks can provide idyllic camping facilities.

Quebec's Atlantic coast, particularly the Gaspé peninsula and the offshore Magdalen Islands, have much in common with Canada's Atlantic provinces — indented coastline, coves and beaches, and small fishing communities — but always with that unique Québécoise flavour.

Ontario stretches 1,600 kilometres (1,000 miles) from east to west, and 1,690 kilometres (1,050 miles) from north to south, covering1,069,000 square kilometres (413,000 square miles) in all. The province is comparatively flat, its highest point being less than 700m (2,300ft) above sea level. The St Lawrence River valley and the lands surrounding the lower Great Lakes are largely given over to agriculture and industrial production. In the centre is the Canadian Shield, with its unique landscape of granite rocks, lakes and trees. Beyond is the Hudson Bay Lowland stretching up to the Arctic Ocean, a sparsely populated area, with forest, scrub, and occasional pockets of agriculture.

Ontario is Canada's commercial and industrial centre. With a population of ten million, it is home to nearly 40 per cent of Canadians. A large portion of Ontario residents live in a narrow band bordering the St Lawrence River and the Great Lakes, reaching from the border with Quebec near Montreal in the east, to Windsor adjoining Detroit in the west. While Southern Ontario retains a lot of agricultural land, the area around Toronto from Oshawa to Niagara Falls (known as the 'Golden Horseshoe'), is a vast urban and industrial megapolis to which immigrants have flocked from all parts of the globe. The cities are new with ever changing skylines, their communities being rich with the cultures from many lands.

Despite the inevitable urban sprawl, visitors are frequently impressed with cleanliness and relative lack of crime in Ontario's cities. Communities have retained large areas of parklands, while natural tourist attractions, including for example Niagara Falls, have been remarkably well preserved. Various periods of Ontario's past are recalled in historic parks and living museums around the province.

The large recreation area to the north and east of the Golden Horseshoe contains several provincial parks, of which Algonquin is best known. Many of the region's vacation resorts are of world-class quality. To the east the St Lawrence River valley has parks, campgrounds, hotels and resorts, and a whole spectrum of recreational opportunities.

Northern Ontario is a sportsman's paradise. Scenery on the road north of Lakes Huron and Superior has a wild and rugged beauty, and national and provincial parks preserve large tracts of country for public enjoyment. Family camping facilities abound, as do hunting and fishing lodges.

The first tour in this chapter covers southern Ontario and Quebec. Most visitors travelling by air arrive in Toronto or Montreal, while motorists from the United States usually cross the border at Detroit, Niagara Falls or entry ports south of Montreal. There is an excursion providing the short link between Detroit/Windsor and Toronto, but otherwise this circular itinerary starts in Toronto. It could, of course, also originate at these other points.

The second tour provides a link between tours originating in Toronto and those in Chapter Three which start at Winnipeg. Except for the final approach to Winnipeg, the tour is confined to Ontario. Travel time in one direction is equal to three nine-hour days. Although the distances are great, driving is not particularly tiring since the route follows the Trans-Canada Highway. Scenery is awe-inspiring in places and there are numerous recreational opportunities along the way to enjoy the outdoors. However, because there is much more to Northern Ontario than can be seen from the Trans-Canada Highway, we have suggested two interesting side-trips by rail.

The return journey takes alternative routes where feasible. It is also possible to return to Toronto through the United States, but distances and driving times are slightly longer.

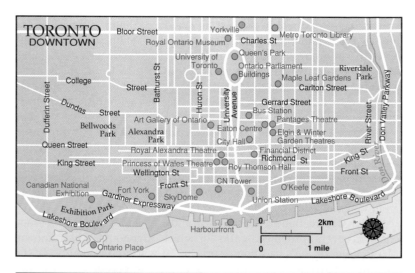

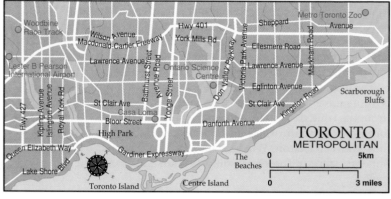

Ontario & Quebec

Toronto

Although origins of Toronto's name are lost in time it is thought to be derived from a native word meaning 'meeting place'. Certainly, aboriginal peoples are known to have come here for centuries to join an overland trail and canoe route between Lakes Ontario and Huron. Etienne Brulé was the first European to arrive (in 1615) and the Toronto Passage soon became well-known to French fur traders. A small store was established in the 1720s; a fortified post was built in 1751. Under early British rule the

Downtown Toronto

post lost prestige, being visited only sporadically by fur traders.

Following the American Revolution of 1775-83, Loyalist families who had supported the British crown fled the newly established United States for areas in the Upper St Lawrence Valley and Lower Lakes. In 1791, their settlements were severed from the old Province of Quebec and incorporated as the Province of Upper Canada. Its first governor, John Graves Simcoe, had plans developed for the provincial capital of York with government offices and a military garrison on the northern shore of Lake Ontario. Growth was slow, and 'Muddy York' was little more than a frontier village of some 700 souls when the War of 1812 broke out between Britain and the United States. Twice raided and burned during this war, York started on a period of rapid growth immediately afterwards.

By 1834, when its population had reached 9,000, York was incorporated as a city and renamed Toronto. Within two decades it was a thriving Great Lakes port, connected by rail to Montreal, New York and Chicago. When the Province of Ontario was founded following Canadian Confederation in 1867, Toronto was named its capital. Farm machinery, iron and steel, and clothing manufacture were among early industries. Commercial enterprises included banks and insurance companies, wholesalers and department stores with branches across the country. Early in the twentieth century, proximity to raw materials and inexpensive electric power from Niagara Falls provided an even greater impetus for industrial expansion. Soon Toronto was a major Canadian metropolis, second only to Montreal in size.

Growth, checked by the Great Depression of the 1930s, revived in World War II. The post-war period brought new industries, including electronics and aircraft production. Also a massive immigration boom, so that by 1951 Greater Toronto had swelled to over one million people. Since then, it has more than doubled and is now Canada's largest city.

Present-day Toronto retains the orderly lay-out developed by Governor Simcoe's surveyors. First-time visitors are usually surprised by the cleanliness of the city streets, and the modern architecture alongside cherished historic sites. They say they feel safe here, and for the most part they are. They like the parks, ever handy scraps of green where they can sit and rest; wooded ravine trails and lakeshore parks where they can work up a head of steam.

Before the arrival of post-war immigrants, 80 per cent of Torontonians were Anglo-Saxon. Then came the influx from Europe and the Caribbean, Asia and other parts of the world. Ethnic neighbourhoods took root and prospered. Now Toronto's Chinatown (Dundas St and Spadina Ave) is one of the continent's largest and most vibrant. St Clair Ave West is known as Little Italy. Danforth Ave has its Greek shops and restaurants. Hop on a Queen streetcar to The Beaches and you will be in a predominently Anglo enclave with one-of-a-kind shops, tree-shaded streets and a board–walk along the shores of Lake Ontario. Some of these communities stage traditional parades and festivals. Their restaurants add tremendous verve to what used to be a very bland dining scene. And every June they all come together with Caravan, a ten days' celebration with pavillions featuring food and entertainment of the countries represented.

Yonge St divides Toronto down the middle, begining at the lakefront and continuing up into Northern Ontario. (At 1,770km, 1,100 miles, it is listed in the *Guinness Book of Records* as the world's longest street.) Since parking is at a premium, and traffic snarls are a nightmare, a bus tour of the city is recommended, following which you can easily get around on your own. Walking north on Yonge St from Union Station, the cross streets you will be most concerned with are Queen, Dundas, Bloor and St Clair. Underground trains run north from Union Station, and east-west on Bloor Street. These are supplemented by surface busses and streetcars to provide efficient public transportation.

The Metro Toronto Convention and Visitors Association does an admirable job in distributing maps and descriptive brochures. For this reason we will do no more than steer you in the direction of some highlights.

Even those not interested in serious shopping will still enjoy Toronto's stores, in part for their interesting locales. Downtown at Queen and Yonge Streets the Eaton Centre has 350 stores, restaurants and cinemas in a bright, climate-controlled, multi-storied complex. The eclectic shops, galleries clubs and cafés on Queen St West attract the young and trendy. Speciality shops and pubs in The Beaches have their loyal fans, and stores at Yonge and Bloor Streets generally cater to upmarket shoppers. Immediately north of Bloor between Yonge Street and Avenue Road, Yorkville is Toronto's most exclusive district. While this is not for the fainthearted or budget-conscious shopper you will want to pay it a visit anyway, for a stroll in the historic lanes and perhaps lunch at a sidewalk café.

All of these can be reached by a network of underground tunnels extending north from Union Station. Climate-controlled and very clean, this is virtually a subterranean city with 5km (3 miles) of walkways, trees blooming in January, 'outdoors' seating for restaurants, countless shops and services, plus access to hotels, cinemas and seven subway stations. So when it is teeming with rain or blowing a gale, or the temperature climbs out of sight, Toronto is a good place to escape the elements.

As expansion continues to march north, the lakefront around which the city was founded has been given a second life. Former wharves, grain elevators and decaying warehouses are now integrated into Harbourfront, a cultural and leisure centre with happenings all-year-round. In summer, footpaths and parklands along the lakeshore here are as busy as those of a seaside resort. Lake activities, more shops, Canada's largest antique market, live theatre, artists at work, cafés and restaurants, free entertainment and imaginative programmes for children all contribute to the holiday flavour.

The lakefront was always a natural gathering place. Back in the 1800s the Canadian National Exhibition was established here as an agricultural fair where Ontario's farmers celebrated the harvest each autumn. Still

❋   going strong, 'the Ex' now embraces international pavillions, midway rides, a fun fair and top performers on stage during the three weeks leading to Labour Day.

As Exhibition promoters look at new ways to keep up attendance, more competition is popping up all around it. Across the lakeshore road, and
❋   linked to the CNE by an overhead walkway, Ontario Place is purpose-built on a series of man-made islands. A childrens' playground, marina, stunning movies on an Imax screen, restaurants and live shows make this a happy summer destination for families.

❋   Dominating the waterfront and city skyline, the CN Tower at 553m (1,815ft) is the world's tallest free-standing structure, featuring indoor and outdoor observation platforms, a revolving restaurant and nightclub.

Ice skating in front of the Old City Hall, Toronto

Close by, SkyDome is the city's newest landmark. This much photographed sports stadium with a retractable roof and integrated hotel is the
home of the 1992 World series winning Blue Jays baseball team. In addition, events are scheduled throughout the year and guided tours fill you
in on statistics. (SkyDome can be reached via a covered walk from Union
Station.)

In the same general area, but a couple of hundred years away, Fort York
was built by the British in 1793, destroyed in the 1812 war and reconstructed immediately after. Its summer programmes illustrate the life and
times of nineteenth-century British soldiers garrisoned at the fort. On
holiday weekends especially, it can be extremely colourful as the red-
coated 'soldiers' go about their business. The Toronto Historical Society
operates several historic homes in the city, giving them a lived-in look
with costumed residents performing chores of the day. Black Creek Pioneer Village at Jane Street and Steeles Avenue is an aggregation of settlers'
buildings essential to a pioneer community, including a former coaching
inn where hot lunches are served in the dining room.

No aspect of Toronto has expanded so dramatically over the past
twenty years as its theatre, which alone brings many visitors to the city.
Offering more live theatre than any other English-speaking city (London
and New York excepted), there were at last count 130 professional theatre
companies in town. Opulent restorations of historic theatres include
Pantages, which stages productions such as *Phantom of the Opera*. Also the
Elgin and Winter Garden, the world's only remaining stacked theatres
and as glamorous now as they ever were in the early 1900s. The Royal
Alexandra is a little jewel, across from the new Princess of Wales Theatre
built to accommodate *Miss Saigon*. Both the National Ballet of Canada and
the Canadian Opera Company perform at the O'Keefe Centre; the Toronto Symphony Orchestra at the Roy Thomson Hall is commended by
experts for its great acoustics.

Toronto has a wealth of outstanding museums and galleries. Best
known are the Royal Ontario Museum (fondly known as the ROM) at
Queen's Park (walk west of Yonge on Bloor and look south). Its Chinese
collection spanning 4,000 years of Asian history is in itself worth the
admission fee. Similarly, the Art Gallery of Ontario on Dundas St West has
the world's largest collection of work by Henry Moore. North of the city
(40km, 25 miles) Kleinburg is a perfect setting for the McMichael Collection of Canadian Art beautifully shown in a rambling log building above
the scenic Humber Valley. Canada's famed Group of Seven landscape
artists are well represented here, as are Indian and Inuit artists. The
gallery has a restaurant, and there are others in town to make this an
enjoyable half-day excursion from Toronto. More Canadian art is displayed in the Ontario Parliament Buildings on Queen's Park, just south of
the ROM. Then, ordinary though it appears on the outside, the Metro
Toronto Library on Yonge St (a few steps north of Bloor) has a wonderful
light-filled interior with greenery cascading from upper balconies, car-

peted walls as well as floors, and special baffles to keep down the noise.

❄   Children will want to visit the Ontario Science Centre, particularly
popular for hundreds of 'hands on' exhibits. (Where else can you have

🦌   your hair stand on end, literally?) Also the Metro Toronto Zoo, recognized
as one of the continent's better zoos. Monorail and electric trains provide
transportation. Even so, with 287 ha (710 acres) to cover there is a lot of
walking involved, so dress accordingly. In winter, zoo trails are groomed
to provide somewhat unusual cross-country skiing.

Toronto's spectator sports can be as much fun for audience enthusiasm
as the game itself. Most first-time visitors want to take in a baseball game
at SkyDome, which is also home to the Argonauts, Toronto's Canadian
Football League team. In winter hockey games at Maple Leaf Gardens
play to sell-out crowds. Big names in tennis compete in international
tournaments at the 10,000-seat National Tennis Centre in York University
each July, and the highlight for horse-racing fans is the Queen's Plate at
Woodbine Race Track.

Participation sports have gained importance in Toronto as most everywhere else. Pay-as-you-play golf and tennis are available. Jogging and
cycling paths are often converted to cross-country ski trails in winter.
(Hop on a ferry from Harbourfront to Toronto Islands for the very best
walking and cycling.) In winter, the handiest public ice rink is right
downtown on Queen Street west of Bay Street in front of the City Hall.

Toronto's Lester B. Pearson International Airport, about 25km (15
miles) northwest of the city centre is served by Canadian carriers as well
as major international airlines on regular and charter routes. Via Rail
provides services to Ottawa and Montreal and beyond, to western Canadian cities and to New York and Chicago. Long distance busses connect
with cities all over the continent.

Accommodation is extensive and varied. A hotel in the Bloor Street area
and another overlooking the harbour is listed in the Additional Information. More domestic and international hotel and motel chains in all price
ranges are found in the downtown, airport, suburbs and lakeshore areas.
There are also many small hotels, hostels, college residences and B & Bs.
Between mid-May and mid-September, the municipality operates two
campgrounds with good facilities suitable for RVs north of the city.

Excursions from Toronto

A number of day trips may be made from Toronto, and the following are
just some suggestions. They can also be incorporated into the longer
itineraries presented later.

• *Niagara Falls (300km/186 miles return)*
This tour takes in the Canadian side of the falls and gorge, with a lunch
stop there, followed by a drive along the Niagara River to Niagara-on-the-
Lake, and return to Toronto via the Welland Ship Canal.

If you do not spend too long at the more time-consuming attractions mentioned, this trip may be accomplished very easily in one day. If you want to see everything though, you may prefer to stay overnight. Also, families with children would like an extra day to visit Niagara Falls' Marineland, a large aquarium with whale and dolphin shows, an adjacent game farm and amusement park. This is not part of the itinerary.

Leave Toronto via the Queen Elizabeth Way (named after the Queen Mother) for Niagara Falls, a distance of about 130km (81 miles). Because Niagara Falls is a major tourist attraction as well as a heavily-used border-crossing point with the United States, there can be delays. Normal driving time is about 1½ hours.

At the large steel-working city of **Hamilton**, the Queen Elizabeth Way crosses the harbour entrance and turns west to lie parallel with the Niagara Escarpment. This huge limestone ridge runs from northern New York State, across southern Ontario, through the Bruce Peninsula and dips below Lake Huron before becoming Manitoulin Island.

The Falls are formed by the Niagara River crossing this huge ridge, carrying the waters of the Great Lakes system between Lakes Erie and Ontario on their way to the Atlantic Ocean. In the 10,000 years since the last Ice Age, the falls have gradually receded some 11km (7 miles) along the path of the gorge from Queenston to their present site.

The steep walls and cataracts of the American Falls on the US side of the river are divided by tiny Goat Island. These falls are about 305m (1,000ft) wide and 64m (210ft) high. Far more dramatic are the Canadian, or Horseshoe Falls, 675m (2,215ft) wide and carrying 90 per cent of the water. These are the world's greatest falls in terms of water volume. Combined flow can be as high as 168 million litres (37 million Imperial gallons) per minute. Depending on season and time of day, some of this is diverted to generate hydro-electric power.

In 1678 a Belgian priest, Louis Hennepin, became the first European to arrive here. He wrote of 'a vast and prodigious Cadence of Water', but it was the Neutral Indian nation which had given Niagara its name, meaning 'The Straight' or perhaps, more romantically, 'Thunder of the Water'.

Following the American Revolution, when the Niagara River became part of the new frontier between the United States and British North America, Loyalists settled on the rich farmlands beside the river. The Niagara Frontier became a prime battlefield when war broke out between Britain and the United States in 1812, and the tour along the river passes sites connected with that war.

The falls became known in Europe and the US through paintings and travellers' descriptions, and by the early 1800s were attracting tourists. Arrival of the first rail line in 1853 brought the beginning of mass tourism, along with all kinds of crude commercialism. In 1887, the Province of Ontario stepped in to curb these excesses by creating Queen Victoria Park —Ontario's first provincial preserve. Today, the city of Niagara Falls (and its US counterpart) retains some tourist traps, but almost the entire 56km (35 mile) riverside area between Fort Erie and Niagara-on-the-Lake is operated as a 1,254 ha (3,099 acre) park, with flower gardens, horticultural school, golf courses, picnic and camping areas, marina, restaurants and several unique attractions.

Approaching **Niagara Falls**, leave Queen Elizabeth Way at Exit 30 and follow Highway 420 into town. The American Falls and the Rainbow Bridge to the US will soon come into view, but continue along the Niagara Parkway to a parking lot beside the mists and rainbows over the Canadian Falls.

In summer a bus system operates in the falls area. Most visitors though prefer to walk through the well maintained park, stopping to enjoy the different vistas as they come upon them and looking over the brink of the Canadian Falls. The upper level of Table Rock House has a restaurant above them and an observation area which provides a broader view. It is also the entrance to scenic tunnels close to the river level, which actually take you behind the thundering waters at any time of the year. A few hundred yards from the Canadian falls a battery of lights is used to illuminate the spectacle after dark. Of several observation towers, the Skylon is favoured as a lunch stop because its revolving restaurant ensures a good view of the falls and gorge as well as the Niagara River rapids and the massive hydro-electric installations upstream.

About a kilometre (⅔ mile) north of the Canadian Falls an incline railway leads to the *Maid of the Mist*, for an exciting boat trip past the American falls and into the great horseshoe which is the base of the Canadian Falls. Loan of waterproof clothing is included in the boat fare. These tours operate between spring and late fall.

Continuing back along the parkway return to the Rainbow Bridge, which you may cross for the views from the American side. (Non-Canadians will require passports and visas.)

The drive through the riverside section of downtown Niagara Falls passes hotels, motels and guest houses in a section described as the world's longest hotel strip. Visitor accommodation comes in all types and price ranges. Some with pleasing views of the falls, together with a campground suitable for RVs, are listed in the Additional Information. Of the numerous tourist attractions you pass on the road, probably a helicopter ride over the gorge and falls will interest once-in-a-lifetime visitors.

The Whirlpool Rapids, on River Road 3km (2 miles) below the falls, has an observation point as well as an aerocar to take passengers over the churning rapids in the gorge below. The Sir Adam Beck Generating Station, 2km (1 mile) beyond, contains a museum of hydro-electric power. The much photographed floral clock here was inspired by a similar clock in Edinburgh and is one of the world's largest.

The Niagara Parks Commission Botanical Gardens are the site of a world-famous residential horticultural school. Its 40 ha (100 acre) campus attracts thousands of tourists and local visitors throughout the growing season. The rose gardens are particularly beautiful, often providing a lovely setting for wedding parties and their photographers.

From here, the drive continues north through the public Whirlpool Golf Course for a further 3km (2 miles) to Queenston Heights Park. There is a prominent monument here to General Sir Isaac Brock, a hero of the War of 1812 who was mortally wounded in the battle of Queenston Heights. This park, with its attractive campsites situated at the southern end of the Niagara Escarpment's Canadian section, provides more good views of the peninsula, particularly from the top of the 64m (210ft) monument. The park is the eastern terminus of the Bruce Trail, a 720km (448 mile) hiking path which follows the escarpment to **Tobermory** at the tip of the Bruce Peninsula.

At the foot of the escarpment, the pretty village of **Queenston** was the end of a portage around the Niagara Gorge before the canals were built.

An exciting boat trip below the Niagara Falls

Now it is no more than a pleasant residential community. The Laura Secord Homestead here commemorates Canada's heroine from the War of 1812. It seems that Laura, a soldier's wife, overheard American officers discussing attack plans and walked 30km (18 miles) through thick brush to warn the British. Her action led to capture of the Americans at the Battle of Beaver Dams. Laura's home is restored to the 1812 period as an example of life at the time of the last British-American armed conflict.

On the approach to Niagara-on-the-Lake, the Fort George National Historic Site is a reconstruction of the principal British post in this area during the period leading to the War of 1812. The fort was captured by the Americans in that war, later retaken by the British and abandoned in 1820.

The town of **Niagara-on-the-Lake**, first settled by Loyalist soldiers and named Newark, was the capital of Upper Canada between 1791 and 1793. Newark was renamed Niagara when the capital was moved to York (Toronto), and around 1900 changed to Niagara-on-the-Lake to avoid confusion with Niagara Falls. The town was a busy transportation centre during the 1850s, joined by steamer service to Toronto, and at the head of the rail line to Buffalo. However, the second Welland Canal, which opened in 1845 (replacing a smaller canal built 16 years earlier), signalled an end to the town's commercial importance. Scheduled steamer and rail services were discontinued in the 1950s.

Although tourism predominates, yacht building, fruit farming and wineries are thriving industries. Its townspeople have restored many of the original buildings and the result is one of the prettiest and well-preserved colonial towns in North America. A stroll along Queen Street takes in one-of-a-kind stores, boutiques and restaurants. Several lovely inns provide gracious accommodation and dining rooms. Even if you cannot stop for a meal, a drink in the lounge of the Prince of Wales Hotel is recommended. The Shaw Festival, held between May and mid-October, presents the works of George Bernard Shaw and his contempories in the splendid Festival Theatre and two smaller theatres. Alternatively the Artpark in nearby Lewiston, NY, offers very inexpensive selections of high-quality drama, musicals, operas, dance, etc.

Leaving Niagara-on-the-Lake, follow Highway 55 to Garden City Parkway; drive under it, turn right and follow signs to the Welland Canal viewing station and museum. Afterwards, follow signs for the Queen Elizabeth Way and return to Toronto.

• *Huronia (300km/186 miles return)*
This trip to Huronia, will take you back in time to the first European community in what is now Ontario, and includes a visit to the shrine commemorating six of North America's martyred saints.

Leave Toronto via Highway 400, drive north to Interchange 121, and then north on Highway 93 to Highway 12 leading to **Midland**. Follow signs to **Ste-Marie Among the Hurons**, which is the first stop.

The Ste-Marie site is a reconstruction of a Jesuit mission founded here in 1639 to minister to the Hurons and other local Indian peoples. What is

Ste-Marie Brought to Life

Visitors stare in dismay as hungry flames consume the chapel, long-house, hospital and wooden pallisades. Then, suddenly, the screen lifts to reveal the recreated mission of Ste-Marie Among the Hurons as it stands today. From the darkened cinema a walk leads to a sunlit compound where Indians and Jesuits once lived side by side, and now costumed actors are eager to show the details.

In the early 1600s a handful of Jesuit priests paddled the waterways from Quebec to spread Christianity among the Huron Indians. At the time more than 30,000 Hurons occupied this peninsula south of Georgian Bay. Farmers for the most part, they lived beside their crops. Jesuits tramping from one village to the next, lived with them.

In 1639, Ste-Marie Among the Hurons was built as a central mission where priests could come to replenish their physical and spiritual needs. This first European settlement inland became remarkably self-sufficient, at its peak supporting sixty priests, servants and *donnés* (volunteer tradesmen).

But trouble brewed between the Indian tribes. Marauding Iroquois and European diseases killed so many Hurons that in one generation they were reduced to 12,000. Eventually the Christians among them moved into Ste-Marie. Others sought refuge between the inner and outer pallisades. Two thousand Hurons died in 1648. The following spring two missionaries were tortured to death, one of them the beloved Father Jean de Brébeuf who founded the mission. Fearing desecration by the advancing Iroquois, the Jesuits set fire to Ste-Marie and in a matter of minutes ten years' work was destroyed.

The recreation shows what a peaceful haven this must have been for Jesuits returning from weeks in the bush. Here they harvested their own crops, raised pigs (brought from Quebec by canoe!) and maintained comfortable living quarters. The Indian compound is also rebuilt; the museum's poignant relics include letters written by resident priests. Try to allow two hours minimum for this visit.

seen today is based on archeological excavations. An audio-visual presentation shows life in the mission during its final days and from there visitors walk into the recreated community.

Across from the mission the Martyrs' Shrine operated by the Jesuits celebrates eight North American martyr priests killed by Indians in the seventeenth century and later canonized. Five of them were tortured to death at Ste-Marie. The shrine, as well as the grounds containing the Stations of the Cross and a miniature of Lourdes Grotto, are open to visitors. A lookout gives an overall view of the Wye River and marsh and the Georgian Bay coastline.

Nearby, the Wye Marsh Wildlife Centre preserves a section of area marshlands with a series of displays, boardwalks and trails, all explained by guides and audio-visual presentations.

Light meals and snacks are available at Ste-Marie and at the Martyrs' Shrine. There are plenty of picnic sites, should you prefer to pack a lunch.

• *Hamilton & Brantford (200km/124 miles return)*
This excursion is to Brantford, a city with historic connections to Ontario's native peoples. Additional stops are at two attractions in the heavy manufacturing city of Hamilton.

Leave Toronto via Queen Elizabeth Way and drive to exit 99, a distance of about 60km (37 miles), then follow signs along Plains Road to **Hamilton**'s Royal Botanical Gardens. While much of this site is parkland with nature trails and a wildlife sanctuary bordering on Lake Ontario, the formal areas — particularly the Rock, Lilac and Rose Gardens — are a joy to amateur gardeners and nature photographers.

Leaving the botanical gardens, follow York Blvd to Dundurn Castle, the nineteenth-century mansion of Sir Allen McNab, Prime Minister of the United Provinces of Canada in 1854-6. This 35-room home has been restored to illustrate life among society leaders in pre-Confederation Ontario. Its Cockpit Theatre presents children's and period entertainments. The admission price includes the Hamilton Military Museum, a collection of military artifacts going as far back as the War of 1812.

Leaving Dundurn Castle follow Dundurn Street, then turn right on King Street to join Highway 403 West towards **Brantford**, a distance of about 35km (22 miles).

Brantford was named after the famous Indian Captain Joseph Brant who led the Six Nations on the British side during the American Revolution. Forced from their territory in upper New York State, they were granted lands on the Grand River. South of the city the Six Nations reservation, reached by Highway 54, has guided tours. Available through its tourism office, they offer insights into the lives and cultures of the six Iroquois peoples here. Native and North American meals are available. In summer the reserve holds various festivals and theatrical productions, so you are well advised to telephone in advance to learn if anything is scheduled during your visit.

Brant's tomb beside Her Majesty's Royal Chapel of the Mohawks is a short distance from the reserve. The 1712 chapel is the oldest protestant church in Ontario, and the only Indian chapel with a royal warrant.

In the same general area, the Bell Homestead is reached via County Rd 24. This home of Alexander Graham Bell is furnished in the period when he lived here, and displays some of his early inventions. The idea of the telephone was conceived in this house. In 1876, the first long-distance telephone call was made from it to Paris, Ontario.

• *Point Pelee National Park via Kitchener & London*
(800km/497 miles return)
This is a long day's drive, covering most of the distance between Toronto and the United States border at Windsor/Detroit. However, the park

Flight of the Butterflies

For years Dr Fred Urquhart, a Canadian zoologist, puzzled over the great mystery of the migrating monarch butterflies, trying in vain to locate their winter home. In 1937 he began tagging Ontario's monarchs and asked spotters in the southern United States to track their flight from Point Pelee. But it was close to 40 years before a resident discovered them in the mountainous country near Mexico City.

At Point Pelee a trolley leaves the visitor centre for the tip every 20 minutes, and from there footpaths lead through a forested area populated by birds and butterflies. When we telephoned the park in mid August we were told that an unseasonably cool spell had precipitated early migration, and 4,000 monarchs had arrived that day. A few days later 5,000 were waiting for take-off, but by the time we got there only 500 clung to the trees. Still it was quite a sight to watch as they rested on the branches of three or four trees, their wings folded so they looked for all the world like dead leaves. Once the sun reached them they opened up to show their familiar white, black and orange markings, then took off as a great colourful cloud. For an up-to-the-minute bird or butterfly count during migration ☎ (519) 322-2371.

offers such unique opportunities to ornithologists and other nature enthusiasts that they will probably consider it worth an overnight stay in the area. It is also a simple detour if you are entering the country through **Windsor**.

Leaving Toronto via Highway 401 west, the drive is through some of southern Ontario's richest farmlands as well as a number of important communities.

Kitchener, about 100km (62 miles) west of Toronto, was named Berlin until World War I. A large chunk of the region's population is of Germanic origin, including Mennonite farmers who can be seen at a colourful farmers' market held here on Saturdays. The town's annual *Octoberfest*, featuring a grand parade with German food and beer, oompah bands and dancing, is always well attended. Several villages north of the city, including **St Jacobs** and **Elora**, are also popular day-trips because of their interesting boutiques, craftspeople and restaurants.

At intersection 232, Highway 59 leads to **Stratford**, an attractive town situated on the River Avon. It is home to the annual Stratford Festival held between early May and mid-November, with an emphasis on Shakespeare's works.

London (population 255,000), 185km (115 miles) from Toronto, was first surveyed in 1793, when it was proposed as the capital of Upper Canada. Situated on the Thames River it shows links with its British counterpart in names like Piccadilly, Pall Mall and Oxford Street. An important commercial and industrial centre, it is site of one of Canada's most respected schools, namely the University of Western Ontario.

Leave Hwy 401 at intersection 48 and travel south for 24km (15 miles) through **Leamington** to County Rd 33 which leads to the gates of **Point Pelee National Park**. The park's well-equipped visitor centre has exhibits and audio-visual presentations about the park and its wildlife. Boardwalks over the marshes and footpaths through the forest take visitors to its most interesting features; canoes and bicycles are available for hire. As well as a nature reserve this tiny national park, only 9.6 sq km (3.7 sq miles), is a favourite destination for day-trippers. Swimming is permitted from the supervised beaches, but there are dangerous currents elsewhere.

What makes it so interesting is that the park occupies Canada's southern-most point, and is on the same latitude as Northern California, Rome and Barcelona. Its ecostructure, therefore, is similar to that of areas south of the Great lakes at the extreme northern range of the jungle-like Carolinian climate zone. About two-thirds of the park are marshlands teeming with wildlife, including many species of ducks and waterfowl, mink and muskrat.

Situated where the Atlantic and Mississippi flyways converge, over 250 species of birds will pass through Point Pelee during a normal spring migration. Experienced bird watchers frequently identify 100 or more in a single day, ranging from tiny humming birds to mighty hawks. Not all of the migrants are birds. They are joined by bats, butterflies, dragonflies, and wasps.

Accommodation is available in Leamington, while the area also has B & Bs which particularly welcome ornithologists. There is no overnight camping here, but the nearby Wheatley Provincial Park has camp sites suitable for tenting and RVs.

• *Kingston via Brighton, Trenton & Picton (600km/373 miles return)*
This is a particularly enjoyable day-trip taking you eastward along the shores of Lake Ontario. Because the total distance via Highway 401 between Toronto and Kingston is 260km (162 miles) and more by travelling the scenic lakeside route recommended, you may choose to take two days for this trip. Or it can be an alternative to the return from Kingston.

To save time, it is suggested that you leave Toronto through the eastern suburbs via Highway 401, and bypass Oshawa, Bowmanville and Port Hope, before joining Highway 2 — the Heritage Highway. This was the major thoroughfare connecting the towns between Windsor, Toronto and the Quebec border west of Montreal before Highway 401 was built in the 1960s. By following Highway 2 you will see interesting old towns dating back to the eighteenth century which are all too often ignored by tourists.

Leave Highway 401 at exit 472, 105km (65 miles) east of central Toronto and turn south to **Cobourg** on Highway 2. It is a town with a typical old-style 'Upper Canada' character, complete with maple-lined streets and distinctive wooden nineteenth-century churches, and was the birthplace of the 1920s movie actress Marie Dressler. In the village of **Grafton**, the Barnum House, now a museum. was built by a settler from Vermont around 1820 and is regarded as one of the finest examples of neo-classical architecture in Canada.

Continue east through Colborne to **Brighton**, a pleasant agricultural centre at the entrance to Presqu'ile Provincial Park. This 809 ha (2,000 acre) park consists of marshes, meadows and woodlands along with a wide sandy beach, hiking trails, picnic areas and extensive camping facilities. An interpretive centre has an aquarium and displays of local animals as well as the many birds seen here during the spring and fall migrations.

Continue along Highway 2 to **Trenton**, at the southern end of the Trent-Severn Canal System. This 386km (240 mile) long waterway connects Lake Ontario with Georgian Bay on Lake Huron through a series of lakes joined by canals and forty-four locks. It is now an entirely recreational waterway and houseboats are rented from some docks and marinas.

Leave Trenton via Highway 33, the Loyalist Parkway which will take you to Quinte's Isle, known administratively as Prince Edward County. The island is in fact a peninsula of rolling farmlands jutting into the lake with a shoreline of dunes and sandy beaches. North Beach and Sandbanks Provincial Parks both have picnic grounds and excellent beaches, although the water is often too cool to really enjoy. Sandbanks also has a campground.

Picton is a pleasant little agricultural town with a deep natural harbour which attracts yachtsmen, power-boaters and other watersports enthusiasts. In summer it is a popular resort community and its annual Quinte Summer Music Festival, held in late July and early August, features some of Canada's top performers. The town has good restaurants, small inns and B & Bs to tempt visitors with time to spare.

Drivers planning to return to Toronto at this point can follow Highway 49 north to Highway 401 (a total distance of about 220km — 137 miles). Those going on to Kingston should continue on Highway 33 taking the small free ferry at **Glenora**. **Adolphustown**, about 3km (2 miles) east of the ferry, has a surprisingly comprehensive United Empire Loyalist Museum, with displays relating to the king's loyal subjects who migrated here following the American Revolution.

The rest of the drive to Kingston continues for about 50km (30 miles)

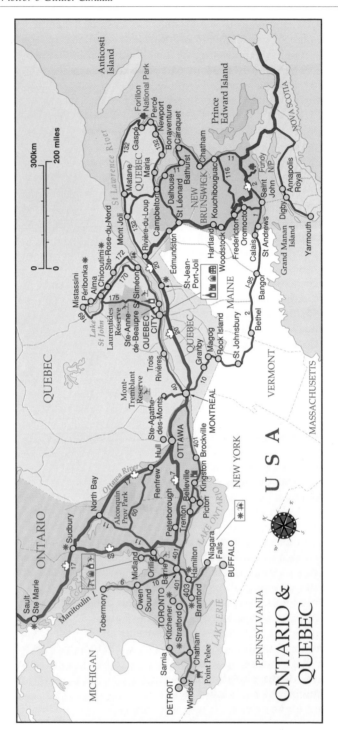

along the lakeshore through parklands and lovely old villages that have become waterside vacation communities.

Toronto to Algonquin Park (280km/174 miles, 2 days)

This is the start of a circular three-week itinerary through eastern Ontario and the Province of Quebec. The first day takes you north of Toronto, to 'cottage country' (so described because of the many summer homes here among lakes and forests of the Canadian Shield), for two nights in one of Ontario's favourite provincial parks.

Leave Toronto via Highway 400 and continue north of Barrie to join Highway 11. **Orillia**, about 120km (75 miles) north of Toronto is situated in the narrows between lakes Simcoe and Couchiching. It is a link in the

The Oxtongue River in flood, Algonquin Provincial Park

Algonquin Provincial Park

Algonquin Provincial Park was established in 1893. Among its 100th birthday celebrations is the opening of a new visitor centre 1 km (⅔ mile) south of Highway 60 at km 43, just east of the Spruce Bog Boardwalk. Set high on a ridge to take full advantage of the valley view, it houses a bookstore, information desks, a cafeteria and new museum containing galleries pertinent to the park. A natural history gallery, for example, features dioramas of the five major habitats. A human history gallery traces man's involvement with Algonquin, from the time of the native peoples, through explorers and European settlement, to present activities.

A new logging museum with a reconstructed caboose camp takes visitors back to the start of area logging about 150 years ago. Succeeding exhibits tell of the men who wintered here, cutting and squaring the great pines, then hauling them to frozen lakes, for spring transportation down the swollen rivers to the Ottawa.

Some 140,000 visitors walk Algonquin's trails each year. For its centennial year more hiking paths have been added, along with the park's first bicycle trail on an upgraded cross country ski route.

The outdoor theatre evening programmes, held at dusk each evening between late June and late September, feature every aspect of the park. Guided walks have been expanded recently to include searches for wildflowers and mushrooms. One of the most popular programmes is the public wolf howl, held at dusk on Thursdays during August. For these you are invited to drive to an area where wolf packs have been located, and there join a naturalist in imitating a howl. If the wolves reply, as they often do, you will remember that starry night in Algonquin Park long after your holiday is over.

Ontario's Autumn Foliage

Autumn visitors to Ontario have a bonus in the fiery display of foliage. The Ontario Ministry of Tourism issues a 24-hour recorded report on colour changes of the leaves throughout the province, when you call 1-800-ONTARIO. They also distribute a free *Fall Auto Tours* book, provincial road map, and brochure detailing traditional Autumn fairs and festivals in Ontario.

Trent-Severn Canal system used by recreational boaters, and a major year-round vacation centre. An impressive bronze statue to explorer Samuel de Champlain who arrived here in the early 1600s now stands in the waterfront park. Nearby, the Stephen Leacock Memorial Home celebrates the life and times of Canada's foremost humourist, whose best known work *Sunshine Sketches of a Little Town* is set in the mythical Mariposa — easily recognizable as early twentieth-century Orillia. Continue on Highway 11 to **Huntsville** (a pretty vacation town with holiday accommodation but by-passed by this route), to join Highway 60 and follow the signs to **Algonquin Provincial Park**. ♣

This 7,600 sq km (3,000 sq mile) natural environment park will give you a true taste of Ontario wilderness, even from the highway cut across its southern sector. The essence of the park is its vast interior reached by over 1,600 km (1,000 miles) of canoe routes. For such a trip you can get all the necessary gear, from canoe and tent rentals to cookware for freeze-dried food, at outfitters in and around the park. (Two of these are listed in the Additional Information.) If that sounds too rugged, the park is a wonderful preserve of lake studded forests, easy walking trails, picnic areas in the tall pines, resorts and campgrounds and even wildlife — all close to the road. Without straying very far you can hear the forest quiet pierced by the haunting cry of a loon, and a lake's stillness broken by the splash of a paddle. You can smell the smoke from cooking fires and the sweet scent of pines, and in Autumn watch as nature paints fiery reds and golds across a canvas of forest greens.

Algonquin Park is rich in wildlife. May and June are the best months for seeing moose beside the highway, especially in early morning and at dusk. Foxes, porcupines, beavers and deer may be seen from the walking trails. The preserve's estimated 2,000 black bears are far less visible than they used to be, and seldom seen on the main highway or its camp-grounds.

Resorts in and around the park offer a wide range of outdoor activities, comfortable accommodation and good dining. Within the park, two re-sorts accessible from the highway blend beautifully with their lakeside/forest settings. Open between mid May and October, both accept lunch and dinner reservations from non-resident guests. The gourmet fare served in Arowhon Pines' dining room has won international acclaim. (The park is 'dry', but if you bring your own wine to Arowhon Pines it will be uncorked and served at your table without charge.) A third lodge within the park has self-catering cottages as well as a meal plan. It is on Cache Lake, reached by boat.

Before setting off for the interior, you are asked to leave your route and schedule in the park office. Eight campgrounds near Highway 60 accom-modate RVs as well as tents, but have no on-site electrical or water hook-ups. Reservations are accepted. In the wilderness proper you can pitch your tent on any island or riverbank.

Algonquin Park to Ottawa (280km/174 miles, 2 days)

Highway 60, through Algonquin Park joins the Trans-Canada Highway (Highway 17) in the Ottawa River Valley. The Ottawa (or Outaouais to the native people who lived here) River forms over a half of the 1,120km (696 mile) border between Ontario and Quebec, but the division is more than administrative. To the north are the woods and lakes of the Laurentian Hills; to the south, much of the forest has been replaced by rich farmlands.

The mighty river, once a prime route for the fur trade, became the centre of Canada's lumber industry during the nineteenth century. Now, there are far fewer logs but hydro-electric dams send power to Toronto, and white-water rafting in the rapids is a popular sport.

Renfrew, near the junction of hwy 60 and the Trans-Canada Highway was first permanently settled by Scottish pioneers, who gave it the name of the Royal Stuarts' ancestral seat in 1848. They turned to lumbering and when the trees were gone the best land became farms. Many of those lumbermen moved on to British Columbia's forests, and today Renfrew is a thriving town which manufactures clothing, magnesium alloys, office equipment and aerospace components.

As you near **Ottawa**, Highway 17 becomes Highway 417, and then Queensway, leading through the city centre. From this approach, the city is seen to be dominated by Parliament Hill's splendid trio of white Gothic buildings topped by green copper roofs and spires overlooking the Ottawa River. Ottawa is Canada's federal capital, but with a population of about 300,000 and a half million in its metropolitan area, it is by no means a large city. Federal government buildings, official residences and embassies, along with the infrastructure necessary to support a national govern-

Relaxing by the lake at Arowhon Pines, Algonquin Provincial Park

ment, are all here. Still the city lacks the usual historic buildings and grand vistas, and even the skyscrapers of European capitals. And therein lies its charm, for this is an eminently liveable city where residents can make themselves comfortable and visitors relax in the casualness of a small town.

The first permanent European settlers were lumbermen who arrived in the area around 1800, and a New Englander named Philemon Wright who built a home that year on the Quebec side of the Ottawa River where Hull now stands. In 1820, Nicolas Sparks cleared a farm in what is now the city core. Importance came with construction of the Rideau Canal in 1826-32. During the War of 1812 British North America's supply lines between Montreal and Upper Canada had been vulnerable to American attack from across the St Lawrence River. A solution was seen in building a canal inland from Kingston on Lake Ontario. Its northern terminus beside the falls where the canal joins the Ottawa River was named Bytown, in honour of Colonel John By who supervised construction.

By the 1830s Bytown had grown to be the Ottawa Valley's premier lumbering centre, and as such rapidly increased in wealth and significance. Incorporated in 1854, and renamed Ottawa, it was selected by

Changing the guard outside the Parliament Buildings, Ottawa

Queen Victoria four years later as the capital of the Province of Canada. From a military and political point of view the city was admirably suited, but with Quebec, Montreal, Kingston and Toronto as serious contenders, the choice astounded everyone. Construction of the Parliament Buildings began in 1859, with work sufficiently well advanced for the government to set up shop when the British North America Act of 1867 designated Ottawa as the capital of the new Dominion of Canada.

Although the Rideau Canal gave Ottawa its early importance, it never had military value, or even a great deal of commercial use. Now it is strictly a recreational waterway, while the banks form part of an elaborate park system joined by driveways, bicycle trails and footpaths. In winter these double as cross-country ski trails, and the canal converts to a 198km (123 mile) long skating rink. Ottawa's parks are especially attractive in May when some three million tulips are in bloom — a gift from Queen Juliana of the Netherlands who stayed here during World War II.

A first-time visitor could easily spend a week in Ottawa's galleries and museums, many of which are within walking distance of downtown hotels and Parliament Hill. If time is limited, the Canadian Museum of Civilization (across the river in Hull) and the National Museum of Science and Technology are a good first and second choice. The National Arts Centre has consistently good theatre, opera, symphony concerts, and in summer outdoor tables are added to its café. In 1988 the National Gallery of Canada moved into a stunning new glass and granite building on Sussex Drive. Art lovers will want two or three hours here, to browse among some of the 40,000 paintings, prints and sculptures, including the largest collection of Canadian art.

Byward Market nearby is a living museum of sorts, since it has been an Ottawa institution for close on 150 years. A wonderfully vibrant, colourful place, it has indoor shops open all year supplemented by outdoor stalls between Easter and Christmas. Merchandise embraces all types of fresh produce in season, meat and baked goods, but there are also bookshops and boutiques, arts and crafts, street entertainers, bars and cafés.

Summer brings entertainers, craft stands, hot dog vendors and something of a carnival atmosphere to the riverside park across from Parliament Hill. (The Hill, incidentally, is one of the few places where 'mounties' wearing their red dress uniform tunics, blue breeches and wide brimmed hats will pose for tourists.)

The three Parliament Buildings, known as East, West and Centre Blocks are open to visitors. Conducted tours of the Centre Block containing the House of Commons and Senate are by far the most interesting. When fire swept through this block in 1961, only the fabulous vaulted ceiling and intricate woodwork escaped. A separate tour will take you up the 93m (305ft) high Peace Tower in front of the Centre Block. It has a carillon of fifty-three bells, beneath which a Memorial Chamber contains four Books of Remembrance naming those Canadians who gave their lives in wars. The chamber walls are engraved with poems, its floor paved with stones from the battlefields of France and Belgium.

Hand-painted Irish linen covers the ceiling of the Commons. The Speaker's chair is a replica of the one in Britain's House of Commons. A 36m (118ft) limestone frieze depicts moments of Canadian history. This and more will be pointed out during your free tour of the Centre Block.

In Summer (daily at 10am, weather permitting) an impressive Changing of the Guard ceremony is performed by soldiers wearing scarlet tunics and bearskin hats such as were last worn in field operations by British troops during the 1884 Nile expedition.

Walking and cycling tours can be arranged through the National Capital Commission Visitor Centre at 14 Metcalfe Street, opposite Parliament buildings. Bus tours of the city, and in summer boat excursions on the Rideau Canal and Ottawa River are both informative and enjoyable. And at any time of year you will want to wander on Sparks Street, a pedestrian shopping precinct where stores include some specializing in native arts and crafts.

The Central Experimental Farm, reached via the canal-side Queen Elizabeth Driveway/Prince of Wales Drive, does not sound like fun but in truth its 500 ha (1,200 acres) of gardens and experimental plots, greenhouses, and barns give amateur gardeners a lot of pleasure.

A drive along Sussex Drive to Rockcliffe Park is about 9km (6 miles) return, passing the Royal Canadian Mint, the Prime Minister's residence (No 24), and Rideau Hall which is home to Canada's Governor General. The park is a pleasant recreational centre with excellent views of the river and the Gatineau Hills.

A favourite short excursion (55km,34 miles) is into the Gatineau Hills, north of Ottawa in Quebec. Leave the city via the Portage Bridge and take Rte 148 for about 2km (1¼ mile), then join the Gatineau Parkway for a circular drive through the beautiful parklands. This drive takes in the Champlain Lookout which affords views over the Ottawa River, and Moorside, once the summer home of Prime Minister William Lyon MacKenzie King (1874-1950). Among King's rather odd collection of architectural ruins are pieces of Britain's Houses of Parliament, bombed in 1941.

Ottawa has airline connections with Canadian and United States' cities. Via Rail operates services to Montreal and Toronto and points east and west. The city has numerous hotels and motels as well as B & Bs, college residences and a youth hostel. The Chateau Laurier, a Canadian Pacific Hotel, has a particularly convenient location close to the Rideau Canal, Parliament Buildings and the National Arts Centre. Also downtown, the Delta Ottawa provides small kitchen units for self-catering in some of its rooms. Less expensive and familiar to European visitors is the Novatel Hotel. The commercial campgrounds listed in the Additional Information are closest to the city and have RV facilities.

Ottawa to Montreal (200km/124 miles, 2 days)

Leave Ottawa via Highway 417 then continue east until it joins the Trans-Canada Highway (Highway 17) and later becomes Quebec Rte 40. Approaching **Montreal** you will see tall downtown buildings dominated by the mountain after which the city was named, and the 83m (272ft) cross which is illuminated at night and visible for 100km (60 miles).

Montreal is a vivacious and sophisticated city. On summer evenings its

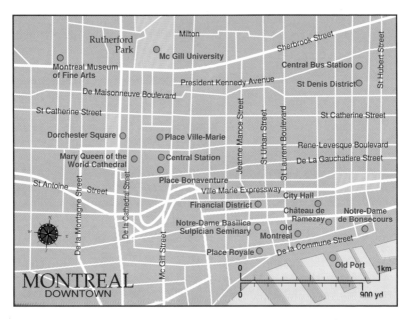

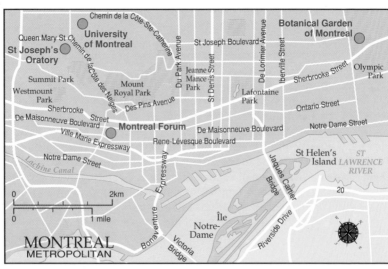

restaurants and clubs spill over to sidewalk tables, and *joie de vivre* permeates the narrow streets of the old sector. Set on an island where the Ottawa and St Lawrence Rivers meet, it is a strategic location in the huge system of lakes and rivers that cover all of eastern North America. Not surprisingly then, native peoples settled here long before Europeans arrived.

In 1535, while on his second voyage of discovery, Jacques Cartier sailed up the St Lawrence River and landed at the Indian village of Hochelaga on the largest island. He established temporary camps and planted a cross at the top of the mountain which he called Mont Réal. Over a century later, in 1642, Paul de Chomedey, Sieur de Maisonneuve, leader of a mission to the Indians, landed here with fifty-three soldiers and settlers to found the colony of Ville-Marie de Montréal, later shortened to Montréal. Among

Place Jacques Cartier in Old Montreal

his tiny entourage were five women, including the nursing sister Jeanne Mance who came with the purpose of establishing a hospital. From the beginning fur trading was the tiny settlement's means of survival. Prosperity arrived at the beginning of the eighteenth century when frequent wars between settlers and the various Indian nations were brought to an end. Montreal became the business capital of New France. As a base for North American discovery it was from here that Du Luth, La Vérendrye, D'Iberville, La Salle and others set out to explore the rest of the continent, as far west as the Rocky Mountains and down the Mississippi River to the Gulf of Mexico.

In 1763, the Treaty of Paris resulted in Montreal becoming part of the new British colony of Quebec. Twenty years later, in the aftermath of the American Revolution, Montreal emerged as the British Empire's gateway to central North America. Prosperity from fur and lumber exports to Britain led to massive immigration, and a period of enormous economic growth. Newly established banks funded canals and harbour construction, steamships, railways and a host of new industries. Upon Confederation in 1867 Montreal became Canada's metropolis, a rival to New York in economic power. Construction of the St Lawrence Seaway in the 1950s made Montreal one of the world's largest inland ports. It was only in the 1970s that Toronto outstripped Montreal as Canada's largest city.

Vibrant and exciting, old-world and charming are adjectives often applied to this, the world's second largest French-speaking city. There is still a large Anglo population here, as well as immigrants from many countries. As a result Montreal can rightly claim to be a bilingual city, and that makes it an easy city to get to know.

First-time visitors could well begin at the Infotouriste centre in Dorchester Square. Once you have an update on attractions and accommodation, you might start with a bus tour or guided walk from here. The centre has maps, audio casettes available for rent as well as information on boat trips around the waterfront, harbour and the Seaway locks.

On a clear day you can put Montreal in perspective with a visit to Mount Royal Park at the top of the mountain, where the chalet look-out presents panoramic views of the city and St Lawrence River against a backdrop of the distant Adirondacks. The park is a favourite with Montrealers because its attractive trails, used for jogging in summer and skiing in winter, are easily accessible from downtown. Motorists must park halfway up and either walk the rest on foot, or ride in a *calèche*, the horse-drawn vehicles seen in Old Montreal.

A tour of Old Montreal, by *calèche* or on foot, is an excursion into city history, steeped in old stone homes and churches, warehouses and neo-classical buildings from the seventeenth, eighteenth and nineteenth centuries. Most of these buildings are still in use, their lower floors often converted to bistros, restaurants and boutiques. A good place to start is Place d'Armes, close to the site of the first battles between settlers and the Iroquois, dominated now by a statue of the city's founder, Sieur de

Maisonneuve. For a long time this was the upper limit of what was a fortified city, before the walls were demolished in the early ninteenth century. As the city prospered this became Montreal's first financial district, and the buildings here now housed Canada's oldest banks and trading companies.

To the south of the square, Notre-Dame Basilica is one of the largest and most beautiful churches on the continent. Everything about it is splendid, from its twin 69m (227ft) towers and neo-gothic architecture to the wood-carving, artwork and stained glass windows depicting the founding of Ville-Marie. If you are interested in symphony concerts, try to attend one in this glorious church. Concerts and recitals on the huge Casavant organ are presented throughout the year and at Christmas time they can be downright magical. Alongside the basilica is Montreal's oldest building, the Sulpician Seminary of 1685, even now a residence for Sulpicians. To the south, near the waterfront, Place Royal is the site of the earliest settlement. Close by is Pointe-à-Callières, where Maisonneuve and his little band landed to found Ville-Marie.

To the northwest, Place Jacques Cartier was the location of one of Montreal's oldest markets, opened in 1804 on the site of the Marquis de Vaudreuil's gardens. Now surrounded by houses, hotels and restaurants in a very pleasing architectural arrangement, the square is filled on summer evenings with noisy outdoor cafés, street musicians, flower vendors and artisans. This is something totally Québécoise, except for Nelson's Column which comes as a surprise. Being such a natural magnet for visitors, the square has an Infotouriste kiosk.

To the south is the Old Port. There are no old buildings here now, but instead a park stretching down to the river. During summer it is scene of daily entertainments: classical, jazz and modern music, as well as dance, mime and so on. There are bicycle rentals and boat tours and the observation tower gives views of the river and waterfront. Children enjoy a playground and theatre.

East of Place Jacques Cartier, Château Ramezay Museum is in the gracious residence of Montreal's governor between 1703 and 1724, which is largely restored to period style. An interesting footnote to history is that this building was the American headquarters when they briefly occupied Montreal during the Revolutionary War. A block to the east, Bonsecours Street is one of the oldest in Montreal. Here, Notre-Dame de Bonsecours is known as the sailors' chapel because its statue of Our Lady stands with her arms outstretched over the river. First built in 1657, it was replaced in 1772 following a fire. Along with the paintings and stained glass windows, it has a collection of *objets d'art*, religious habits, and various ship models donated by seafarers to make this a particularly interesting museum. The church even has a rooftop observation deck looking out over the river. Located at 415 Bonsecours, Les Filles du Roy is one of several restaurants in the area specializing in traditional Quebec cuisine. The name recalls 800 seventeenth-century women sent under royal sponsorship to New France, complete with trousseaus and dowries, as prospective brides to the male settlers. Almost all found husbands in short order.

There is much more to see in Old Montreal, but by now you may be ready for a change of pace with a sampling of modern Montreal. A few blocks to the north and west, St Catherine is the main shopping street. Many of its stores are connected through their lower floors to the underground city, a network of shopping malls and walkways which also incorporate hotels, Metro stops and the main railway station. It is all self-contained and climate controlled so that some Montrealers claim never to step outdoors in winter.

Montreal has 5,000 restaurants which range from traditional French, through Québécoise and typical North American to any number of ethnic varieties. There are also wonderful patisseries and delicatessens. After dark, downtown Montreal sparkles with theatre, concerts, operas and ballets. Cabarets, dinner theatres and clubs come in all styles — New Orleans jazz, Montmartre can-can, Beirut belly-dance and Munich beer hall — so take your pick. There are dance clubs for the enthusiast and nightfall invariably brings the cafés and discos in Vieux Montréal to life. The St Denis district, considered to be Montreal's Latin Quarter, has more cafés, bistros, clubs and ethnic restaurants close to the University of Quebec's Montreal campus. The bars and pubs around McKay, Bishop and Crescent Streets to the west of McGill University are always busy with young people.

The Botanical Garden of Montreal should be on any visitor's 'must see' list. Located on Sherbrooke East, beside the impressive Olympic Stadium, it is a brief walk from Pie 1X Metro Station. Encompassing 73 ha (180 acres), the garden is in size second only to London's Kew Gardens, having some 26,000 species in its thirty gardens and ten greenhouses. The Chinese garden, prefabicated in Shanghai and assembled here by Chinese craftsmen in 1990, covers 2.5 ha (6 acres). It is a delightful combination of pavillions, water and rocks, trees and shrubs that no visitor should miss. The unique Insectarium has a large collection of the world's insects, live and preserved, complete with audio-visual presentations and so many computerized interactive displays that visitors acquire a lifetime's knowledge of the subject in an hour or so. While here you will want to tour the Montreal Biodome, an extraordinary living museum of the natural sciences and the environment which covers four complete ecosystems. It was opened in 1992 to celebrate the city's 350th anniversary.

Île Ste-Hélène, reached by Metro, was site of Expo 67. Now this outdoor complex has a swimming pool and picnic grounds in summer, skiing and snow-shoeing facilities in winter. Its amusement park, La Ronde, operates thirty-five rides including the world's largest roller coaster.

The Montreal Museum of Fine Arts located on Sherbrooke close to downtown is Canada's oldest art museum. Among its diverse collection are important examples of Canadian paintings, sculpture, furniture and silverware. In the past, the museum has successfully attracted some excellent travelling art shows, so check on current happenings.

Without doubt ice hockey is Montreal's number one spectator sport. Visitors here during the October to May season should try to take in a game at the Forum, home of the beloved Montreal Canadiens. It is worth a visit for the crowd's enthusiasm alone. In summer, major league baseball is featured in the Olympic Stadium and harness racing at Blue Bonnets Stadium is a local tradition. The Grand Prix Molson du Canada, part of the Formula One circuit and held every June on Île Sainte-Hélène, is just one of many international sporting events featured in Montreal.

Montreal is an easy city to get around. Streets are laid out in a grid pattern, either parallel to the river, or crossing at right angles. To simplify language matters, Montrealers usually confine themselves to street name, omitting the words 'street', 'rue', 'boulevard', etc. Numbering starts at a new 100 with each block, the lowest numerals being close to the river or east and west of St Laurent which divides the city. It all comes together in an address locator map, available free from Infotouriste. Public transport includes the Metro, with its rubber-wheeled trains and architecturally acclaimed stations, which has four inter-connected subway lines to all parts of the island and to the river's south shore.

Montreal is served by international airlines providing world-wide connections and direct flights from the United States and Europe. Domestic airlines provide connections with all major Canadian centres, Via Rail services Toronto, Ottawa, Halifax and other points east and west. Several shipping companies offer summer cruises of the lower St Lawrence River and the coasts of the Atlantic Provinces and New England.

Of the many downtown hotels, the Queen Elizabeth and Bonaventure Hilton are two with direct access to the underground city and the Metro. L'Hôtel de l'Institut, a government-operated training institution, is situated in the St Denis district and has very affordable rates. There are less expensive hotels and motels in the suburbs and close to the airports. Montreal has a good selection of B & Bs as well as college residences and hostels. The Additional Information lists one of the campgrounds to the southwest of the city which is suitable for RVs.

Excursions from Montreal

Among the excursions from Montreal are two one-day outings to resort areas frequented by Montrealers and other perennial visitors, where some stay for a weekend or their annual vacations.

• *Mont-Tremblant (300km/186 miles return)*
This drive goes into the **Laurentians** (Les Laurentides), a hilly section of the Canadian Shield immediately north of Montreal. Very enjoyable at any time of the year, it is particularly colourful in late September when the foliage is at its best. The Laurentians are Montreal's cottage country, and in addition to private accommodation, the region claims to have the highest concentration of holiday resorts in North America. Certainly

there are numerous facilities for golf, tennis, equestrian activities, and watersports on the lakes. Hikers, campers and naturalists generally love this region. Then, with over 100 ski lifts and tows, and trails for cross-country skiers, it is a major winter sports centre. As you might expect, the area is well-endowed with inviting small inns, cafés and restaurants, as well as summer stock theatres and that uniquely Québécoise institution, the *boîte à chansons*, where performers sing traditional and popular songs.

To get to the Laurentians, leave Montreal via Rte 15 (Autoroute des Laurentides). This highway is paralleled most of the way by the slower Rte 117, which could be taken on the return journey. About 40km (25 miles) north of Montreal, and after passing Mirabel Airport, you will come to **St-Jérôme** known as Gateway to the Laurentians. This was home to the legendary Curé Antoine Labelle. It was his untiring efforts at colonization during the late nineteenth century that led to the founding of so many villages named after saints. **Ste-Adèle**, about 20km (13 miles) further north is a pretty town with good visitor facilities.

Another 20km (13 miles) north, at **Ste-Agathe-des-Monts**, the auto-route merges with Rte 117. Ste Agathe (population 8,500) located on lac des Sables is the Laurentian's largest town. This is a well-known sailing centre with popular beaches. Many prosperous Montrealers have sum-mer homes here, and visitors will readily find excellent restaurants and inns. Continuing on via Rte 117, you pass through a number of smaller communities before arriving at the village of **Mont Tremblant** in the shadow of Mont Tremblant (960m, 3,150ft), the highest point in the Laurentians. This very attractive village (population 700) is surrounded by several lake-side resorts. It is a favourite ski centre. One lift operates all year, providing a super lookout for fall colours. Mont Tremblant Park, which covers 1,248 sq km (482 sq miles), contains over 500 lakes as well as countless rivers and streams. Summer activities include fishing, hiking and horse-back riding. Of the park's campgrounds, those at Lake Monroe and Lake Provost have extensive facilities and are suitable for RVs. The large northern section is a wild-life reserve.

• *The Eastern Townships (300km/186 miles return)*
This drive goes east from Montreal parallel with the United States border and into the Eastern Townships — L'Estrie. It is part of the route followed when returning from the Atlantic provinces after leaving the United States (page 69) and could be included in that itinerary, time permitting.

The area was settled by Loyalists who came here after the American Revolution, and the term Eastern was used to differentiate from the Western Townships in what is now Ontario. During the 1820s to '40s these settlers were joined by Irish immigrants, and as industry expanded by French-speaking Canadians. By the beginning of the twentieth century, the region was populated largely by francophones. Even so, it retains many British and early American characteristics and most residents are bilingual.

Now generally called L'Estrie (meaning 'Kingdom of the East'), this is a region of rolling hills, woods, orchards and rich farms, so similar to lands to the south that it is sometimes described as Quebec's New England. Lakes and rivers enhance the tranquil scenery, and the hills make for excellent skiing. It is a natural year-round playground for the residents of Montreal and Quebec City. Here are fine old hotels and modern resorts, and golf courses, along with cosy village bistros and elegant restaurants. Leave Montreal via Rte 10 (Autoroute des Cantons de l'Est). **Granby**, to the north of the highway, about 60km (37 miles) from Montreal, has large zoological gardens and a collection of fountains from various parts of the world. However your objective is **Magog** named after nearby Lake Memphremagog (Abenaki Indian for 'expanse of water'). It is still an industrial city (population 13,600) but also a major resort centre. To the north Mount Orford Park just north of Rte 10 is reached via Rte 141. The summit of Mount Orford (852m, 2,795ft) is served by ski-lift all year round. It provides great views of the surrounding farmlands and vacation country, with the Appalachian Mountains to the south. In summer park visitors can golf, hike and canoe. The Orford Arts Centre is an important summer attraction, particularly during its festival featuring art exhibitions, concerts of popular and classical music presented by well-known performers, English and French language films and theatre.

South of Magog at **St-Benoît-du-Lac** the beautiful Benedictine abbey, created by an architect member of the order, provides a retreat for men and women looking for a few days of quiet contemplation. Its gift shop sells cheese and cider produced by the monks. **North Hatley**, to the east of Magog via Rte 108 is outstanding among this region's resort communities. The lake-side village first attracted wealthy Americans who came here in the 1920s to escape prohibition. Now many of those homes have been converted to resorts, inns and B & Bs. The village is renowned for its art galleries and shops, its cafés and restaurants, and during summer English-language performances at the Piggery Theatre.

Montreal to Quebec City (260km/162 miles, 2 days)

This journey via Rte 40 between Montreal and Quebec City usually takes less than three hours but you may prefer to travel on the slower riverside road (Rte 138). Known as the old Chemin du Roi, it was first built in 1734 to link Montreal and Quebec City. The long narrow fields (*rangs*) so obvious from this road reflect the way that the land was originally divided to give each farm river frontage, yet keeping the properties close together for mutual protection.

About halfway you will pass through the town of **Trois-Rivières** (population 60,000) so-named when explorers mistook the three channels in the St Maurice River delta for separate rivers. Samuel de Champlain ordered a fort to be built here in 1634 to control the fur trade, and protect the friendly Algonquin from attack by the Iroquois. In 1663 it became the seat of local government, and during the nineteenth century was a major lumber town and port. Hydro-electric dams built on the St Maurice in the

1930s led to pulp and paper manufacture, and now Trois-Rivières is among the world's largest suppliers of newsprint.

Les Forges du St-Maurice is a national historic park recording regional history with an emphasis on New France's first iron-founding industry. Established in 1730, it operated until the local iron ore deposits gave out over 150 years later.

Following the itinerary you approach **Quebec City** from the west on Rte 40, branching onto Rte 540 and then to boul Laurier (Rte 175). This road leads to the historic area of old Quebec City. Driving can be difficult in this city's steep and narrow streets and since most attractions can be easily reached on foot, it is best to park and walk. Buses are convenient and taxis plentiful. Because of its heavy emphasis on tourism, almost everyone you come in contact with will be bilingual. All commercial signs, however, are in French.

First, some historical background. In 1535, when Jacques Cartier initially arrived at the St Lawrence River narrows below the steep bluff of what he named Cap Diamant, he encountered the native village of Stadacona. This belonged to the latest group of Indian hunters, fishermen and farmers who had occupied the site for thousands of years.

The diamonds after which Cartier named the cape turned out to be worthless quartz. France lost interest in its New World discoveries until the fur trade was responsible for Samuel de Champlain's voyage of 1608. Realizing the site's strategic value Champlain built a trading post at the foot of Cap Diamant, and so founded the city. The cliff-top was developed

Château Frontenac Hotel dominates the skyline in Quebec City

as the heavily fortified military and administrative capital of New France, leaving the lower riverside section as the merchantile district. The city's position enabled it to repulse attacks during the Anglo-French wars of the late seventeenth and eighteenth centuries, but it was finally taken in 1759. Six years later Quebec City became the capital of the new British colony of Quebec. In 1775, it was successfully defended for the last time when American revolutionary forces under Benedict Arnold (before he joined the British) were repulsed. The city walls were strengthened but never needed again. During the later eighteenth and nineteenth centuries, Quebec City prospered as a shipbuilding, manufacturing, and a transportation centre shipping lumber and later wheat.

Today, as capital of the Province of Quebec with a population of 166,500 and a total of a half million in the metropolitan area, it is an administrative and cultural centre. Tourism is a vital industry that capitalizes on the city's unique location, its 400 years of history, and of course its Gallic charm.

Quebec City, designated a UNESCO World Heritage treasure, is the continent's only walled city north of Mexico and contains its largest collection of seventeenth- and eighteenth-century buildings. A tour of the old city could begin at the tourism information centre just to the left of the Porte St-Louis entrance to the walled city. There, conducted tours on foot, by bus, or by *calèche* can be arranged. If you are making your own way, start with a stroll down rue St-Louis past some of the city's heritage buildings, now converted to shops, small hotels and restaurants, to the Place D'Armes. Under the French regime this square was the city's

The St Lawrence River, Quebec City

Eating Out, French Canadian Style

Quebec's traditional dishes frequently have their origins in Normandy and Brittany, where settlers to the New World had their roots. Meals were typically made from heavy, high energy foods that would sustain hard-working and frugal farm families through the long cold winters. Ingredients were what could be grown, hunted or fished, supplemented by molasses and spices. In consequence staple foods included potatoes, pork, fish, maple sugar, blueberries, and beans — and corn originally acquired from the Indians.

In Quebec and French Canadian communities across Canada, the following is familiar fare:

Cipaille	a deep-dish pie with six layers of meat, poultry, and vegetables separated by pastry, also called six-pâté
Fèves au lard	baked beans
Frites	French fries, chips
Gibelotte	fish hash
Ouananiche	land-locked salmon
Pâté-Chinois	a form of shepherd's pie
Pot-en-pot	fish and potato pie
Poutine	french fries topped with cheese curds and gravy or barbecue sauce
Ragoût de boulettes	pork and meatball stew
Soupe à la gourgane	dried bean soup
Soupe aux pois	yellow pea soup
Tarte au sucre	maple sugar pie
Tarte aux bleuettes	blueberry pie
Tortière	meat pie, usually filled with ground pork and veal, but it originally had small game filling.

Grande Place, the site of military parades and civic gatherings. On one side is the former Palais de Justice, and on the other the majestic Château Frontenac Hotel named after one of New France's most celebrated governors. Beside the hotel, Dufferin Terrace is a broad promenade overlooking the St Lawrence River, Lower Town and port.

At its south end Dufferin Terrace joins the Governors Promenade, a stairway and footbridge leading to the Citadel and National Battlefields Park. The huge star-shaped Citadel which stands on the Cap Diamant promontory was built between 1820 and 1852 on the site of earlier French fortifications. The Citadel still functions as the Governor General's Quebec residence and as a military installation. The grounds and some buildings are open to the public, with guides conducting tours in both French and English. In summer the parade square is scene of a daily changing of the guard ceremony, presented by soldiers of the French-speaking Royal

22nd Regiment (corrupted by Anglos to the 'Van Doos') wearing traditional guardsmens' red tunics and bearskin busbies. At other times cannon firings and the evening retreat ceremony can be seen. Anyone with a deeper interest in military history will enjoy the Artillery Park National Historic Site, just inside the city walls at the Porte St-Jean. This is an installation used in various military capacities from the 1700s until 1964.

National Battlefields Park encompasses the Plains of Abraham, where British troops under General James Wolfe climbed Cap Diamant's face on 13 September 1759 and defeated the French under the Marquis de Montcalm. The battle, which left both generals dead, led to the fall of Quebec, and eventually to the loss of France's North American possessions. Also fought within the park was the lesser-known battle of Ste-Foy, in which the French General Lévis defeated British troops under General Murray the following year, but failed to retake Quebec and perhaps change the course of history. An interpretation centre explains both battles in detail. Also in the park, the Quebec Museum contains a sizeable fine arts collection dating from the seventeenth century to present day.

Returning to Dufferin Terrace take the funicular, or brave the Casse-cou (Breakneck) steps to the Lower Town, the riverside area which is the oldest part of Quebec City (also reached by road). Here Place Royale was the site of Champlain's 1608 settlement and the beginning of France's colonization of North America. The Royal Battery, built in 1691, was used in the defence of Quebec against the British and has now been turned into a park. Although restored seventeenth- and eighteenth-century buildings have been converted to residential and commercial use, the general appearance reflects the area in 1759 before the British occupation. The buildings house interesting restaurants, boutiques and craft shops. Ferries sail from here to Lévis on the river's south bank, from where you can photograph the traditional postcard views of Old Quebec City.

A pleasant riverside walk leads to the Port of Quebec historic site in Louise Basin. There, an information centre on rue St-André has a series of exhibits, models and audio-visual shows tracing Quebec City's role both as a seaport and ship-building centre. The Agora is a large amphitheatre which features theatrical presentations, classical and modern music concerts. And although still a commercial port, part of the harbour is now a marina and base for tour boats.

There is of course more to this gracious city. It has good theatres, a symphony orchestra and some of the country's best restaurants, but it is the picturesque, the quaintness, the historical buildings and the Frenchness retained against all odds, that endears it so to visitors.

The Grande Allée, part of Rte 175 leading from Ste-Foy, is one district with plenty of visitor accommodation. Restaurants reflect Quebec's ardent love of good food with French and ethnic cuisines, and traditional Québécoise dishes. In fine weather, rue du Trésor, on the north side of Place d'Armes, is a busy little alley where artists work and show their paintings, prints and jewellery for sale.

Winter is fun time in Quebec City. Especially in February when the Carnaval de Québec attracts a half million visitors for parades, games, competitions, fireworks displays and general revelry, all led by its master of ceremonies, the 3m (20ft) snowman, Bonhomme.

Quebec City has hotels and motels belonging to chains as well as independents, in the historic area and in the suburbs. Château Frontenac is listed in the Additional Information because of its location, and also a much smaller and less expensive neighbour. It is convenient to stay in the western suburb of Ste-Foy so a motor hotel here is listed as well. Quebec City has B & Bs, college residences and youth hostels. The campgrounds listed are fairly close to the city and are suitable for RVs.

Quebec City to La Malbaie (150km/93 miles, 1 day)

If it were not part of a longer itinerary, this fairly short drive down the lower St Lawrence to the middle of the Charlevoix Coast could serve as a day trip from Quebec City. It takes you along the north shore of the St Lawrence, through a region of time-worn hills and cliffs, ancient fishing and farming villages. The area has long attracted some of Canada's leading artists and has been a favourite vacation spot since the nineteenth century. Leaving downtown Quebec City, take Rte 440 almost until it becomes Rte 138, but at this point there are two diversions.

The Pont de l'Île leads to **Île d'Orléans**, a picturesque island so rich in Quebec's heritage that it has been declared an Historic District. In the early seventeenth century the island's fertile soil attracted large numbers of settlers, and its population soon matched that of both Montreal and Quebec City. The influence of settlers in New France from Normandy and Brittany is still seen in the architecture of villages, churches, farms and mills. Agriculture remains vital to island economy, and visitors will delight in the strawberries, cream and maple syrup, offered along with other fresh farm produce at roadside stands.

A tour of the island is about 70km (43 miles) long. Just north of the bridge, **St-Pierre's** church which dates back to 1718, retains much of its early decor. The more elaborate **Ste-Famille** church with its three bell towers was consecrated in 1749, and **St-François** at the north end has the wild vineyard that led Jacques Cartier to call the island 'Île de Bacchus' before it was renamed in honour of France's royal family. Especially interesting is **St-Jean**, once a village of river pilots and navigators with most of its seafarers' houses dating from the mid-nineteenth century. The pretty old-fashioned village of **Ste-Pétronille** (at the south end) has long been a favourite with artists. In 1759 this was Gen Wolfe's headquarters for his assault on Quebec City. Small inns and B & Bs around the island are understandably popular.

On the north side of the highway, Montmorency Falls are in a park just above the point where the Montmorency River flows into the St Lawrence River. At 83m (272ft), they are about one and a half times as high as Niagara, and among the most impressive in North America, particularly

Mont Ste-Anne is noted for its World Cup class skiing

White-water rafting is one of Quebec's many outdoor sports

in winter when spray deposits form a huge conical 'sugarloaf' at the base. There are viewing platforms at both upper and lower levels, and the park also contains the redoubt built by Gen Wolfe for his seige of Quebec City.

About 35km (22 miles) east of Quebec City, **Ste-Anne-de-Beaupré** is a village named after the mother of the Virgin, who it is said will heal the sick of heart, mind and body. Believing that she saved shipwreck victims off nearby Cap Tourmente, seafarers erected a chapel to her in 1658, during which time legend has it that a crippled workman was miraculously cured. Built too close to the river, it was reconstructed further inland, then replaced by a stone church in 1676. Attracting pilgrims from the beginning, the church was enlarged several times before being replaced by the first basilica in 1872. After this was destroyed by fire the present Roman-style basilica with twin towers, rich wood-carvings and stained glass windows was built in 1923. Each year it receives over a million pilgrims who come to walk the Stations of the Cross and see the Scala Santa which represents an opera house in miniature, but contains a replica of the twenty-eight steps climbed by Christ to the judgement seat of Pontius Pilate. A 107-room inn accommodates pilgrims wanting to stay for more than a day, while a hospital takes care of any requiring medical attention. There are several motels in the immediate area.

Mont Ste-Anne Park, 5km (3 miles) east of Ste-Anne-de-Beaupré, is a large provincial park with facilities for golf and hiking in summer. Its real fame is for downhill skiing, on slopes registered on the World Cup circuit.

For the next 60km (37 miles) or so the highway cuts inland to **Baie-St-Paul**, a picturesque town where the Gouffre River flows into the St Lawrence. Baie-St-Paul is enhanced by its 200-year-old houses, art galleries and *ateliers*. The Panorama exposition, held here between mid-June and mid-September brings together artists from all along the Charlevoix Coast. Surrounding hills give lovely views of the countryside, the Lower St Lawrence River and the Île-aux-Coudres. Air currents above them make this a favourite venue for hang-gliding and sailplane enthusiasts. The Gouffre River is well-known for its salmon fishing.

Île-aux-Coudres, named by Jacques Cartier after the hazel trees he found here, can be reached by hourly ferry from the little village of **St-Joseph-de-la-Rive** on Rte 362. Settlement came slowly and it was the middle of the eighteenth century before a parish was established. Some original buildings can be seen at The Mills of Île-aux-Coudres in St-Louis. Islanders who lived by farming, fishing and whaling had to be self-sufficient, which meant making their own clothing and linens. Local weavers still produce and sell traditional bed-covers, table linens and rag rugs. Several operate small inns and B & Bs.

La Malbaie, so called by Champlain when his ships were grounded by the tide here, is one of three small communities grouped around the bay where the little Malbaie River flows into the St Lawrence. This area has been a favoured North American vacation spot since the middle of the nineteenth century. Located at the top of a cliff high above the river at

Pointe-au-Pic, Manoir Richelieu was built by Canada Steamship Lines in 1899 at a time when the company operated smart white painted steamships rather than the huge red-hulled bulkers now seen on the seaway. The *manoir*'s guest book in those days listed North America's truly rich and famous, including United States President Taft. The present château-style Manoir Richelieu, built in 1928, is still a good family resort. Recently restored to original splendour it has a spa, golf course, tennis courts and swimming pool, and caters to a spectrum of winter sports. **Cap-à-l'Aigle**, so named by Cartier after the eagles that nested here, provides more heady views of the river and its shoreline.

The Malbaie area has delightful little inns, one of which is listed here, and some memorable restaurants. Here, as elsewhere on the Charlevoix coast, you will find chalets, studios and houses for rent (contact Quebec Tourism for details). The campground listed has full RV services.

La Malbaie to Tadoussac (70km/44 miles, 1 day)

This short journey gives plenty of time to complete the drive along the Charlevoix coast and then take a short whale-watching trip along the St Lawrence River. **St-Siméon**, 33km (20 miles) east at the junction of Rtes 138 and 170, is terminus for the ferry service to Rivière-du-Loup on the south shore of the St Lawrence. Les Palisades to the north of here is a provincial nature appreciation centre with splendid views of the Rivière Noire valley. Presentations on local wildlife are given in French. St-Siméon is a centre for hunting and fishing, with outfitters providing the necessary equipment and supplies.

Close to the south bank of the Saguenay River where it meets the St Lawrence, **Baie-Ste-Catherine** is a base for whale-watching cruises. The Pointe-Noire Coastal Station has a belvedere looking out over the river, as well as displays and presentations describing the whale species living offshore.

Tadoussac reached by a frequent free ferry service across the Saguenay River also has whale watching cruises, including some associated with GREMM, a research organization with an interpretive centre and naturalists who accompany the safaris. In addition to whale-watching cruises Tadoussac is a base for excursions on the Saguenay River, subject of the next drive.

The cold waters where the Saguenay flows into the St Lawrence are rich in krill and the small fish on which the whales feed. While thirteen species of whales, including dolphins, porpoises and orcas (killer whales) live in the St Lawrence River and its estuary, minke, finback and beluga are seen most frequently in the waters off the Saguenay. The 500 belugas who live here year round are the only such group outside of the Arctic. It is believed they have been living in the Saguenay for 12,000 years. Now sadly their numbers are reduced by pollution. Although the huge finbacks, second largest of all the whales, are less numerous in the area, a dozen or so, including calves with their mothers, may be seen in a single expedition.

Tadoussac was an Indian meeting place long before Jacques Cartier arrived in 1534, and it soon attracted Europeans. Pierre Chauvin established Canada's first trading post here in 1600, and this is where Samuel de Champlain concluded the first treaty with Indians in 1603. The first mission was founded in 1615 and by 1647 the Jesuits had built a chapel in Tadoussac. Virtually everything was destroyed during an Iroquois attack. A wooden chapel built in 1747 still stands. It, and the reconstruction of that first trading post, are open for visitors.

The most prominent building in the town is the Hotel Tadoussac, a long white structure with bright red roof built in the 1940s. It is on the site of an hotel where white cruise ships deposited vacationing passengers a century ago. The resort is set in well-maintained gardens beside a sandy beach, and guests can enjoy golf, tennis and a heated swimming pool, as well as facilities at a nearby hunting and fishing club. In addition to this hotel, the town has small inns and a hostel. The campground has full RV services.

Tadoussac to Chicoutimi (400km/249 miles, 1 day)

This drive of roughly 400km (249 miles) takes you along the north shore of the Saguenay Fjord and then right around Lake St John before stopping overnight in Chicoutimi. If the weather is fine and you have time to spare, you may want to stay a second night and take a day-long cruise down the fjord from Chicoutimi.

The Saguenay Fjord was formed some 70 million years ago when part

Gathering maple syrup, Quebec

of the Canadian Shield collapsed to form a deep trench, and then more recent Ice Age glaciers gouged out rocks and debris to leave a valley. As ice melted the sea flooded in to create a fjord 106km (65 miles) long and about 2km (1¼ mile) wide. The fjord, in places 300m (1,000ft) deep, is bordered by precipitous cliffs reaching to 510m (1,675ft) high at Cape Eternity. Almost the entire shoreline is incorporated into a conservation area operated by Quebec province with facilities for hiking, fishing, camping and cross-country skiing.

When Jacques Cartier arrived here in 1534 with his king's instructions to look for gold as he searched for a route to the Orient, he eagerly listened to tales of a rich 'Kingdom of the Saguenay'. Although the kingdom was all fantasy, the river was already a well-known Indian trading route to the area around Lake St John. Jesuit missionaries explored it during the 1600s and lumbering became important in the 1800s, but real riches were elusive until the first hydro-electric dam was built in 1925. Then came a huge aluminum smelter at Jonquière and several pulp and paper mills. The Saguenay is now one of Quebec's major industrial centres.

Leaving Tadoussac via Rte 172, you will drive though forested hills parallel with the fast-flowing Ste-Marguerite River, known for its salmon and trout fishing. The first stop is **Ste-Rose-du-Nord**, about 90km (56 miles) along. Called the Pearl of the Saguenay, this pretty riverside village has a well known small inn and restaurant and some B & Bs. Further along **St-Fulgence** gives dramatic views of the fjord from the peak of its Mont Valin. The return journey provides an opportunity to view the Saguenay fjord from the south side. Hiking trails lead from **L'Anse St-Jean** to Cape Eternity and to Cape Trinity where a huge statue of the Virgin is an historic monument traditionally saluted by passing ships with the playing of *Ave Maria*.

Although a bridge west of St-Fulgence leads directly to Chicoutimi, the itinerary continues on past Alma to Rte 169 and the northern shore of Lake St John. The industrial town of **Alma** invites visitors to tour the smelters and pulp and paper manufacturing plants.

The almost circular Lake St John is an ancient glacial basin, that was at one time an arm of the sea. Fed by a number of rivers it empties, via hydro-electric stations, into the Saguenay River. It is an excellent source of land-locked salmon. The north shore in particular is enjoyed by hunters and fishermen, hikers and climbers. Fertile countryside to the south is occu-pied by prosperous dairy farms.

Between the lake and the Péribonka River, Pointe Taillon Park has a beach, camping facilities, hiking and cycling trails. In **Péribonka**, the Louis-Hémon Museum honours the author of the pastoral romance and one of Quebec's most celebrated literary works *Maria Chapdelaine*. The museum features the farm central to the book, and the house where the French expatriate Hémon worked. Interpretation is in French.

This is blueberry country. **Mistassini**, which claims to be the world's blueberry capital, holds a festival in August when the countryside is literally shaded blue by ground-hugging berries waiting to be harvested. At this time inhabitants sell the fresh-picked fruit, *au naturelle* or choco-late-dipped. Pies, cakes, cheesecakes (using local cheeses) and confec-tions, wines and even liqueurs made from the fruit are available all year.

Val-Jalbert preserves the remains of an early twentieth-century com-pany town which used power harnessed from the Ouiatchouan Falls and local timber to produce pulp for paper-making. The town and the thun-dering falls are attractive and make a worthwhile visit . The power plant and pulp mill, hotel and school, as well as stores and workers' homes are open to the public. Visitors may rent accommodation in the houses and there are picnic grounds and campsites. Tours are available in French, or in English for groups by prior arrangement.

Chicoutimi is a further 70km to the east via Rte 170. This city (popula-tion 60,000) is an industrial and administrative centre, and a deep-water port whose present prosperity can be traced to mid-nineteenth-century lumber mills, and to the hydro-electricity that brought paper mills and aluminum smelters. The region does, however, retain strong links with the past. Each February it holds the Carnaval-Souvenir festival when inhabitants don clothes the style of a century ago, to participate in the cultural and recreational events of their forefathers. The Pulpmill is the oldest archeological industrial site in Quebec. Once the world's largest, it closed in 1930 and is now a museum with tours conducted in French, and in English for groups by prior arrangement. French summer theatre and other entertainments are featured.

Two Chicoutimi motels and an RV campsite are listed in the Additional Information. There are also small inns and B & Bs in the region and hostels in Péribonka and Chicoutimi.

Chicoutimi to Rivière-du-Loup (150km/93 miles, 1day)

This short journey leads back to the St Lawrence and then across by ferry to the south shore. Should you choose to return from here to Quebec City, follow Rte 175 through the huge Laurentian Wildlife Reserve and the Jacques Cartier Conservation Park.

Following this itinerary, leave Chicoutimi via Rte 170 and drive direct to St-Siméon for the ferry to Rivière-du-Loup. An early start will give time for a diversion to L'Anse-St-Jean (page 119) for another view of the Saguenay Fjord, or a whale-watching expedition to the mouth of the Saguenay from Rivière-du-Loup (see also page 26). Overnight accommo-dation close to the ferry dock and the river is suggested, or the municipal campground which has RV services. An alternative is to continue along the coast before stopping for the night at, say Rimouski, 107km (66 miles) to the east, where plentiful accommodation includes a hostel.

Rivière-du-Loup to Percé (600km/372 miles, 2 days)

This drive, following Rte 132 along the coastline of the St Lawrence River estuary and then the Gaspé Peninsula to Percé, is within sight of water for most of the way. The scenery changes constantly, from limestone cliffs to rugged rocks and shingle beaches, pretty coves and small fishing communities where cod is sun-dried on racks as it has since settlers arrived from Northern France and the British Isles centuries ago.

About 50km (30 miles) to the east, the picturesque provincial park at **Bic** preserves a stretch of Lower St Lawrence coastline, with a rich variety of inlets, marshes and woods, plenty of birdlife and resident seals. The park has a beach, hiking and camping and nature interpretation programmes. **Rimouski** (population 29,000) a little further on, is the region's administrative capital and site of a major oceanographic research centre. Its port provides freight and passenger services to Quebec communities along the north shore of the Gulf of St Lawrence. **Matane** is a thriving community and terminus for ferry services to the north shore. The shrimp fishery is so important to the economy that it is the focus of a festival held at the end of the season, in late June. It is also a centre for salmon fishing. Outfitters cater to visiting fishermen, and while downtown you can watch salmon leaping the dam during their summer migration. Matane, and a number of other coastal communities along the route, provides access to provincial parks and reserves in the peninsula's interior.

Forillon National Park at the northern tip embraces 240sq km (93sq miles) of remarkably varied terrain. Most spectacular are the layered and worn limestone cliffs and long pebble beaches of the coastline. Even so the salt marshes, cliffside arctic vegetation and boreal forests inland are as interesting to nature enthusiasts. Among their resident wildlife are some 200 different bird species, bear, moose, deer, foxes and mink. Seals live on the beaches and rocks, and up to a dozen species of whales can be seen offshore. The park has an interpretive centre, naturalist-guided walks, and campgrounds, two of which are suitable for RVs. Coastal villages offer fishing and diving charters, seal and whale-watching expeditions.

Gaspé (population 17,000), situated at the head of a huge natural harbour, is the region's administrative centre. The 9m (30ft) granite cross which commemorates Jacques Cartier's landing here in 1534 to found New France is worth seeing. So is the modern wooden cathedral, the only one of its kind in North America, with a large stained glass window and fresco presented by the French Republic. The Gaspésie Museum displays maps and artifacts of the region, with emphasis on the area's maritime heritage from the Vikings and Basques to the present time. An impressive monument to Jacques Cartier stands in the grounds.

Percé is a further 32km (21 miles). Once a sizeable fishing centre and the largest port in the vicinity for traders from northern France, southwest England and the Channel Isles, it now depends on its beautiful setting to attract tourists. The highway approach from either the north or south opens up spectacular vistas of the town, with the pierced rock formation and Bonaventure Island offshore. Better still, take one of the hiking trails to the top of Mont Ste-Anne, and then call in at the town's interpretation

Fisherman cleaning cod at Percé

centre to see regional exhibits and presentations. The pierced limestone rock, looking from some aspects like a ship at sea, is 439m (1,440ft) long and up to 88m (290ft) high. At one time it was even longer, with as many as four natural arches. There were two when Cartier landed, but now there is only one, with a 30m (98ft) wide opening. You can walk on the sandbar out to the rock at low tide, or for a different angle walk to the top of Mont-Joli a short distance from the town centre.

Bonaventure Island, a brief boat-ride offshore, is a major bird sanctuary and summer home to 50,000 gannets along with puffins, cormorants, murres, and a half dozen other species. Boats leave Percé every 20 minutes or so in summer to circle the island before leaving passengers at the landing stage. Both the island and rock are designated as a provincial park. There is an interpretation centre close by Bonaventure's dock and naturalists escort visitors hiking across the island to view birds nesting on the cliff-tops. Or, you can go off on your own to enjoy the sandy coves. No overnight camping is permitted so be sure that you do not miss the last boat back to Percé. This gives you time for an evening stroll along Percé's pier and beachside boardwalk.

Percé's restaurants serve good meals in both casual and sophisticated restaurants. Speciality shops and artists' studios, a museum and a French-language summer theatre all provide interest for visitors. The Percé Bay Underwater Park with headquarters in town has offshore diving facilities and instruction. There are lots of motels and small inns and at least one B & B. Motels listed in the Additional Information are on the waterfront

Visitors learning about Bonaventure Island's bird sanctuary

with views of the rock and Bonaventure Island. In the same location, the smaller inn has a very good restaurant. The provincial campground in town is suitable for RVs.

Percé to Quebec City (720km/447 miles, 1 day)

The return drive to Quebec City follows Rte 132 along the Gaspé Peninsula's south shore, crosses north to the St Lawrence Estuary and then turns west. The road, hugging the Gaspé's gentle south coast, passes sheltered bays and rivers favoured for their salmon fishing, as well as through fishing and farming villages and resort towns, founded by the different ethnic groups that populate this region.

Although the peninsula's population is now largely French speaking, names like Chandler, Newport and New Richmond reflect times when Loyalists settled here in 1784 following the American Revolution. The resort community of **Bonaventure** about halfway along the coast on Chaleur Bay, was founded by Acadian families expelled from Nova Scotia. A museum records their heritage. Near **Maria** is a Micmac Indian reservation with an unusual church in the shape of a wigwam. **Carleton**, another seaside resort town, was founded by Acadians.

Following Rte 132 inland, you will cross the peninsula to reach the north coast at **Mont Joli**, and then retrace the road to Rivière-du-Loup. From there Rte 132 continues along the coast to Lévis and beyond, passing through riverside towns which include St-Jean-Port-Joli (see page 26). Rte 20, the Trans-Canada Highway, is of course much faster. With only limited accommodation in Lévis, it is better to cross the river and spend the night in Quebec City (see page 114).

Quebec City to Toronto (800km/497 miles, 3 days)

This the start of a three-day journey to Toronto with overnight stops in eastern Ontario. It begins by crossing back to the south shore and taking Rte 20 to Montreal, a distance of about 250km (155 miles). There is little to detain you on this stretch.

Travelling from the east and passing through Montreal, it is best to stay on Rte 20 then enter the city through the La Fontaine tunnel. Continue on to Rte 520 (Autoroute Metropolitaine) until it rejoins Rte 20 which leads into Ontario's Highway 401. (Signs for Toronto make this quite easy.) Close to the Ontario/Quebec border are tourist information centres operated by both provinces. Continue along Highway 401 and stop overnight in the Cornwall area, about 115km (70 miles) west of Montreal.

Cornwall (population 46,000), Ontario's most easterly city, has a bilingual population. It is linked with Rooseveltown, New York state, by an international bridge and is headquarters of the St Lawrence Seaway Authority. It is chosen as an overnight stop because it is close to places to visit next day. Campers should drive on to the St Lawrence Parks Commission campground at Morrisburg.

The final leg of this journey is parallel with the St Lawrence Seaway, a section of the Great Lakes Waterway. Jointly operated by the United States and Canada, it gives large ocean-going ships access to the continent's interior via the Great Lakes. The Welland Canal and the huge locks at Sault Ste Marie were already in place before the Seaway was completed in 1959 but there was only a small, shallow, canal around the river rapids between Montreal and Lake Ontario. During construction of the Seaway, this was replaced by a series of canals and seven locks which lift vessels a total of 65m (213ft). The project also included a hydro-electric dam forming the artificial Lake St Lawrence. To make way for this, roads and railways and 500 buildings had to be moved to higher ground. They include some with important links to the late eighteenth-century Loyalist settlers of Upper Canada's St Lawrence valley.

The best of these buildings were assembled on the new riverbank near **Morrisburg** to form **Upper Canada Village**, a living museum which recreates life around the 1860s. Encompassing thirty-five buildings its houses range from a family's first crude log cabin, to handsome dwellings with imported furniture enjoyed two generations later. The village also has a doctor's house, two churches, a school, smithy, steam-powered grist-mill, woollen mill, a fully operational farm, and hotel which serves meals of the period. Horse-drawn wagons and a canal boat give rides. The village strives for authenticity; homes are furnished to a theme, while demonstrations and interpretations are given by appropriately costumed residents.

Within walking distance of Upper Canada Village, Crysler Farm Battlefield Park commemorates a battle in the War of 1812 in which a British/Canadian group defeated a much larger force of American invaders. There is a beach and picnic area, and in summer lovely flower gardens.

If the village and park has been visited by midday, the afternoon can be pleasantly passed on the scenic 150km (93 mile) riverside drive along Highway 2 to Kingston. About 20km (12 miles) west of Upper Canada Village, **Iroquois** is the largest town that was relocated to make way for the seaway. Nearby Iroquois Lock has a lookout and information centre where the seaway's operation is fully explained.

At **Brockville**, the road becomes the Thousand Islands Parkway. In reality there are far more than 1,000 islands, although the early French explorer who gave them this name was not to know it. Much of the riverbank is parkland administered by the St Lawrence Parks Commission. **Mallorytown Landing**, centre of the **St Lawrence Islands National Park** has a beach, picnic area, campground and an information centre. The park also contains seventeen islands and eighty rocky islets accessible by boat. **Ivy Lea** is at the Canadian end of the international bridge connecting Ontario with New York State. From the 1000 Islands Skydeck lookout tower, the river and islands combine to present a glorious view below. **Gananoque** is the centre for river cruises past some magnificent vacation homes on private islands in both Canada and the United States. Most famous of these is Heart Island's Boldt Castle. Built by the owner of New York's Waldorf Astoria Hotel for his wife, the castle was abandoned unfurnished and unoccupied after her untimely death. Incidentally, it was Boldt's personal chef Oscar who named his salad dressing in honour of the 1,000 islands.

Kingston (population 54,000) is a further 30km (19 miles) west at the eastern end of Lake Ontario. The city's history goes back to 1673, when the French chose it as site of their Fort Cataraqui fur trading post. Later as Fort Frontenac it became base for more exploration and forays against the Iroquois and the British. The fort was taken by the British in 1758. In 1784, it became a centre for Loyalist migration from the United States and was named King's Town in honour of King George III. From there Kingston became the administrative centre for settlements at the eastern end of Lake Ontario and the upper St Lawrence. While the town was unharmed in the War of 1812, a growing military presence stimulated the economy, establishing it as a premier trading and shipping centre. Construction of the Rideau Canal added to this prosperity. Fort Henry, originally built during the War of 1812 and garrisoned by British troops to guard the entrance to the St Lawrence River, was rebuilt in 1836 to defend the canal.

Kingston became the largest town in Upper Canada and was capital of the United Provinces of Canada for three years from 1841. Queen's Uni-

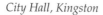

City Hall, Kingston

versity, now one of Canada's most prestigious schools, was founded in 1841. Expecting Kingston to become capital of the new Dominion of Canada, citizens were outraged when Queen Victoria chose Ottawa. Even so, the city continued developing as a government and military centre and a major lakes shipping port. The advent of railways reduced the city's commercial importance, then with little threat from the United States some military bases closed. Until World War II, when the area started to attract more industry, nothing much happened in Kingston.

Today, it is a good-looking city of weathered stone buildings and tree-lined streets, with pleasant, prosperous suburbs. Fort Frontenac as well as the Martello Tower, Customs House and old railway station represent different periods in the city's history. Past expectations of greatness as the national capital are portrayed in the neo-classical City Hall built in 1843-4. Close by is St George's Cathedral, and links with the military past continue with the Royal Military College, the National Defence College and extensive armed forces' installations, which are very much in evidence. Fort Henry is a now a military museum. During the tourism season it is manned by the Fort Henry Guard, trained, uniformed and equipped as British troops of 1867. The guard is changed every hour, on the half hour. Gun salutes, military drills and evolutions are carried out daily. The impressive sunset ceremony which takes place at 7.30pm on Mondays, Wednesdays and Saturdays during July and August, weather permitting, is included in the admission.

Belleview House National Historic Site was for a while the home of Sir John A. MacDonald, Canada's first Prime Minister. One of Kingston's more interesting houses, it was built in the style of an Italian villa for a local merchant in the early 1800s and immediately dubbed the Pekoe Pagoda by uncharitable neighbours. A museum next door traces the career of MacDonald, who came from Scotland with his family at the age of five.

In summer, the Chamber of Commerce operates a one-hour trackless train tour of the downtown area, starting from Confederation Park opposite City Hall. More information on Kingston is available from the tourist bureau on Ontario Street.

On the Via Rail line, Kingston is about halfway between Toronto and Montreal. It is also the departure point for three- to seven-day cruises operated by St Lawrence Cruise Lines. Kingston has good hotels and motels, including the handsome Hochelaga Inn. Other hotels listed in the Additional Information have been selected for their waterfront location.

After visiting Kingston leave for Toronto, a distance of 260km (162 miles) via Highway 401 west, or if time permits, follow the route described in the day trip from Toronto (pages 92-3).

Northwest Ontario

Toronto to Sault Ste Marie (690km/429 miles, 1 day)

This second itinerary from Toronto goes north on Highway 400 to join the Trans-Canada Highway (Highway 69 at this point), about 140km (87 miles) from the city. In this vicinity, downhill and cross-country skiing are popular winter sports in such centres as Moonstone and Horseshoe Valley. Soon after joining Highway 69, at Port Severn, the Trent-Severn Canal System is crossed close to the point where it enters Georgian Bay. This is a land of deep blue lakes, foaming rivers — trees, trees and more trees, and the wild landscape of the Canadian Shield.

This too is 'Cottage country' to families from Southern Ontario and the United States, who own vacation properties on the lakefronts and on Friday evenings create huge traffic hold-ups when heading to their weekend hideaways. Fishing camps, outfitters, guides and floatplane services are designed to get you to otherwise inaccessible lakes. Resorts offer every sports and leisure activity, comfortable lodge and cottage accommodation and usually good dining. Exceptional accommodation is provided at The Inn at Manitou on Lake Manitouwabing, a gold shield Relais & Chateaux hotel, features a tennis clinic, full spa and European and Canadian cuisine unmatched in holiday country. There is also an exciting childrens' camp for the arts here, with youngsters from several countries.

Picnic sites along the highway are usually in picturesque spots. There are also half a dozen provincial parks with recreational and camping facilities. About 80km (50 miles) south of Sudbury the route crosses the French River, once a canoe route followed by the fur traders. Now enjoying the status and protection of a provincial park, it offers great fishing. With trout, bass, pike, sturgeon and other species awaiting the challenge, it can truly be described as an anglers' paradise. Some area resorts are luxurious, others have fairly primitive accommodation, but all provide everything the fishing enthusiast could wish for, including guides who have spent a lifetime in these waters and know where the big ones hide.

Sudbury, about 390km (240 miles) north of Toronto, lies in a great geological basin, the origins of which are probably a meteorite strike millions of years ago. This left a rich cache of metallic ores which were first discovered during railway construction in the 1880s. Regional mines produce gold, silver and platinum, as well as cobalt and 85 per cent of the world's nickel. Pollution from the mines had turned the surrounding countryside into something resembling a moonscape, but recent land-reclamation schemes are having a beneficial effect on the environment. The Big Nickel, a giant (9m, 30ft) replica of the 1951 Canadian coin, marks an exploratory mine converted to an educational centre open for tours. Science North is a more fascinating educational centre, devoted to science and in particular to northern development and technology.

In addition to its mining activity, Sudbury (population 92,000) is an administrative centre and gateway to Ontario's Northland. Although the itinerary continues along the Trans-Canada Highway to Sault Ste Marie, an interesting side-trip is by Polar Bear Express, the train from Cochrane to Moosonee on James Bay, a huge inlet of the Arctic Ocean.

Cochrane is 380km (235 miles) north of Sudbury via Highway 144, which runs north from the Trans-Canada Highway about 15km west of Sudbury. Follow Highways 101, 67 and 11 to Cochrane, from where the train leaves at 8.30am and returns late the same night. Overnight accommodation in Cochrane is fairly limited, so reserve in advance. Parking is available at the station and a campground close to town is suitable for RVs.

There is no highway to **Moosonee**, just this ribbon of steel through dense bush and marshlands for a train journey that covers 299km (186 miles) and takes about 4½ hours. Day-trippers have time to visit the town and take a 15-minute boat trip operated by local Crees across to **Moose Factory**, the island site of the Hudson's Bay Company's second fur trading post in North America. Built in 1673, it was the first English settlement in Ontario. St Thomas Church here is interesting for the beaded moose-hide altar cloths and Cree-language prayer books. Also holes in the floor permitting flood waters to flow in, so that the church will not float away during the spring thaw.

In Moosonee, boat and bus tours are available, as are short floatplane flights over James Bay. Moosonee also has flights to Polar Bear Provincial Park, a 24,000sq km (9,300sq mile) wilderness park accessible only by charter aircraft and with written permission from the park authorities.

Having travelled this far, it is a pity to return to Cochrane the same day. If you stay the night there is time to see everything and perhaps enjoy the northern lights. All of the tourism-oriented facilities here are synchronized to train schedules, allowing plenty of time to visit the Revillon Frères Museum displaying artifacts of the local rival to the Hudson's Bay Company, and to see Indian crafts for sale in the James Bay Educational Centre. Accommodation is provided in the town, and the Northern Ontario Railway has various hotel and travel programmes from either Toronto or Cochrane. Campers can arrange with Cree boatmen for transportation to the Tidewater Provincial Park.

Visitors taking the side trip to Cochrane and Moosonee will rejoin the itinerary at the Trans-Canada Highway (Highway 17) just west of Sudbury. The distance then to Sault Ste Marie is approximately 305km (190 miles), passing through lumbering and mining communities with resorts and outfitters where hunting or fishing excursions can be arranged. At **Serpent River** Highway 108 leads 42km (26 miles) north to **Elliot Lake**, a uranium mining town with more hunting and fishing opportunities. The municipal office, open weekdays, has a mining and nuclear energy museum.

Sault Ste Marie (population 81,000) lies on the north side of the St Mary's river which connects Lakes Huron and Superior. Joined by an international bridge with its neighbour of the same name in Michigan, it

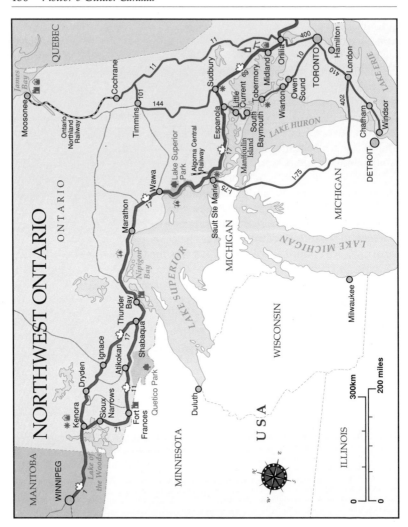

is an industrial centre with a large steel-works and pulp-mill.

Known generally as 'The Soo' from the French pronunciation of *sault*, or rapids, the river was a gathering place for native peoples long before the French explorer Etienne Brulé arrived in 1622. A mission was established in 1668 and the Northwest Company built a fur trading post here in 1783. Five years later they dug a small canal to avoid portaging around the rapids. It was destroyed during the War of 1812, and since then increasingly larger locks have been built. On the American side they handle a larger annual tonnage than any other comparable locks in the world, and are an important part of the Great Lakes Waterway. The smaller Canadian lock is a heritage site operated by Parks Canada. Close by you can see a reconstruction of that first canal. The MS *Norgoma*, the last overnight passenger ship to be built for the Great Lakes, is now a museum. Boat tours of the locks are conducted from the museum's dock.

The Algoma Central Railway will take you from Sault Ste Marie on a picturesque day trip that is especially colourful in late September when the foliage is at its most glorious. The 183km (115 mile) journey passes through ravines and forests, providing a unique opportunity to see the interior wilderness of Northern Ontario. A 2-hour stop in the Agawa Canyon allows time for a picnic and a walkabout. Box lunches can be ordered and full meals are served in the train's dining car. Train reservations are available only at the station on the day before departure, which is just as well because there is little point in this adventure in poor weather.

Sault Ste Marie has hotels and motels, mostly by the Trans-Canada Highway. Those in the Additional Information are close to the waterfront, locks and railway station but the RV campground is north of town.

Sault Ste Marie to Thunder Bay (720km/447 miles, 2 days)

This drive follows the Trans-Canada Highway (Highway 17) around the northern rim of Lake Superior, on the so-called North of Superior Route. Roughly 120km (75 miles) north of Sault Ste Marie, the highway runs for about 80km (50 miles) through Lake Superior Provincial Park, a natural environment park with beaches, picnic and camp grounds. Ancient Amerindian pictographs can be seen at Agawa Bay, a pleasant beach near the south gate. **Wawa**, a few kilometres from the north gate was a trading post in the late seventeenth century and has been site of a number of gold-

Cochrane, gateway to the north

Winnie the Pooh

North of Superior, and Sault Ste Marie, there is a town called White River. One day in 1913 a trapper came upon an orphaned bear cub in the woods, and brought her into town. The following summer Lt Harry Colebourn, an army veterinarian, was travelling from Winnipeg to Quebec. When his train stopped at White River, he purchased the small black bear and named her Winnipeg after his hometown. It was, of course, soon shortened to Winnie. As if that was not enough excitement for a young cub, Winnie was taken to England by Lt Colebourn and became a mascot of the Second Canadian Infantry Brigade on Salisbury Plain.

When the brigade was sent to France in December 1914, Winnie went to live in the London Zoo. There she was adored by all — gave rides to youngsters, performed tricks, and ate goodies from childrens' hands. Young Christopher Robin Milne was so keen on Winnie that he named his own teddy after her. (No matter that teddy was light brown, and a boy.) The rest is history. Christopher Robin's father A. A. Milne, along with illustrator Ernest Shepard, made the namesake immortal in his books, and to this day Winnie the Pooh books and bears are sold in toyshops everywhere.

As for the real characters in this story, Lt Colebourn visited Winnie several times before she died in 1934. A statue was erected for her in London Zoo, bearing a plaque that reads 'She gave her name to Winnie-the-Pooh and A. A. Milne and Ernest Shepard gave Winnie-the-Pooh to the rest of the world.' In 1992 a bronze statue of Winnie was unveiled in White River, so the town can now be known for more than its record-breaking cold winter weather.

rushes. Wawa, 'wild goose' in the Ojibwa language, is a rest stop for large numbers of these birds during their migrations. For this reason you will see an enormous goose sculpture beside the highway.

Marathon, a gold mining town and site of a paper mill, is also the gateway to Pukaskwa Provincial Park, the interior of which is accessible only on foot or by canoe.

In the Nipigon Bay area, and especially Kama Bay, is some of the most beautiful forest and shoreline scenery on the entire North Of Superior Route. About 40km (25 miles) west of **Nipigon**, the Ouimet Canyon is a 150m (500ft) wide, 110m (350ft) deep volcanic fissure with solid rock sides and convenient viewing platforms. Another 20km (12 miles) brings you to Sleeping Giant (Sibley) Provincial Park, a peninsula ending in an 11km (7 mile) long rock formation, which at a distance can actually resemble a giant person lying on his side. According to Ojibwa legend, the Great Spirit of the Deep Sea Water turned to stone after his secret silver mine was revealed to the white men by a Sioux scout. Probably this should not be totally dismissed as folklore, since miners did make enormous fortunes from silver found here in the 1860s. The park, about 40km (25 miles) east of Thunder Bay, has excellent recreational facilities and a campground suitable for RVs.

Close to the eastern approaches to **Thunder Bay**, the Terry Fox monument dominates a highway lookout over Lake Superior. Fox, who lost a leg due to cancer at the age of 18, set out from Newfoundland in 1980 to run the entire width of the country. After covering 5,373km (3,399 miles) at 40 km (25 miles) per day and raising $1.7 million for cancer research, he had to give up at this point. Since his death annual runs have been held in thirty-three different countries, raising over a $100 million for charity.

The Thunder Bay area was home to Paleo-Indian hunters perhaps 10,000 years ago, and was inhabited by the Ojibwa nation when seventeenth-century explorers arrived here to set up a fur trading post. In 1803, the Montreal-based North West Company established Fort William, a busy trading post at the mouth of the Kaministiquia River. Within the next 20 years Fort William was to become the most important settlement in the interior of North America and the centre of the company's trading empire. In 1821 the North West Company amalgamated with the Hudson's Bay Company and the fort's value gradually declined to the point of closure in 1883. Settlement around it had been growing, encouraged by lumbering, the discovery of silver, and the building of docks at nearby Prince Arthur's Landing, later to become Port Arthur. Railway construction brought tremendous expansion in the late nineteenth century, and so did the grain, forest products, coal, iron ore, potash and sulphur which arrived here by train for transfer to huge lake steamers.

The twin cities of Fort William and Port Arthur were amalgamated in 1970, taking the name of the bay on which they were situated. Today, Thunder Bay (pop 113,000), is Canada's third largest port, loading ships plying the Great Lakes and St Lawrence Seaway. Huge grain elevators which hold the grain before shipment are a waterfront feature popular with photographers. Thunder Bay is also a major pulp and paper manufacturer while secondary industries includes the manufacture of railway rolling stock.

Early trading post roots are remembered at **Old Fort William**, a recon- struction on the Kaministiquia River at Point de Meuron, 14km (9 miles) from the original site. One of Canada's top living museums, its programmes show the interaction of Scottish-born Montreal traders, French Canadian *voyageurs* and Indian trappers who would meet here each June for a 'Rendezvous.' Now, costumed inhabitants and tour guides explain daily life within the fur trade society, and the early nineteenth-century material culture as experienced at Fort William. More of Thunder Bay's history is depicted in Centennial Park's reconstructed 1910 logging camp and museum.

Kakabeka Falls Provincial Park, 29km (18 miles) west of Thunder Bay on the Trans-Canada Highway, contains the spectacular falls where the

Kaministiquia River plunges 39m (128ft) into a narrow gorge. In this region steeped in Objiwa legend we are told of the lovely Princess Green Mantle who led a procession of enemy warriors over these falls, thereby saving her nation but sacrificing her own life. If you look carefully, you might just see Green Mantle in the mist.

Bus and boat tours of Thunder Bay take in Old Fort William. City attractions include a museum and art gallery and the Canada Games Complex with an Olympic pool and a 73m (237ft) waterslide. Ski resorts attract winter visitors to four downhill ski areas and well-maintained cross-country ski trails.

Thunder Bay is about 55 km (34 miles) from the United States border at Grand Portage, MN. Of the city's hotels and motels two quite close to Old Fort William are listed. The KOA campground is near your route but campers can also continue on for two nights at the Kakabeka Falls Provincial Park, where there is a full service campground.

Kakabeka Falls, west of Thunder Bay

Thunder Bay to Kenora via Fort Frances (550km/342 miles, 1 day)

This drive from Thunder Bay to Kenora, 205km (127 miles) east of Winnipeg via Highway 11, is the southern alternate route of the Trans-Canada Highway in this region. It is about 70km (42 miles) longer than the more direct Highway 17 route, which is reserved for the return journey. This drive goes through rugged bush country with few communities, so it is a good idea to keep an eye on the fuel gauge.

Leave Thunder Bay via the Trans-Canada Highway (Highway 11/17) and take the southern (Highway 11) branch roughly 50 km (30 miles) west at Shabaqua Corners. Some 140km (85 miles) along is **Atikokan**, centre of a popular wilderness recreation area and entry point for the nearby Quetico Provincial Park. Accessible only by foot and canoe, this park extends as far as Minnesota's Boundary Waters Canoe Area on the United States border.

Another 120km (75 miles) brings you to Rainy Lake, then the Noden Causeway, a series of bridges leading into **Fort Frances**, with wonderful views of the area. Fort Frances, named after the wife of the Hudson's Bay Governor Sir George Simpson, was the successor to Fort St Pierre, the fur trading post first established by Pierre de la Vérendrye in 1731. The small Fort Frances Museum presents displays on the Indian era before the Europeans arrived, the fur trade and later settlement. Admission includes the lookout tower. Now, the town (population 9,000) is largely dependent on pulp and paper manufacturing. It is also a major tourist centre for boating, fishing and hunting. Connected by bridge to International Falls, Minnesota, it is a transit point for Central Canada, via Duluth, Chicago and Detroit.

On leaving Fort Frances, follow Highway 71 north beside Lake of the Woods. This lake, with a surface of 4,349sq km (2,702sq miles), more than 14,600 islands and an enormously convoluted coastline, is only one of the thousands of lakes here in the southwest corner of Northern Ontario. Obviously then, it is a thriving vacation centre for the residents of Manitoba, northwest Ontario and bordering American states.

Sioux Narrows is a typical example of the region's tourism industry. Off season, it is a quiet village of 375, plus 500 Ojibwa who live on the nearby Whitefish Bay Reserve. In summer, the population swells to 5,000 as visitors flock here to boat docks, campgrounds, cottages, fishing lodges and first-class resorts. Also here is Sioux Narrows Provincial Park with a beach, picnic areas and full-service campground.

At **Kenora**, 80km (50 miles) to the north, Lake of the Woods flows into the Winnipeg River. This was an important native settlement long before French explorers arrived, and La Vérendrye built the fur trading post of Fort St-Charles here in 1732. History since then has been turbulent at times, with battles among Indian Nations, between white men and natives, riotous railway builders and Prohibition whiskey smugglers. It was the Grand Trunk Railway, and its insatiable demand for timber that brought boom times. Then came the mills which ground western grain to flour for easier shipment, and a couple of gold-rushes. Surprisingly, Kenora once shipped two-thirds of the world's caviar. All of this, and much more can be learned at the very interesting Lake of the Woods Museum. In the museum's shadow is St Alban's Cathedral, smaller than most parish churches yet serving a diocese of 640,000sq km (247,000sq miles). A visit is worthwhile for its stained glass windows alone. Because of the large Indian population close by, the town is an excellent source of native artwork. An annual regatta held in early August attracts entrants from Canada, the United States and Europe. Two hotels close to Kenora town are listed in the Additional Information. One campground listed is nearby, the other is near the intersections of Highways 17 and 71. Kenora is connected (through Minaki) with Via Rail and plane to Winnipeg, Toronto and Thunder Bay.

Minaki, a pretty village on the Winnipeg River, about 50km (30 miles) north of Kenora and reached from the Trans-Canada Highway, is the site of Minaki Lodge. This resort began when Canadian National's predecessor, the Grand Trunk Railway, started building luxury accommodation for its passengers. Now, as then, recreational opportunities for guests include golf and tennis, pools, theatre, boating and some of the best fishing they will probably ever encounter. Passenger trains between Toronto and Winnipeg stop here on request.

The main lodge's lofty log centre hall with massive stone fireplace, furs and stuffed creatures will take you back to the early days and more prosperous times. Since the Ontario government spent millions of dollars on its restoration and in building an access road some 20 years ago Minaki Lodge has changed management several times. Accommodation is comfortable, in log bungalows and modern additions. Service and cuisine at the lodge can be variable.

From Kenora, the Trans-Canada Highway (Ontario Highway 17) continues about 50 km (30 miles) before becoming Manitoba Highway 1. Soon after crossing the border, the countryside takes on a dramatic change as the rocks, lakes and forests of the Canadian Shield give way to Prairie grasslands. It is a further 140 km (87 miles) to the outskirts of Winnipeg. A signpost along this stretch of road tells when you have reached the longitudinal centre of Canada.

Winnipeg to Manitoulin Island (1,610km/1,000 miles, 3 days)

The section of the itinerary from Winnipeg to Manitoulin Island, retraces a large part of the road that was followed on the westward journey from Toronto. However, this time take Highway 17, the northern segment of the Trans-Canada Highway, from east of Kenora to the point about 50km (30 miles) west of Thunder Bay where Highways 11 and 17 join. Thunder Bay and Sault Ste Marie are logical stops for the next two nights. On the third day leave the previous route, driving south through Manitoulin Island to the ferry connecting with the Bruce Peninsula. From there, the loop is completed by continuing on to Toronto.

Leaving Winnipeg, follow the Trans-Canada Highway (Highway 1) until it crosses the border and becomes Ontario Highway 17. Proceed through Kenora, continuing on this highway when it reaches the junction with Highway 71.

The road continues to parallel the Canadian Pacific Railway route, the original trans-continental line built following Confederation. Although there are more spectacular stretches in the Rocky Mountains, the builders probably found this section the most challenging as deep muskeg bogs swallowed whole segments of line, and locomotives sank from sight. Now, enormous trains haul raw materials to Thunder Bay and points east. The rocks and lakes and the muskeg are still here, making for superb scenery and great fishing and hunting.

About 120 km (75 miles) east of Kenora is **Dryden** (population 5,500). This town owes its start to gold miners and then to a farmer who, after discovering fertile soil, established a permanent settlement here. It is now a lumber town with pulp and paper manufacturing, as well as a tourism centre with good camping, hunting and fishing.

Ignace, about halfway between Kenora and Thunder Bay, started as a railway town. Presently engaged in mining and lumbering, this is another centre for hunting and fishing. Highway 599 leads to Pickle and Central Patricia Lakes, 292km (181 miles) away, and the most northerly points in Ontario that can be reached by road.

Since you pass through other Northern Ontario cities and towns already encountered, they require no further comment, except to mention an alternative itinerary through the United States from Sault Ste Marie to Southern Ontario. To follow this route, cross into Sault Ste Marie, Michigan, via the International Bridge, which leads straight into Interstate 75. Follow the highway to Flint, Michigan. From Flint take Interstate 69 and Interstate 94 to Port Huron and the international Bluewater Bridge. Cross the bridge to Sarnia, Ontario (total distance in the United States is 560km, 348 miles). From **Sarnia**, drive on Highway 402 for 100km (62 miles) to London, and join Highway 401, 185km (115 miles) west of Toronto. Sarnia, a petrochemical centre, is 160km (100 miles) north of **Windsor** which is the automobile manufacturing city neighbouring Detroit and a major entry point into Canada. On the shores of Lake Huron, about 50km (30 miles) north of Sarnia, the Pinery Provincial Park and the **Grand Bend** recreational area generally, are very popular weekend and vacation destinations for area residents. Point Pelee National Park (described on page 92) is within easy driving distance of both Windsor and Sarnia.

The scheduled itinerary through Canada from Sault Ste Marie continues on to Espanola. There, turn south on Highway 6 and carry on for 53km (33 miles) to Little Current on **Manitoulin Island**. This island, probably the world's largest island on an inland lake, is 176km (109 miles) long and between 5 and 80 km (3 and 50 miles) wide. Its rocky shoreline and scattering of interior lakes make the island a favourite with sailors and fishermen. It had long been a native settlement when the first Jesuit missionaries arrived in 1648, but their mission was short lived and European habitation was sporadic until it became a centre for Indian Administration in the 1830s. Most of the island was purchased from the Indians in 1862. The Indian reservation at **Wikwemikong** has a pow-wow each August which attracts native dancers from all over North America. With a total of six reservations on the island, this is a good place to purchase native arts and crafts. Visitors spending time on Manitoulin Island will enjoy the Assiginack Museum, SS *Norisle* and the Heritage Park at **Manitowaning**. The museum's focus is an old stone building, once the island's jail. There is also a home furnished in early twentieth-century style, a smithy and a schoolhouse. At one time, the old *Norisle* sailed on the ferry service to Tobermory.

Poultry farming, sheep ranching and commercial fishing are major occupations here. Tourism is extremely important, with small resorts and businesses specializing in camping, fishing, boating and scuba diving. Listed in the Additional Information are two resorts and a campground with RV facilities close to the ferry terminal. Details of other resorts are available through Travel Ontario.

Ferries operate between Manitoulin's South Baymouth and Tobermory from April to October. This 2-hour mini-voyage passes close to the scenic Georgian Bay islands, and is so enjoyable that passengers often sail in both directions without disembarking.

Tobermory to Toronto (300km/186 miles, 1 day)

At the northern tip of the Bruce Peninsula **Tobermory** is a great little holiday town with two harbours, called Big Tub and Little Tub. First settled in the 1870s, largely by Scottish immigrants, its major industry was lumbering until the forests were demolished. Fishing was important before stocks declined. But it is the scenery and shipwrecks in the treacherous waters offshore that have brought Tobermory's current prosperity as a recreational centre. The cold, clear, fresh waters have perfectly preserved nineteenth-century and early twentieth-century sail and steam vessels. Now, they are an attraction in Fathom Five National Marine Park, which is Canada's only such park. Dive clubs come here from all over the Americas, while local shops and boats cater to snorkellers and scuba divers. In summer the marina is always crowded, and a pleasant evening walk is past the yachts and cruisers berthed there.

Tourists will enjoy the park's visitor centre where this unique environment is described. Glass-bottom tour-boats allow non-swimmers to view the wrecks. There are also boat rides to Flowerpot Island, named after two large rock pillars. On Flowerpot you will find walking trails, interpretive displays and a few wilderness campsites.

Tobermory is the headquarters of Bruce Peninsula National Park, incorporating 270sq km (104sq miles) of the last remaining wild areas of the Niagara Escarpment, on both sides of the peninsula. Eroded cliffs and caves of the escarpment that led to the formation of Niagara Falls are within the park's boundaries. So are marshlands, clay plains and sand dunes where the rock formations slope down under Lake Huron. Hikers, botanists and nature lovers generally are attracted by the variety of trees and ferns and the forty-nine species of orchids found here. The park is open all-year-round for hiking, camping and cross-country skiing. The Bruce Trail, a 720km (447 mile) walking trail connecting Tobermory with Queenston on the Niagara River, begins in the park and runs down the eastern side of the peninsula.

Because Tobermory receives so many visitors the town has good restaraurants, interesting craft shops and speciality stores. A suitable resort and a motel are listed. The campground, close to town, is one of several in the upper Bruce Peninsula.

This itinerary concludes with the 300km (186 mile) drive to Toronto, following Highway 6 down the Bruce Peninsula, through the resort town of Wiarton to Owen Sound and then via Highway 10 to Highway 401. The drive is through fertile farmlands, a landscape startlingly different from that on the Trans-Canada Highway towards Manitoulin Island.

Given a little more time you might enjoy driving south via Highway 21 along the shores of Lake Huron from the Bruce Peninsula to Ipperwash, before turning inland towards Toronto. This road takes you through enjoyable vacation communities, including Southampton, Goderich and Grand Bend, and past a half dozen lake-side provincial parks with long strands of clean, sandy beaches, picnic sites and campgrounds.

Additional Information

Places to Visit

Adolphustown, Ont
United Empire Loyalist Museum
Hwy 33
Open: Tuesday to Sunday, late June to Labour Day
☎ (613) 393-2869

Brantford, Ont
Six Nations Tourism
Oshweken, Ontario
Open: Monday to Friday, weekend tours by arrangement
☎ (519) 445-4528

Mohawk Chapel
Mohawk Rd
3km south of Brantford, via Colborne St
Open: daily July & August, closed Monday and Tuesday, rest of year
☎ (519) 445-4528

Bell Homestead
94 Tutela Heights Rd (reached via Colborne St and County Rd 24)
Open: daily, mid-June to Labour Day, closed Mondays rest of year
☎ (519) 756-6220

Chicoutimi, Que
The Pulpmill
300, rue Dubuc
Open: daily mid-June to mid-September
☎ (418) 543-2729

Fort Frances, Ont
Fort Frances Museum
259 Scott St at Hwy 11
Open: daily, mid-June to Labour Day
☎ (807) 274-7891

Gaspé, Que
Gaspésie Museum
80 boul Gaspé
Open: daily
☎ (418) 368-5710

Hamilton, Ont
Dundurn Castle
York Blvd at Dundurn Park
Open: daily
☎ (416) 522-5313

Royal Botanical Gardens
Plains Road
Open: daily
☎ (416) 527-7962

Kenora, Ont
Lake of the Woods Museum
Main St, S at Memorial Park
Open: Monday to Saturday, July to
Labour Day, Tuesday to Saturday rest of
year
☎ (807) 468-8865

Kingston, Ont
Fort Henry
Hwys 2 & 15
Open: daily mid-May to Labour Day
☎ (613) 542-7388

Belleview House National Historic Site
35 Centre Street
Open: daily June 1 to Labour Day
☎ (613) 545-8666

Manitoulin Island, Ont
Assiginack Museum
Hwy 6 at Manitowaning
Open: daily June to Labour Day
☎ (705) 859-3902

Midland, Ont
The Martyrs' Shrine
Open: daily late-May to mid-October
☎ (705) 526-3788

Ste Marie Among the Hurons
5km east on Hwy 12
Open: daily late-May to mid-October
☎ (705) 526-7838

Wye Marsh Wildlife Centre
Beside Ste-Marie
Open: daily
☎ (705) 526-7809

Montreal, Que
Botanical Garden of Montreal
4101 Sherbrook East
Open: daily
☎ (514) 872-1400

Château Ramezay Museum
280 Notre Dame East
Open: daily June to Labour Day, closed
Monday rest of year
☎ (514) 861-7182

Montreal Museum of Fine Arts
1379 Sherbrooke West
Open: all year Tuesday to Sunday
☎ (514) 285-1600

Notre-Dame Basilica
116 Notre-Dame West
Open: Monday to Saturday between
June 25th and Labour Day
☎ (514) 849-1070

The Old Port
Waterfront between St-Laurent and Berri
Open: daily, most entertainment is
between May and September
☎ (514) 283-5256

Moosonee, Ont
Polar Bear Express
Ontario Northland Railway
c/o Union Station,
65 Front St E, Toronto,
Ontario M5J 1E6
Operates Saturday to Thursday from
June 21 to Labour Day
☎: Toronto 965-4268
elsewhere 1-800-268-9281

Morrisburg, Ont
Upper Canada Village
Hwy 2 11km east of Morrisburg
Open: daily, mid-May to mid-October
☎ (613) 543-3704

Niagara Falls
& Niagara-on-the-Lake, Ont
Fort George National Historic Site
Niagara Parkway south of Niagara-on-
the-Lake
Open: daily, mid-June to Labour Day
☎ (416) 468-4257

Laura Secord Homestead
Partition St, Queenston
Open: daily mid-June to Labour Day
☎ (416) 262-4851

Maid of the Mist boats
5920 River Road at Clifton Hill Rd
Operations daily spring to fall
☎ (416) 358-5781

Marineland
7657 Portage Rd S,
Open: daily, closed Fridays in winter
☎ (416) 356-9565

Niagara Parks Botanical Gardens
Niagara Pkwy, 8km north of Niagara Falls
Open: daily
☎ (416) 356-8554

Table Rock Scenic Tunnels
Table Rock House, beside Canadian
Falls
Open: daily ☎ (416) 358-3268

Skylon Tower
5200 Robinson St
Open: daily
☎ (416) 356-2651

Whirlpool Rapids Aerocar
River Road
Operations daily, early May to late
November
☎ (416) 356-2241

Shaw Festival Theatre
Niagara-on-the-Lake
☎ (416) 468-2172

Orillia, Ont
Stephen Leacock Memorial Home
Off Hwy 12b on Old Brewery Bay
Open: daily mid-June to Labour Day,
closed weekends April 15 to mid June
and Labour Day to mid-December
☎ (705) 326-9357

Ottawa, Ont (& Hull, Que)
Canadian Museum of Civilization
100 Laurier St, Hull, Que
Open: daily May 1 to Labour Day,
Tuesday to Sunday, rest of year
☎ (819) 776-7000

Central Experimental Farm
Prince of Wales Dr at Maple Dr
Open: daily
☎ (613) 995-5222

National Arts Centre
Confederation Square
Open: daily
☎ (613) 996-5051

National Gallery of Canada
380 Sussex Dr
Open: daily May to Labour Day,
Tuesday to Sunday, rest of year
☎ (613) 990-1985

National Museum of Science and Technology
1867 St Laurent Blvd
(2km south of Queensway)
Open: daily, May 1 to Labour Day,
Tuesday to Sunday, rest of year
☎ (613) 991-3044

Parliament Buildings
Open: daily
☎ (613) 993-1811

Péribonka, Que
Musée Louis-Hémon
700 rte Maria Chapdelaine
Open: daily May to Labour Day, Tuesday to Sunday rest of year
☎ (418) 374-2177

Quebec City, Que
Artillery Park National Historic Site
2 rue D'Auteuil
Open: daily May to October, closed
weekends rest of year
☎ (418) 648-4205

The Citadel
côté de la Citadelle, off rue St-Louis
Open: daily
☎ (418) 648-3563

National Battlefields Park
390 rue De Bernieres (reception and
interpretive centre)
Open: daily early June to early September
☎ (418) 648-4071

Ste-Anne-de-Beaupré, Que
Basilica of Ste-Anne-de-Beaupré
Centre of town, off Rte 138
Open: daily
☎ (418) 827-3781

Sault Ste Marie, Ont
Algoma Central Railway
Agawa Canyon Tour departs daily
between early June and mid- October.
Some winter excursions
☎ (705) 254-4331

MS Norgoma Museum Ship
Norgoma Dock at Foster Dr
Open: daily, June to September
☎ (705) 942-6984

Sudbury, Ont
Big Nickel Mine
5 km west on Hwy 17W
Open: daily May to mid-October
☎ (705) 522-3701

Science North
Ramsey Lake Rd & Paris St
2 km from Hwy 69
Open: daily
☎ (705) 522-3700

Tadoussac, Que
GREMM
Tadoussac Marina
Open: daily mid-June to mid-October
☎ (418) 235-4421

Old Chapel
Off Rte 138, Tadoussac
Open: daily late June to Labour Day
☎ (418) 235-4324

Pointe Noire Coastal Station
Rte 138,
south of Baie Ste-Catherine ferry dock
Open: daily late June to Labour Day
☎ (418) 237-4383

Thousand Islands Area, Ont
1000 Islands Skydeck
Hill Island
via Thousand Islands International Bridge
Open: daily, mid-May to October
☎ (613) 659-2335

Boldt Castle
Heart Island
Open: daily mid-May to early October
☎ (315) 658-4721

Thunder Bay, Ont
Old Fort William
Broadway Avenue, south off Hwy 61
Open: daily
☎ (807) 577-8461

Centennial Park
Arundel St off Boulevard Lake Park Rd
Open: daily
☎ (807) 683-6511

Toronto, Ont
Art Gallery of Ontario
317 Dundas St W
Open: daily in summer, closed Mondays
September to May
☎ (416) 977-0414

Black Creek Pioneer Village
1000 Murray Ross Parkway, Downsview
Open: daily
☎ (416) 736-1733

CN Tower
301 Front St W
Open: daily
☎ (416) 360-8500

Fort York
Garrison Road off Fleet St, near CNE
Open: daily
☎ (416) 392-6907

McMichael Canadian Art Collection
Islington Ave and Major MacKenzie Dr,
Klienburg
Open: daily May to October, closed
Mondays rest of the year
☎ (416) 893-1121

Metro Toronto Zoo
Meadowvale Rd,
Scarborough (5 km north of Hwy 401)
Open: daily
☎ (416) 392-5900

Ontario Parliament Buildings
Queen's Park
☎ (416) 965-4028

Ontario Place
955 Lakeshore Blvd
Open: daily mid-May to Labour Day
☎ (416) 965-7917

Ontario Science Centre
770 Don Mills Road
Open: daily except Mondays
☎ (416) 225-0146

Royal Ontario Museum
100 Queen's Park Crescent (at Bloor St W)
Open: daily
☎ (416) 586-5551

Trois-Rivières, Que
Les Forges du St-Maurice National Historic Park
10,000 boul des Forges
13 km north of Trois-Rivières
Open: daily, except December and January
☎ (819) 378-5116

Val-Jalbert, Que
Val-Jalbert Historic Village
Rte 169, 10km east of Roberval
Open: daily May to September
☎ (418) 275-3132

National, Provincial & Municipal Parks

Ontario
Algonquin Provincial Park
PO Box 219, Whitney, Ont
Open: all year
☎ (705) 633-5572
reservations (705) 633-5538

Bruce Peninsula National Park
PO Box 189
Tobermory, Ontario NOH 2RO
Open: all year
☎ (519) 596-2233

Fathom Five National Marine Park
PO Box 189
Tobermory, Ontario NOH 2RO
Open: April to mid-November
☎ (519) 596-2233

Kakabeka Falls Provincial Park
Trans-Canada Hwy 32km
west of Thunder Bay
☎ (807) 577-4231

Point Pelee National Park
Hwy 33, 10km south of Leamington
Open: daily
☎ (519) 322-2365

Polar Bear Provincial Park
For permission to enter, write to
District Manager,
Ministry of Natural Resources,
Box 190, Moosonee, Ontario POL 1Y0
☎ (705) 336-2987

Presqu'ile Provincial Park
Brighton, Ontario
Open: daily
☎ (613) 475-2204

Quetico Provincial Park
South of Hwy 11 near Atikokan
(no road access)
☎ (807) 597-2735

Sandbanks Provincial Park
Hwy 33, then County Rd 12
18km west of Picton
☎ (613) 393-3319

Sioux Narrows Provincial Park
Hwy 71, 5km south of Sioux Narrows
☎ (807) 226-5223

Sleeping Giant (Sibley) Provincial Park
County Road 587
south of Trans-Canada Hwy
☎ (807) 933-4332

St Lawrence Islands National Park
Hwy 2, Mallorytown
☎ (613) 923-5261

Tidewater Provincial Park
Charles Island, Moose River
☎ (705) 336-2987

Wheatley Provincial Park
Hwy 3, 13km east of Leamington
☎ (519) 825-4659

Quebec
Bic Provincial Park
On Rte 132, south of Bic
☎ (418) 722-3811

Bonaventure Island and Percé Rock Provincial Park
Open: daily June 24 to October 15
☎ (418) 782-2721

Forillon National Park
Rte 132
Open: daily June 1 to Labour Day, some activities all year round
☎ (418) 368-5505

Jacques Cartier Conservation Park
☎ (418) 622-4444

Laurentian Wildlife Reserve
☎ (418) 848-2422

Mont-Tremblant Park
Entrances via Rtes 117 and 125
☎ (819) 688-2281

Mount Orford Park
Rte 141, north of Magog via exits 115 & 118
☎ (819) 843-6233
Arts Centre (819) 843-3981/1-800-567-6155

Percé Bay Underwater Park
199 Rte 132
Open: daily May to September —
permit required
☎ (418) 782-5403

Pointe Taillon Park
Rte 169 near Péribonka
☎ (418) 695-2644

Saguenay Park
☎ (418) 272-2267

Accomodation, Campgrounds & Outfitters

Algonquin Park, Ont
Arowhon Pines
Arowhon Pines Rd, off Hwy 60
General Delivery, Huntsville P0A 1K0
☎ (705) 633-5661
(416) 483-4393 in winter

Algonquin Outfitters
RR 1M, Dwight, Ontario, P0A 1H0
☎ (705) 635-2243

The Portage Store (outfitters)
Canoe Lake, Hwy 60,
Algonquin Park, Ontario P0A 1K0
☎ (705) 633-5622

Chicoutimi, Que
Hotel Des Gouverneurs
1303 boul Talbot, 2km south on Rte 175
☎ (418) 549-6244
1-800-463-2820

Journey's End Motel
1595 boul Talbot 3km south on Rte 175
☎ (418) 693-8686 1-800-668-4200

Camping de la Carrière
Rte 172, 2km north on road to St-Honoré
☎ (418) 543-9269

Cochrane, Ont
Northern Lites Motel
Cochrane, south on Hwy 11
☎ (705) 272-4281

First Canada Inns Cochrane Station Hotel
200 Railway St Cochrane
☎ (705) 272-3500 1-800-267-7899

Drury Park (campground)
2km north on 2nd St
☎ (705) 272-4361

Cornwall, Ont
Best Western Parkway Inn
1515 Vincent Massey Dr
from Hwy 401 exit 789
☎ (613) 932-0451

Journey's End Motel
1625 Vincent Massey Dr
from Hwy 401 exit 789
☎ (613) 937-0111
1-800-668-4200

Kenora, Ont
Inn of the Woods
470 First Ave S
☎ (807) 468-5521

Kenora Travelodge
800 Hwy 17E, 1km east
☎ (807) 468-3155

Anicinabe Park (campground)
6th Ave S
☎ (807) 468-6878

Heritage Place KOA Kampground
Hwy 17, 16km east
☎ (807) 548-4380

Kingston, Ont
Holiday Inn
1 Princess St
☎ (613) 549-8400

Ramada Inn
1 Johnston St
☎ (613) 549-8100

Hochelaga Inn
24 Sydenham St
☎ (613) 549-5534

Lake Ontario Park (Municipal)
Campground
King St W at Portsmouth Ave
☎ (613) 542-6574

KOA Kingston
North of Hwy 401 exit 611, via Hwy 38n
to Cordukes Rd, then 1km east
☎ (613) 546-6140

La Malbaie, Que
Manoir Richelieu
181 rue Richelieu, Pointe-au-Pic
☎ (418) 665-3703
1-800-463-2613

Auberge Les Trois Canards
49 côté Bellevue, Pointe-au-Pic
☎ (418) 665-3761

Camping Chutes Fraser
500 chemin de la Vallee
5km north of Hwy 138
☎ (418) 665-2151

Manitoulin Island, Ont
Gordon's Lodge
Hwy 540B, 3 km north of Gore Bay
☎ (705) 282-2342

Rockgarden Terrace Resort
Lake Mindemoya, Hwy 542
☎ (705) 377-4652

South Bay Resort (Campground)
2km north of ferry terminal
☎ (705) 859-3106

Leamington, Ont
Journey's End Motel
279 Erie St South
☎ (519) 326-9017
1-800-668-4200

McKellar, Ont
Inn at Manitou
McKellar Centre Road,
McKellar, Ontario, P0G 1C0
☎ (705) 389-2171
(416) 967-3466 in winter

Minaki, Ont
Minaki Lodge
Hwy 596, 50km north of Trans-Canada Hwy
☎ (807) 224-4000

Montreal, Que
Queen Elizabeth Hotel
900 Rene Levesque West
☎ (514) 861-3511
1-800-441-1414

Bonaventure Hilton International
1 Place Bonaventure
☎ (514) 878-2332
1-800-268-9275

L'Hôtel de l'Institut
3535 St Denis
☎ (514) 282-5120
1-800-361-5111

Camping Pointe-des-Cascades
2, chemin du Canal (off Rte 20, exit 29)
☎ (514) 455-2501

Moosonee, Ont
Moosonee Lodge
☎ (705) 336-2351

Polar Bear Lodge
☎ (705) 336-2345

Morrisburg, Ont
Riverside-Cedar Park (Campground)
6 km east of Morrisburg on Hwy 2, from
Hwy 401, exit 758
☎ (613) 543-3287

Niagara Falls, Ont
Michael's Inn
5599 River Road
☎ (416) 354-2727

Skyline Foxhead Hotel &
Skyline Brock Hotel
5875 & 5685 Falls Ave
☎ (416) 374-4444
1-800-263-7135

Niagara Falls KOA Kampground
8625 Lundy's Lane (Hwy 20)
6km west of Niagara Falls
☎ (416) 356-2267

Niagara Glen-View Tent & Trailer Park
3950 Victoria Ave at River Road
☎ (416) 358-8689

Niagara-on-the-Lake, Ont
Prince of Wales Hotel
Junction of Picton and King Sts
☎ (416) 468-3246

Pillar and Post Inn
48 John St at King St
☎ (416) 468-2123

Shalamar Campground
Niagara Pkwy 8km south
☎ (416) 262-4895

Ottawa, Ont
Chateau Laurier Hotel
1 Rideau St
☎ (613) 232-6411
1-800-441-1414

Delta Ottawa
361 Queen St
☎ (613) 238-6000 / 1-800-268-1133

Novotel Hotel-Ottawa
33 Nicolas St
☎ (613) 230-3033 / 1-800-221-4542

Camp Hither Hills
Hwy 31, 22km south of Hwy 417,
Bronson St exit
☎ (613) 822-0509

Poplar Grove Campground
Hwy 31, 24km south of Hwy 417,
Bronson St exit
☎ (613) 821-2973

Percé, Que
Hotel La Normandie
222 Rte 132
☎ (418) 782-2112
1-800-463-0820

Hotel Le Mirage du Rocher Percé
288 Rte 132
☎ (418) 782-5151

Auberge du Pirate
Rte 132, near centre of town
☎ (418) 782-5055

Baie-de-Percé Camping
1650 rue Sir Louis Jette
☎ (418) 643-4875

Picton, Ont
Merrill Inn
343 Main St
☎ (613) 476-7451

Quebec City, Que
Le Château Frontenac
1 rue des Carrieres
☎ (418) 692-3861
1-800-441-1414

Le Château de Pierre
17 av Ste-Genevieve
☎ (418) 694-0429

Hôtel le Châteaubriand (Ste-Foy)
boul Hochelaga, off Rte 73, exit 136
☎ (418) 653-4901

Camping Municipal de Beauport
2 rue Fargy
from Rte 40, exit 321 16km north of city
☎ (418) 666-2228

Quebec City KOA
684 chemin Oliver
Rte 20 exit 311, 5km south of Pierre
Laport Bridge, after crossing from city
☎ (418) 831-1813

Rivière-du-Loup, Que
Auberge de la Pointe
10 boul Cartier
☎ (418) 862-3514

Journey's End Motel
85 boul Cartier
☎ (418) 867-4162
1-800-668-4200

Camping Municipal de la Pointe
Rte 132, La Pointe
☎ (418) 862-4281

Ste-Rose-du-Nord, Que
Auberge le Presbytère
136 rue du Quai
☎ (418) 675-2503

Sault Ste Marie, Ont
Bay Front Quality Inn
180 Bay St, Sault Ste Marie
☎ (705) 945-9264

Holiday Inn
208 St Mary's River Dr
☎ (705) 949-0611
1-800-HOLIDAY

Sault Ste Marie KOA Kampground
501 Fifth Line
9km north of town on Hwy 17
☎ (705) 759-2344

Tadoussac, Que
Hotel Tadoussac
165 rue Bord de l'Eau
Open: May to mid-October
☎ (418) 235-4421
1-800-463-5250

Camping Tadoussac
Rte 138, 2km north of ferry
· ☎ (418) 235-4501

Thunder Bay, Ont
Valhalla Inn
1 Valhalla Inn Rd
4 km west of junction Hwys 17/11 and 61
☎ (807) 577-1121
1-800-268-2500

Journey's End Motel
660 W Arthur St, just east of junction
Hwys 17/11 and 61
☎ (807) 475-3155
1-800-668-4200

Thunder Bay KOA Kampground
Spruce River Road, 11km east on Trans-Canada Hwy (Hwy 17/11)
☎ (807) 683-6221

Tobermory, Ont
Bruce Anchor Motel
Hwy 6 at Front St, Tobermory
☎ (519) 596-2555

Tobermory Lodge and Motel Resort
Harbourfront, 2km from ferry dock
☎ (519) 596-2224

Lands End Park (Campground)
Hay Bay Rd, 2km west of Tobermory
☎ (519) 596-2523

Toronto, Ont
Four Seasons Hotel
21 Avenue Road
☎ (416) 964-0411
1-800-268-6282

Harbour Castle Westin
One Harbour Square
☎ (416) 869-1600
1-800-228-3000

Indian Line Campground
Finch Avenue, west of Hwy 427
☎ (416) 678-1233

Albion Hills Campground
Hwy 50, 8 km (5 miles) north of Bolton
☎ (416) 880-4855

Ferry Services

St-Siméon to Rivière-du-Loup
Service operates April-September. At least three sailings each way daily, seven in July-early August.
☎ (418) 862-9545

Manitoulin Island, Ont
Service between Tobermory and South Baymouth has six sailings July-early September, at least two for the rest of season late-April to late-October.
☎ 1-800-265-3163

Cruise Line (St Lawrence & Ottawa Rivers, Rideau Canal)
St Lawrence Cruise Line Inc
253, Ontario St
Kingston, Ontario, K7L 2ZT
☎ (613) 549-8091

Local Tourist Authorities

Kingston, Ont
Kingston Area Visitor and Convention Bureau
209 Ontario St,
Kingston, Ontario K7L 2Z1
☎ (613) 548-4415

Montreal, Que
Greater Montreal Convention and Tourism Bureau
1555 Peel St, Suite 600,
Montreal, Quebec H3A 1X6
☎ (514) 873-2015

Ottawa, Ont
National Capital Commission Visitor Centre
14 Metcalf St
Mailing address: 161 Laurier St,
Ottawa, Ontario K1P 6J6
☎ (613) 239-5000 1-800-465-1867

Toronto, Ont
Metropolitan Toronto Convention and Visitors Association
207, Queen's Quay West,
Toronto M5J 1A7
☎ (416) 203-2500
1-800-363-1990

3

THE PRAIRIE PROVINCES

The prairie provinces, consisting of Manitoba, Saskatchewan and Alberta, stretch from Ontario's border close to the longitudinal center of Canada, to the crest-line of the Rocky Mountains. Although they are named after the prairies, these grassland plains in fact cover only the southern part of the region. North of this belt is a band of rolling parkland, with trees and a good agricultural soil. Slanting northwest beyond that is the Canadian Shield, and the land of rocks, lakes and boreal forest which covers its surface.

More often than not, the prairies are thought of as being flat and monotonous. In fact, they ascend in distinct steps, as they climb nearly a mile in height from the Hudson Bay lowlands to the Rocky Mountains. Ranges of hills rise above the plains and broad river valleys cut into the clay soil. In places river valleys form the 'Badlands', where erosion has sculpted layers of clays and rocks into moonscapes.

Before the Europeans arrived, these grassy plains and parklands were home to millions of buffalo and to nomadic Indian nations. Travellers on the Trans-Canada Highway which frequently parallels the original Canadian Pacific Railway line, will see how white man's arrival transformed the landscape. The buffalo are long gone, as are most of the Indians. Now this is the domain of cattle, wheat and other crops, along with potash mines and oil-wells, large and small communities.

Agriculture has brought its own landscape to the prairies. Groupings of grain elevators and seed bins punctuate the horizon. In summer the fields are a mass of colour: greens that gradually lighten and turn gold as the wheat ripens, the blue and white flax flowers, and yellow of the rapeseed. On uncultivated roadside land, wildflowers attract clouds of equally colorful butterflies. Hillsides now support some of largest grazing herds in the world, while feedlots fatten cattle prior to shipment.

Cities and towns are unique, reflecting the people and the way the prairies were developed. Onion-domed churches are a reminder of the eastern European immigrants. Along with eastern Canadians, Britons and Americans and many other nationalities, they were attracted by the prospect of land, free to anyone willing to bring it into production.

Some communities can trace their origins to fur-trading posts. The major prairie cities — Winnipeg, Brandon, Regina, Saskatoon, Calgary, and Edmonton, as well as many a small town — grew up around railway points. At first, the downtown core surrounded the railway station and yards, with residential areas beyond. Today skyscrapers dominate city centres and the railways, which concentrate on freight, have relocated in the suburbs. Few passenger services remain.

Visitors will find the prairies rich in recreational facilities. Some of those deep prairie valleys with their rivers and lakes are natural vacation playgrounds. National and provincial parks preserve the land as it was before the white man's arrival. Their facilities run the whole gamut from well-appointed resorts and hotels to wilderness campsites.

Travellers interested in Canada's history will find much to absorb them on the prairies. Legendary nomadic peoples who roamed the plains before discovery by Europeans are depicted in several museums. So is the history of the first white explorers, French from Quebec and English from Hudson Bay, who established fur-trading forts. You will hear about the French-speaking Métis whose rebellion led to Manitoba' foundation, and of the huge migrations from Europe brought here by the newly completed railways. And the North West Mounted Police, that remarkable band of men who maintained some sort of order throughout this transition.

Manitoba is a great deal more than prairies. One sixth of the surface is covered by inland waterways. To the north is the province's own Arctic coastline, some 400 miles (645 km) of Hudson Bay shore with the wheat port of Churchill connected to the south by railway. It is this watershed that shaped Manitoba's early history when Hudson's Bay Company explorers and traders sailed from England, travelling the river systems and founding such trading centres as Fort Garry on the site of present day Winnipeg.

Today those same waters are an important recreational resource, and Winnipeg is an interesting city, with an ethnic diversity reflected in its visitor attractions and entertainments.

Saskatchewan, along with Alberta, was carved out of the Northwest Territories in 1905 and is the only Canadian province with entirely straight, man-made, borders. Predominently agricultural, Saskatchewan also has important petroleum and potash deposits. Visitors will enjoy the wide open spaces stretching to the horizon, where the sky seems to cover the earth like a giant upturned bowl. Prominent attractions include the cities of Regina and Saskatoon as well as the Cypress Hills, the Qu'Appelle River Valley, Prince Albert National Park and various provincial parks.

Alberta's western boundary is formed by peaks of the Rocky Mountains. Although the eastern region is quite similar to the other prairie provinces, the west is one of Canada's most scenically varied areas. Large segments of the Rockies have been set aside as national parks, which attract overseas visitors in all seasons. In these parks there is a choice of world-class resorts, idyllic campgrounds and a whole spectrum of accommodations in between.

Farming, cattle ranching, and more recently petroleum, have trans-

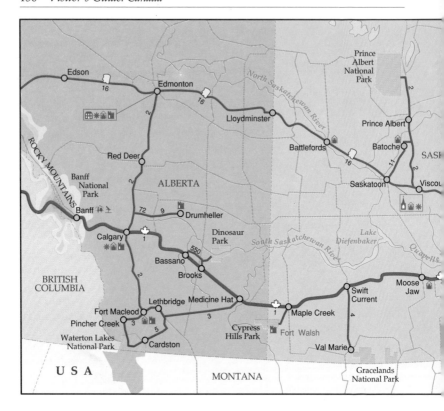

formed Alberta into one of Canada's wealthiest regions. Calgary and Edmonton are shiny new cities portraying a Texan-style prosperity with lavish visitor facilities.

Large chunks of provincial wealth have been channelled into imaginative museums and exhibits. One of the most recent contains dinosaurs reconstructed from bones found in and around the province's Badlands. Another tells the story of ancient buffalo hunters through dramatic presentations and exhibits.

This tour originates in Winnipeg, usually reached from Europe via Toronto, Calgary or Vancouver, and by road from the US via border crossings to the south. Some visitors will arrive in Winnipeg by rail from Toronto or Vancouver via Edmonton and Saskatoon.

Winnipeg (2 days)

The forks of the Red and Assiniboine Rivers, near the centre of present-day **Winnipeg**, have been visited or inhabited by humans for at least 6,000 years. The first European, La Vérendrye, arrived here in 1738 and built the fur-trading post, Fort Rouge. This was succeeded by the North West Company's Fort Gibraltar in 1804. The small Red River Settlement which grew beside the fort was largely populated by French-speaking contrac-

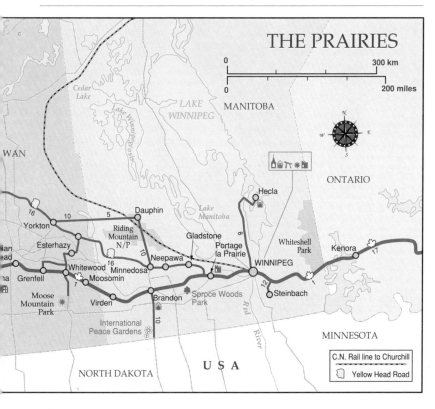

tors, former company employees and their Indian wives and children —
the first of the Manitoba Métis. The Hudson's Bay Company established
its Fort Garry close by in 1821 and that same year a group of Scottish
settlers, dispossessed by the Highland Clearances, arrived under the
sponsorship of Lord Selkirk.

Canada's purchase of the Hudson's Bay Company lands in 1869 stimulated immigration from eastern Canada, the United States and the British
Isles. This influx led to the Métis' rebellion under Louis Riel and to the
founding of a miniscule Province of Manitoba. The Canadian Pacific
Railway arrived in 1885, carrying large numbers of immigrants encouraged by prospects of free prairie land. They came from the United Kingdom and from the crumbling Russian and Austro-Hungarian Empires.
Many travelled no further than Winnipeg, and by 1891 its population had
reached 26,000. Golden years followed as the city went through a period
of urban growth unmatched anywhere else in Canada. By 1916, with a
population of 163,000, Winnipeg was Canada's fourth largest city and the
Prairies' great distribution centre. But that was not to last.

The 1920s and '30s brought disaster to the Prairies in the form of
drought, grasshopper plagues, falling grain prices and world-wide depression. Winnipeg's growth resumed after World War II, but by then its

Louis Riel

Hero, saint, murderer, mad-man — he was called them all. Leader of the Métis (people of mixed French/Indian heritage), Riel was born in St Boniface across the river from central Winnipeg in 1844, and his body is buried there. An educated man who studied for the priesthood and then the law, he led his people in the 1868 rebellion when government surveyors staked out plots of land belonging to the Métis. The Métis set up their own government (the first step in the founding of Manitoba) and executed one of the surveyors.

Anticipating reprisals, Riel fled to Montana, where he became a school-teacher for ten years. Meantime, many Métis moved to Saskatchewan, and when government surveyors again moved in to stake out their land they implored Riel to return as their leader. A second uprising concluded at Batoche (see page 162), scene of the last battle on British soil. Hardly a fair fight, it saw 300 Métis with inferior weapons ranged against 800 militia. Riel was tried as a traitor and hanged at the NWMP barracks in Regina. Now, each summer his trial is re-enacted in that city and it is almost always performed to a full house.

previous monopoly as distribution centre was challenged by Calgary, Edmonton, Saskatoon and Regina. Even so, this is a prosperous city of nearly 600,000 and home to more than half of Manitoba's population. Now as in the past, Winnipeg's economy is based largely on transportation, and today there are also secondary industries.

Culturally, it has been richly endowed by its ethnic population. Winnipeg is home to many of Canada's writers and artists; it has a prestigious ballet company, a symphony orchestra and an opera association, a renowned art gallery and thriving theatre. There are two major universities as well as colleges and specialized schools. Various ethnic groups have built interesting cathedrals, churches and cultural centres. The city is enhanced by parks and amateur sports facilities. Football, ice hockey and curling are major spectator sports.

In many ways, this is the most diverse of Canada's Prairie cities. Although often overlooked it is definitely well worth a two-day stay, and perhaps more as a base from which to explore neighbouring attractions.

There is nothing intimidating about Winnipeg's size because the simple grid layout, broad avenues and ample parking make it easy for motorists and pedestrians. Bus tours are enjoyable as are boat excursions on the Red and Assiniboine Rivers, including one to Lower Fort Garry. The city also has a public bus system. Most visitor sites are within walking distance of Portage and Main Street, a few blocks north of the confluence of the Red and Assiniboine rivers. This intersection of wide streets, long claimed to be the windiest in the country, is now sheltered by tall bank towers and underground walkways.

North on Main Street the Manitoba Museum of Man and Nature is without doubt one of the finest interpretive museums in Canada. Its seven galleries bring visitors quickly through billions of years, from the beginnings of the universe to formation of the Earth and the geological changes that took place in Manitoba. Other galleries depict the Prairies and the province's Arctic shoreline when the first humans arrived. *Nonsuch* is a replica of the ship that sailed from England in 1688 in search of furs, and led to formation of the Hudson's Bay Company. The full-sized replica which sailed from England in 1970 is now berthed alongside a recreated seventeenth-century London dock. The museum's most fascinating exhibits relate to the fur trade, and the company that ruled northern and western Canada and parts of the United States for two centuries.

This museum shows the dependence of the Plains Indians on the buffalo, and of the animals' disappearance which coincided with European settlement. Lives of early immigrant farmers are illustrated with displays and artifacts. A fascinating Urban Gallery portrays life here in 1920 when the city was at its most prosperous.

Returning southwards, the Exchange District and Old Market Square are part of a heritage district comprising fifteen blocks of late nineteenth-century warehouses, banks and business premises. Carefully restored they are converted now to shops, restaurants and nightspots. South of Portage Avenue on Main Street a tiny patch of park encloses the stone gateway of Upper Fort Garry. Across from it, the Fort Garry Hotel is one of Canada's historic railway hotels, handsomely restored with a European-style casino occupying its seventh floor.

The Forks National Historic Site behind the railway station (across Main Street), incorporates former railway lands at the junction of the Red and Assiniboine Rivers. This site commemorates peoples who have contributed to the transformation of the Canadian west: natives who hunted, fished and traded here, French explorers, Métis and Scottish settlers, trading company employees and railway builders. Close to the river forks, former railway warehouses have been converted to accommodate a produce market, crafts shops, cafés, snack bars and restaurants. There is also an interpretive centre, and riverside grassy areas with two amphitheatres and a small boat dock.

St Boniface across the Red River is a bilingual community which recalls the city's French and Métis founders. The Basilica here is the oldest in western Canada, originally built in 1818 and replaced several times following fires. The last was destroyed in 1968, leaving only the façade and part of the walls which enclose the present structure. Louis Riel, Manitoba's founder, is buried in the churchyard. Next door, the St Boniface Museum is housed in Winnipeg's most historic structure, built for the Grey Nuns in 1848. It is now devoted to Franco-Manitoban history which of course includes Louis Riel. Both the museum and basilica face Taché Promenade, a pleasant riverside walk with excellent views of the Winnipeg skyline.

Winnipeg's Assiniboine Park Zoo is a great attraction

The Forks, a popular place to meet and relax in Winnipeg

To explore most of Winnipeg's other landmarks requires the use of a car or public transportation.

About ten blocks west of the city centre, the Manitoba legislature building stands in spacious grounds on the banks of the Assiniboine River. Built of local limestone, this neo-classical building was completed in 1919. Inside, flanking the grand staircase are two huge bronze buffalo representing the province's emblem. Atop the dome, the gilded 'Golden Boy' clutches a wheatsheaf and holds the torch which illuminates Manitoba's future. Within the grounds statues reflect the province's diverse founding peoples: Queen Victoria, Lord Selkirk, Pierre de La Vérendrye and Louis Riel. Assiniboine Park, 5km (3 miles) to the west, is a 152 ha (375 acre) park encompassing various sports and recreational facilities, formal flower gardens and an excellent zoo — all of which are free.

Lower Fort Garry National Historic Park, about 32km (20 miles) north of Winnipeg, via Hwy 9, is reached by driving north on Main Street until it crosses the Winnipeg by-pass and becomes Hwy 9. This site on the banks of the Red River contains the stone fort built by the Hudson's Bay Company in 1830. It replaced an earlier fort at the Forks, which was subjected to regular flooding by the Red River. Governor George Simpson intended his new fort as company headquarters in Rupert's Land, and a fitting home for his new bride. However, located too far from the Red River settlement, it was not a success. Later, when the company sold its lands to the new Dominion of Canada, the fort took on a number of different roles. In 1873, this was where soldiers were sworn into a new force to be known

An Indian celebration at the Forks National Historic Site, Winnipeg

as the North West Mounted Police. Later it became a penitentiary, an asylum and then a country club. Now restored to the mid-nineteenth-century fur-trading period, costumed guides provide interpretation. In addition, the reception centre contains historical displays and audio-visual presentations on the fur trade and the Red River Settlement.

Winnipeg is connected by buses and airlines to all major Canadian cities and many place in the United States. It is on the main Via Rail trans-continental passenger service and terminus of the line to Churchill in Northern Manitoba. In the Additional Information the Hotel Fort Garry is included for its historical connections, and another for its convenient location. Winnipeg also has many less expensive hotels and motels, as well as B & Bs, a university residence and hostel. The campground is suitable for RVs. Bird's Hill Provincial Park, some distance away but very pleasant, also has full services.

Excursions from Winnipeg

• *Falcon Beach via the Royal Canadian Mint & Steinbach*
(250km/155 miles return)
Falcon Beach in the Whiteshell Provincial Park is a popular summer weekend destination for Winnipeggers. Located on the Ontario border it is reached via the Trans-Canada Highway (Manitoba Hwy 1), so could also be visited during a drive between Winnipeg and Kenora, Ontario.

Leaving downtown Winnipeg as Hwy 1 crosses Lagimodiere Boul, you will see the glass-sided futuristic building of the **Royal Canadian Mint**. In addition to producing Canada's coinage, this modern plant makes coins for foreign countries. Galleries are designed for visitors to view the manu-facturing process, while collections and exhibits explain the history of Canada's coinage.

Steinbach, 16km (10 miles) south of the Trans-Canada Highway on Hwy 12, is the site of a heritage village with buildings moved here to commemorate the Mennonites who came from the Ukraine in 1874. A windmill dominates the village of some twenty buildings laid out in the Mennonites' traditional pattern. Farmhouses, smithy, printshop, general store and combined church/schoolhouse are all furnished to period. Displays of antiques and manuscripts, as well as traditional household artifacts and vintage farm equipment will be of interest. A cafeteria serves Mennonite fare in a converted livery stable. The Pioneer Days Festival, held on the first weekend of August features agricultural methods of Mennonite pioneers.

Falcon Beach is hub of the 2,590sq km (1,000sq mile) Whiteshell Park, a busy place on summer weekends because of its recreational facilities. These include a wide sandy beach and lake for swimming, boats for hire, tennis courts, a golf course and riding stables. Resorts, fishing lodges and a fully serviced campground accommodate overnighters. A variety of habitats range from the great rocks of the Canadian Shield to black spruce swamps and Prairie grasslands, 200 lakes and a dozen rivers. This is a good place to relax on the beach with a picnic, or explore further by walking on one of the interpretive trails.

• *Hecla Island via Gimli (350km/217 miles return)*
This drive goes north along Hwy 8, beside the lower section of Lake Winnipeg to another of Manitoba's Provincial Parks. En route it passes some of Winnipeg's favourite weekend spots, including **Winnipeg Beach** situated in a small provincial park. This town has a number of motels, restaurants, stores and campgrounds. **Gimli**, about halfway between Winnipeg and Hecla Island, is the largest Icelandic community outside Iceland. It features a giant Viking statue and a museum tracing the community's history which focuses on the local fishing industry.

Hecla Island Provincial Park, reached via causeway from **Riverton**, is a collection of rocky, wooded islands. Park wildlife includes a large moose population, wolves, foxes and lynx, as well as 180 species of bird. Located on the continent's Central Flyway, its marshes provide a summer home to 50,000 migrating wildfowl. Brochures and maps in the reception centre show what is where. One brief walk is on a wooded trail to the viewing tower, where you might see a moose or two at dusk or dawn. **Hecla** village has been partially restored as the small community established by Icelanders on the shores of Lake Winnipeg over a century ago. They came to Canada following eruption of Mt Hecla in their original homeland, and harsh as it looks, life here held far more promise than what they left behind. Gull Harbour within the park is a modern resort where you can have a good lunch if you are on a day trip, or stop overnight for some extra time out. The campground is suitable for RVs.

• *Churchill (by air or rail)*
Churchill, on Hudson Bay is Canada's only Arctic port. Inaccessible by road it is served by air and a tri-weekly Via Rail service from Winnipeg. The 1,697km (1,054 mile) train journey takes 36 hours, the flight a little over 2 hours.

Located at the mouth of the Churchill River the community has a short but flourishing tourist season. Summer visitors are attracted by its very remoteness, its carpets of wild flowers above the tree line, wildlife that includes caribou herds and belugas, and fantastic fishing opportunities. Autumn though is the busiest time for tour operators, when they take small groups in tundra buggies to see the polar bears, who create havoc for residents but provide a unique experience for visitors.

Churchill also has interesting historical sites. First inhabited by Europeans in 1685 it was discovered by the Dane, Jens Munk, in 1619. The first permanent settlement was the Hudson's Bay Company's Fort Churchill named after John Churchill, a company director who later became Duke of Marlborough. A second fort was built and destroyed by the French in 1782, after which the original Fort Churchill was re-established as a trading post. The present town traces its origins to the completion of the railway and harbour facilities in 1931. While the ice-free season is limited to three months, the port is 1,600km (1,000 miles) closer to Europe than is

Polar bear and cubs near Churchill, Hudson Bay

The interpretative centre at Riding Mountain National Park

Montreal, so it has advantages as a port for shipping Prairie wheat. Although viewing the wildlife is the main reason for coming here, the town's reception centre has exhibits on the fur trade and Hudson's Bay Company posts. Here you can get information on two of the area's historic sites, Cape Merry where Captain Munk landed, and the remains of Fort Prince of Wales which is reached by boat. A wonderful Inuit museum traces the local history of the fur trade. More importantly it describes cultures of the native peoples from this region, starting with the pre-Dorset inhabitants of 1,700BC and progressing to the present-day Inuit.

Because transportation, accommodation and tours are limited, and the tourism season brief, it is advisable to book a package with one of the tour organizations well in advance. Two are listed in the Addditional Information. The whale-watching season is July and August. For polar bears you should be here in October or early November — and bring warm clothes.

Winnipeg to Riding Mountain National Park (280km/174 miles, 2 days)

This drive takes you northwest of Winnipeg to Riding Mountain National Park. Leave the city via the Trans-Canada Highway (Hwy 1) and drive 75km (47 miles) to **Portage la Prairie**. La Vérendrye arrived in 1738 and for fifteen years it was his base for exploring the Prairies to the west. The name goes back to the time when it was a resting area in the short portage between the Assiniboine River and Lake Manitoba. Now irrigation from the Assiniboine River has made it central to one of Manitoba's richest vegetable-growing regions.

In Portage La Prairie, turn north and continue along Hwy 16 to pass through Gladstone and Neepawa, then **Minnedosa** which has several times been chosen as Manitoba's loveliest town. Turn north on Hwy 10 here, to the gates of **Riding Mountain National Park**.

The visitor centre in **Wasagaming** gives complete descriptions of the park's natural and human history. The 2,978sq km (1,150sq mile) preserve is part of the Manitoba Escarpment, a tilting shelf of shale with its highest edge 756m (2,480ft) above the plains on the park's north and east sides. Abrupt enough to be called a mountain, it was named by men travelling west who exchanged their canoes for horses at this point. The park embraces three distinct ecological zones: some of the last remaining eastern deciduous forest in Manitoba, boreal forest and parklands of mixed forest and grasslands. Park wildlife includes moose, elk, deer and bears, a herd of bison and numerous beavers and wildfowl.

Nature fans will enjoy the short hiking trails, back-country treks, canoe routes and wilderness camping areas. Others come to the park for swimming and boating, golf, tennis and horse-back riding. Winter brings downhill and cross-country skiing, snowshoeing, snowmobiling, ice-fishing, and some camping.

Located on the shores of Clear Lake, Wasagaming is the park's hub containing the aforementioned reception centre, stores and small restaurants, a filling station and the world's largest cinema constructed entirely of logs. Two rather different places to stay are listed in the Additional Information. There are others in Wasagaming and at Onanole, close to the park gates. One of several campgrounds with RV services is within walking distance of Wasagaming.

Riding Mountain National Park to Prince Albert National Park (640km/398 miles, 2 days)

Drive north through Riding Mountain park on Hwy 10 to **Dauphin** named in honour of the French king's son by La Vérendrye who arrived here in the 1730s. Settlers from Ontario in the 1880s were followed by three major waves of Ukranian immigrants. Canada's annual National Ukranian Festival (held in early August), features colourful national costumes and traditional foods, folk song and dance.

Leave Dauphin via Hwys 10 and 5, which upon crossing the border becomes Saskatchewan Hwy 10, and continue to **Yorkton**. This town was founded in 1882 by settlers from Ontario who were joined by immigrants from Eastern Europe when the railway arrived in 1889. Today the city (population 15,000) is centre of a rich grain-growing area. The Yorkton branch of Saskatchewan's Western Development Museum (one of four such provincial museums) recreates the lives and times of settlers of many ethnic groups in Western Canada. St Mary's Ukranian Catholic church, the first Ukranian brick-built church in Western Canada, has a dome ceiling painting regarded as one of the finest in North America.

Leave Yorkton via Hwy 16 and approximately 250km (158 miles) later is the intersection of Hwy 2, just beyond Viscount. Continue north on Hwy 2 to **Prince Albert**. This city (population 32,000), named after Queen Victoria's consort was founded in 1866 as a Presbyterian mission. The growing population of British descent was joined by those of French, Ukranian, and German ancestry, but the boom collapsed when the Canadian Pacific Railway adopted a more southerly route. Today Prince Albert is an administrative and agricultural service centre and the gateway to northern Saskatchewan's lumbering industry.

Prince Albert National Park's townsite on Lake Waskesiu, 88km (55 miles) to the north, is reached via Hwy 2. The park covers 3,875sq km (1,496sq miles) of rolling hills, lakes, streams and bogs, bridging the aspen parkland of central Saskatchewan with the province's vast northern boreal forest. An exciting treasure house for naturalists, it is home to elk, deer, moose, caribou, foxes, wolves, bears, badgers, beavers and 200 bird species. The rare bald eagle is sometimes seen here, while Lavallee Lake has a white pelican nesting ground. There is also a small bison herd in a paddock close to the park's southeast entrance. An interpretation centre introduces visitors to these creatures and to the author/conservationist Grey Owl, whose restored cabin and grave can be reached by a hiking trail then by boat or canoe.

Prince Albert National Park has 100km (60 miles) of hiking trails, wilderness camping areas and canoe routes. The fishing is great, espe-

> ## The Legend of Grey Owl
> As the son of a Scottish father and Apache mother, Grey Owl cut a fine figure with his lean features, braided black hair and buckskin clothes. For years he worked as a trapper in Quebec, until his Iroquois wife Anahereo brought home two tiny beavers orphaned by one of his snares. On befriending the young beavers, he gave up trapping, and was on his way to becoming Canada's best known conservationist.
> Grey Owl published his first article on conservation in 1929, and had four books to his credit within nine years. He lectured in North America and Britain, spending his last seven years as the resident naturalist of Prince Albert National Park. There, in a wilderness accessible only by canoe, he built a log home and shared it with his beavers. Following a strenuous lecture tour in 1938, Grey Owl developed pneumonia and died at the age of 50.
> Shortly afterwards, it was discovered that this legendary Canadian was actually an Englishman named Archibald Belaney. Without a drop of Indian blood in his veins, he had been born in Hastings and raised there by his grandmother and two maiden aunts. During an unhappy childhood he read about Canadian Indians living off the land. At the age of 17 he apparently decided to become one of them. Emigrating to Northern Ontario he learned wilderness survival skills from the Ojibwas, and called himself Grey Owl. Nobody guessed his secret, not even his wife.
> Rocked by news of the fraud, Grey Owl's admirers soon forgot his valuable contribution to conservation. Now, with the subject on almost everybody's mind, it is his work and not his pedigree that is remembered. The cabin where he lived with his beavers is visited by hundreds every summer.

cially for trout, pike and walleye. In winter, cross-country skiing, snowshoeing and ice fishing are popular. Waskesiu Lake townsite has country club style leisure facilities, shops and restaurants. Here is one of Canada's finest golf courses as well as tennis courts, lawn bowling, lake swimming and boat rentals. Trail-riding stables have programmes for beginners; bicycles are available for use in town and on the trails.

Accommodation in and around the townsite includes self-catering cottages, resorts and lodges. A campground, one of several in the park suitable for RVs, is close to town. All in all Prince Albert National Park gives a relaxing few days with little or no driving.

Prince Albert National Park to Saskatoon via Batoche (200km/124 miles, 2 days)
This drive to Batoche retraces Hwy 2 to Prince Albert then continues for about 60km (37 miles) south to the intersection with Hwy 225. Follow that

�֎   road to Batoche National Historic Park on the banks of the South Saskatchewan River.

The village of **Batoche** became the unofficial capital of the Métis buffalo
hunters and farmers who settled here in the 1870s when they were forced
to leave Manitoba's Red River Settlement. It also became the scene of great
tragedy. After some fifteen peaceful years, grievances against the central
government mounted, particularly over the question of land ownership.
The Métis called upon their old leader Louis Riel for guidance. His
petition to Ottawa was ignored, and soon the local Crees (who had their
own complaints) joined the Métis. Increased tensions culminated in the
North West Rebellion in the spring of 1885.

The government hastily organized a force under General Frederick
Middleton. Fighting took place along the banks of the South Saskatchewan River, with the greatly outnumbered Métis under the military
leader Gabriel Dumont fighting a guerrilla war. It ended with Middle-
tons's successful seige of Batoche. Riel was tried and hanged at Regina.
Cree chiefs Poundmaker and Big Bear were imprisoned and died soon
after their release. Dumont escaped to the United States, but returned to
Batoche where he is buried.

The park's interpretive centre has an excellent audio-visual presentation on the complex history of Batoche through the eyes of settlers and
rebellion leaders. Displays include scenes from the battle, military equipment and other artifacts. You can follow the battle through on-site markers and some restored buildings, while costumed guides explain events of
the fight for Batoche.

Saskatoon is about 90km (56 miles) from Batoche, via Hwys 225, 312
and 11. Named after a Cree word for the succulent berry growing here,
Saskatoon was founded as a Temperance colony in 1883 by settlers from
eastern Canada and Great Britain. They were followed by immigrants
from Eastern Europe and Scandinavia, and when the railway arrived in
1890 Saskatoon became a hub of western Canada's transportation system.
Situated in the heart of Saskatchewan's rich grain belt it is the province's
largest city (population 185,000), and regional centre for the northern
Prairies.

Some of its most pleasing vistas are seen from parklands bordering the
South Saskatchewan River, most especially the low west bank which is
site of the château-style Bessborough Hotel, Anglican and Roman Catholic cathedrals and Knox United Church. From the higher east bank all
seven bridges can be seen astride the river connecting the city's two
halves, giving Saskatoon its nickname 'City of Bridges'.

Saskatoon's University of Saskatchewan has an attractive riverside
campus. There the Diefenbaker Centre has a museum on recent Canadian
history and one of the country's most colourful prime ministers. Across
the river, the Mendel Art Gallery & Civic Conservatory in its parkland
setting is certainly worth visiting. Ukranian culture is well represented in
both the Ukranian Museum of Canada close to the Mendel Art Gallery,

An Indian dancer at Wanuskewin Heritage Park, near Saskatoon

Indian gathering, Wanuskewin Heritage Park

and the Ukraina Museum beside the Ukranian Catholic Cathedral.

Saskatoon's branch of the Western Development Museum is of exceptional interest to anyone concerned with Saskatchewan in the early 1900s. Its Boomtown 1910 replicates a small prairie town of this era when settlers had brought their farms into full production, crops were bountiful, prices high and such communities prospered. A separate display focuses on mail-order shopping, so important to rural life until the 1970s. The museum also features a fine assembly of classic cars, antique farm machinery and equipment.

Wanuskewin Heritage Park, 5km (3 miles) north of the city, is a new 100 ha (248 acre) archeological park showing 8,000 years of North American prehistory and native Indian culture. It has a modern reception centre and prehistoric sites such as tipi rings, buffalo jumps and pounds, and habitation areas clustered within a kilometre of each other.

Saskatoon supports a symphony orchestra and several theatre groups. It has good restaurants, hotels and motels, B & Bs, a hostel and YWCA residence. Two downtown hotels are listed in the Additional Information. Both campgrounds listed offer full services for RVs. The city has direct air services and bus connections to most major Canadian cities. It is on Via Rail's trans-continental service.

Saskatoon to Edmonton (530km/329 miles, 2 days)

Drive west from Saskatoon via Hwy 16 towards **North Battleford**, a distance of 140km (87 miles). Battleford and North Battleford (collectively known as 'The Battlefords', with a combined population of 18,000) are a service centre for the surrounding region which depends upon agriculture and petroleum development. Battleford was one of the earliest settlements in western Canada. In 1876, while little more than a fur-trading post it was selected as the capital of the vast North West Territories, but six years later the territorial capital was moved to Regina. When the new Canadian National Railway by-passed Battleford, the neighbouring community of North Battleford was born and it soon became a city.

Fort Battleford National Historic Park is a reconstruction of the North West Mounted Police district headquarters to which white settlers fled during the North West Rebellion (see page 162). Poundmaker surrendered here after Batoche, and here Canada's last public execution saw eight Indians hanged. The reception centre displays artifacts from the period, including Poundmaker's war club and rifle, and a Gatling gun used by government forces.

North Battleford is site of the Western Development Museum's Heritage Farm and Village. With the 'Story of Agriculture' as its theme, it is the reconstruction of a 1925 Saskatchewan village with pioneer farmhouses, churches, NWMP post, bank, barbershop and drugstore. In summer, there are demonstrations of 1920s farming equipment and techniques together with various agricultural displays.

It is a further 140km (87 miles) through rich agricultural lands and heavy oil country to **Lloydminster**. The main street, Meridian Avenue, marks the 110th meridian, as well as the Saskatchewan/Alberta border, which means that Lloydminster (population 17,000) has city status in both provinces.

After another 250km (155 miles) via Hwy 16 is **Edmonton**, Canada's most northerly major city and Alberta's capital. Situated between the productive farmlands of southern Alberta and the vast resources of the northern regions, it has over 2,200 oilwells within a radius of 40km (25 miles). Accordingly it is acknowledged as Canada's oil capital.

The city is situated in the North Saskatchewan River Valley on a site which has attracted human habitation for at least 5,000 years. European settlement started when the Hudson's Bay and North West Companies built trading forts here in 1795. When these companies merged in 1821, Fort Edmonton (probably named after a district in London) became centre of the western fur trade.

Edmonton underwent a major boom when it became a supply centre for the Yukon Gold Rush in the late 1890s. The railway was completed this far in 1905 and Edmonton was named as capital of the new province of Alberta that same year. Development of aviation saw this city become a gateway to the resource-rich north. A further economic boost arrived during World War II when it served as supply base for construction of the Alaska Highway (see page 226). However, its present prosperity can be traced most directly to nearby Leduc, where in 1947 the location of oil was the first of many discoveries.

Edmonton (metropolitan area population 675,000) has used its wealth to create a vibrant, handsome and cosmopolitan city in the heart of the northern Prairies. Its people have invested heavily in the arts and in preserving their heritage, so visitors will find plenty to do and see in this warm-hearted city.

A bus or walking tour provides an excellent introduction. These are available from tourism offices at the Convention Centre located at 97th St and Jasper Ave, at the airport and beside major highways approaching the city. A particularly pleasant stroll is along the Heritage Trail, starting from the Convention Centre then continuing along the escarpment overlooking the North Saskatchewan River to the Alberta Legislature Building. The trail combines a series of interpretive galleries describing the city's past, and goes to some of the more dramatic viewpoints. Much of the city has been set aside for public pleasure. The river banks are preserved as Canada's largest urban park, embracing sports and recreational facilities and many kilometres of all-year-round trails. There are striking buildings, such as the imposing atriums of the Muttart Conservatory. AGT Vista 33's viewing gallery atop the government telephone tower gives panoramic views of the area as far as Refinery Row beyond the eastern suburbs.

Allow several hours for Fort Edmonton Park which traces development of the city through full-sized replicated streets from different periods. The history lesson starts with the rebuilt Hudson's Bay Company fort of 1846, staffed by costumed 'residents'. This leads to historical streets portraying Edmonton in 1885, 1905 and 1927. A restored steam train and street car carry visitors to various sections of the park. Shows, festivals and musical performances are featured at weekends and holidays, which attract large crowds.

❋   For a completely different experience, West Edmonton Mall is an extraordinary complex, part shopping centre and part amusement park. Spread over 45 ha (111 acres) are 800 stores, a competition-sized skating rink, two lakes — one for bathing, complete with surf, and the other for submarine rides! It even has its own hotel.

❖   The Provincial Museum of Alberta, in a building erected in 1967 to commemorate Canada's Centennial is a good place to learn more about Alberta before moving on. Four large galleries illustrate the province's heritage with displays on palaeontology and geology, zoology and human habitation from its earliest times.

During Edmonton's Klondike Days (held over ten days each July) citizens turn back the clock to relive the Klondike Gold Rush with parades, costume parties, contests, gold-panning, old-time casino gambling and general merriment.

Edmonton has direct airline connections with most other Canadian cities as well as with Los Angeles, Chicago, London and Frankfurt. There are bus connections with other North American cities; Via Rail's passenger service connect to Vancouver and Winnipeg. It is a large city, but has a driver-friendly layout, or there are buses and a light rail transit line.

This is a city with good theatres, an opera association, ballet company and symphony orchestra; it has excellent restaurants and first-rate hotels. The Hotel Macdonald is one of the traditional railway hotels, recently reopened following restoration. Moderately priced accommodation includes B & Bs and a hostel. The Additional Information also lists the full service campground closest to downtown.

Edmonton to Drummheller (280km/174 miles, 1 day)

This drive ventures into the Alberta Badlands with an overnight stop there before going on to Calgary. An alternative route is to join up with the Western Canada itineraries by driving the Yellowhead Hwy (Hwy 16) from Edmonton to Jasper (see page 192), a distance of 360km (224 miles).

From Edmonton head south on Hwy 2. Soon after leaving the city's suburbs, the road passes close to the site of Leduc Number One, the well which gushed black oil on 13 February 1947 and led to the prosperity that now characterizes Alberta. **Red Deer**, 150km (93 miles) to the south, was settled in 1882 when some Scots appear to have confused the abundant local elk for the red deer of their homeland. A modern city (population 48,000), it services the agricultural and petro-chemical industries.

Continue south on Hwy 2 for about 100km (62 miles) then turn east on Hwy 72 to Hwy 9, which leads into **Drumheller**. The area around Drumheller, located on the Red Deer River, was first settled by ranchers in 1897.

The townsite was later purchased by a Colonel Drumheller who started coal mining operations in the valley. When the railway arrived in 1912 the town grew quickly with coal as its economic base, but when oil and gas replaced coal in the late 1940s the mines closed. The small city (population 6,500) diversified as an agricultural centre, and tourism based on its unique location has become increasingly valuable.

Drumheller lies in the strange and rugged Red Deer Valley Badlands. Part of this area has been developed as the Dinosaur Trail and the East Coulee Drive, circular routes 48 and 25 km (30 and 15 miles) long which originate in Drumheller. Valley walls clearly show the multi-layers of 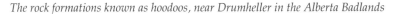 sediment which built up into clay, shale and rock over billions of years before the Rocky Mountains were formed, encasing the fossils of sea creatures and land animals. The arid terrain is dotted with cactii and hoodoos — mushroom-shaped columns of clay and soft rock capped by harder rocks — shaped by wind and water over 10,000 years. You will see the remains of recent coal mines and small mining communities, and the dozens of donkey-head pumps topping the oil-wells.

Perhaps the best overall view is from the lookout above Horsethief

The rock formations known as hoodoos, near Drumheller in the Alberta Badlands

Canyon where rustlers used to hide stolen horses while they altered the brands. Travelling along this upper level, you will see the impressive Tyrrell Museum of Palaeontology below. The museum is named after a young government geologist who, when searching for coal in 1884, came upon the petrified skull of a creature later named Albertosaurus. Opened in 1985, the museum is an astonishing combination of ancient dinosaur skeletons and state-of-the-art technology —the authors regard it as one of Canada's top five museums. In 11,200sq m (120,000sq ft) its displays, computer terminals, mini-theatres and indoor garden describe the evolution of life over 3.5 billion years. Its central theme is a collection of dinosaurs, with 800 specimens from around the world including thirty-five complete skeletons stalking through dioramas in the Dinosaur Hall. The preparation laboratory gives a fascinating peek into the techniques used to make fossils ready for display.

Within the museum grounds self-guided hiking trails explore the surrounding Badlands. Close by, the Midland Provincial Park has more trails leading to the site of a former coal mine with exhibits about coal-mining in the area. Fossil and gem enthusiasts will enjoy the city's museum and a number of local stores cater for rockhounds.

Drumheller offers escorted tours, along with recreational opportunities such as golf, tennis and swimming. Canoe rentals are available on the river. There are motels, some B & Bs and a full service campground on the Dinosaur Trail.

Drumheller to Calgary (40km/87 miles, 2 days)

The drive south via Hwy 2 to **Calgary** takes about 90 minutes. Located at the confluence of the Bow and Elbow Rivers, where the Prairies give way to the foothills of the Rockies and the mountains themselves provide a distant backdrop, this is a dazzling city.

Land around Calgary has been settled by humans for the last 12,000 years. European history started with the North West Company's David Thompson, who wintered near here in 1787. White buffalo hunters arrived in the 1860s and traders from the United States built fortified posts to exchange what was literally 'rot-gut' whiskey with the Indians for buffalo hides. This vile trade led to the establishment of Fort Calgary (named after a bay in the Scottish Hebrides) by the newly-formed North West Mounted Police in 1875.

The settlement that grew up around this fort mushroomed into a town, and then a city after the Canadian Pacific Railway arrived in 1883 and laid out the present townsite. Cattle ranching and meat packing dominated the economy, followed by cash-crop farming. When oil was discovered at nearby Turner Valley, it led to Alberta's first refinery built here in 1923. As more petroleum finds followed, so Calgary stood ready to reap the tremendous rewards resulting from them. Now it has a population of close to 700,000 and covers 671 sq km (259 sq miles) which in area at least makes it Canada's second largest city.

While building an ultra-modern metropolis for today, Calgary remembers its past in stirring recreations and museums and re-enactment of times when this was indeed the wild, wild, west. For the history of the Canadian west, and in particular of its native people, you will want to visit the Glenbow Museum located in the same complex as Calgary's Convention Centre. Also visit Heritage Park, claimed to be Canada's largest living museum, 5km (3 miles) south of the city centre on a site overlooking the Glenmore Reservoir. Seen as a functioning town, it has among other things its own newspaper, a bakery selling oven-warm bread, a log church still used for weddings, and costumed citizens who talk convincingly of their life here. Visitor transportation is by way of a steam train, horse-drawn bus and electrical streetcar. Allow time enough to sample some Alberta beef and homemade pie in the Wainwright Hotel, ride an old-fashioned carousel, wander along the 1910 street, and you will definitely capture the spirit of western pioneers.

The Fort Calgary interpretive centre on the fort's original Bow River site, gives an insight into the formative years of the North West Mounted Police as well as the city's early days. From the fort, a pedestrian bridge leads to St George's Island, and the modernistic buildings of its zoo and prehistoric park. Zoo habitats are designed to simulate conditions the animals would experience in the wild; the prehistoric park recreates an era of volcanoes, hoodoos and dinosaur inhabitants of this region millions of years ago.

As expected in this prosperous city shopping opportunities abound, encouraged by an absence of provincial sales tax. Five downtown malls are inter-connected by pedestrian walkways. So provided you do not become irretrievably lost, you can happily shop all day without braving wintry blasts outdoors.

Calgary has modern theatres and concert halls. Restaurants have come a long way in recent years as city chefs continue to win international culinary awards. According to the season, sports fans will want to watch a football or ice hockey game played by local teams, and of course winter brings excellent skiing in neighbouring mountain resorts.

Still the city's biggest visitor attraction by far is the Calgary Stampede and Exhibition. This is the time when shopkeepers are all decked out in cowboy or pioneer costumes. There is dancing in the streets, big and little parades, impromptu entertainment, free pancake breakfasts — and all this before you get into the Stampede grounds. If you plan to visit Calgary at Stampede time you are urged to book show tickets and accommodation well in advance. This is one time of year when the city population expands to overflowing.

Streets laid out in a simple grid plan combine with the convenience of busses and a light rail transit service to make this an easy city to get around. Just remember that it is in four sections: east and west divided by Centre Street and north and south by the Bow River and Memorial Drive.

There are airline connections to most Canadian cities as well as to many

The Calgary Exhibition and Stampede

Billed as 'The Greatest Show on Earth' the Calgary Exhibition and Stampede began in 1912, and with a $16,000 purse brought competitors from all over North America. Now a combination of agricultural exhibition, fun-fair and rodeo, it is held in the 52 ha (130 acre) Stampede Park for ten days in July. Kicking off with a two hours Grand Parade, it has the whole city involved with street entertainers and dances and pancake breakfasts cooked by the roadside.

Afternoon rodeos feature calf and steer roping, bareback and even bull riding. Wild cow milking can be hilarious, while the evening chuckwagon races are full of action and suspense. These involve four wagons each pulled by four horses and flanked by four mounted outriders. The race starts with a figure eight, followed by a mad dash round the track to the finish line — usually with crashing wheels and a tangle of horses. (The wagons are a modification of the food wagons once used to take lunch to cowboys out on the range

during round-up.) A musical show following the chuck-wagon races is included in the ticket price.

Elsewhere in the grounds you will find an Indian Village, agricultural shows, a giant casino, more entertainment and lots of western-style hospitality. The day ends with a grand fireworks display and the amusement park is open to midnight. Try to allow one full day to see the Stampede, preferably two.

United States, South American and European destinations. Long distance bus services include those connecting with Via Rail's trans-continental trains through Edmonton.

Two downtown hotels representing the upper and mid-price ranges are listed in the Additional Information. In addition to these, many more hotels and motels are located downtown, at the airport and along the Trans-Canada Highway. Calgary also has B & Bs and hostels. The full service campgrounds listed are close to the Trans-Canada Highway, with great views of the Rockies. Calaway Park adjoins a large amusement complex which may be attractive to families.

Excursions from Calgary

- *Banff (130km/81 miles return)*

Calgary is a departure point for the Western Canada itinerary, which starts with the scenic drive to Banff described on page 189. If you are not taking the Western Canada tour, this short trip would be very enjoyable.

- *Fort Macleod, Head-Smashed-In Buffalo Jump, Waterton Lakes National Park (600km/373 miles return)*

This drive visits the Waterton Lakes National Park on the United States border, first stopping at heritage sites around Fort Macleod. The return drive retraces the same route, or as an alternative, go east to Medicine Hat, then continue back across the Prairies as described on page 174.

Leave Calgary via Hwy 2 south and drive to **Fort Macleod**. The town dates from 1874 when 150 men of the recently-formed North West Mounted Police, commanded by Assistant Commissioner James Macleod, marched 1,126km (700 miles) in three months from Manitoba's Lower Fort Garry in search of the infamous whiskey traders' Fort Whoop-up. Needless to say, by the time the mounties arrived and built their first headquarters on an island in the Oldman River the whiskey traders had long since disappeared. In 1877 Macleod negotiated a treaty with the Blackfoot Indians which led to a peaceful settlement of land in the southern part of what, in 1905, became the province of Alberta.

The Fort Macleod Museum is a representation of the fort erected on the present site in 1883, after the island location was flooded. In addition to exhibits relating to the police force, the fort replicates a police post during the early settlement period. The town of Fort Macleod has retained enough historic buildings to warrant walking tours, arranged at a booth beside the museum.

Head-Smashed-In Buffalo Jump, about 18km (11 miles) from Fort Macleod, preserves a traditional native hunting site. Designated a UNESCO World Heritage Site its museum describes ancient buffalo hunts, where optical illusions created by steep cliffs in the midst of a rolling landscape were used to stampede buffalo to their deaths. (This too would be on the authors' 'Canada's Top Five Museums' list.) An interpretation centre adeptly uses exhibits and audio-visual presentations to illustrate the relationship between the buffalo and lives of the Plains

Head-Smashed-In Buffalo Jump

At one time as many as sixty million buffalo (or bison) roamed the Prairies, and to the Plains Indians who hunted them with all the planning and precision of a military manoeuvre they meant life itself.

Three to four hundred hunters and their families would gather for the annual hunts which took advantage of their prey's weak eyesight to lure them to their deaths.

Drive lanes to funnel the beasts into a narrow channel were outlined with tree boughs for several miles from the cliff's edge. Next, young runners in buffalo or wolf skins, often imitating the bleat of a lost calf to attract the herd's female leader, led them into a lane selected to keep hunters downwind. It is thought that the first of the herd realized their mistake as they neared the jump, but with hundreds more buffalo thundering behind them they could not turn back.

Head-Smashed-In Buffalo Jump is known to have been in use 5,500 years ago. Designated a World Heritage Site it is in the same league as the Pyramids, the Parthenon and Stonehenge. It was named just 150 years ago after a young Blackfoot Indian who hid beneath the cliff to witness the herd crashing at his feet. When the hunt was over his body was recovered with his head totally crushed.

Plains Indians used every part of the buffalo. They sewed hides to make tipis and clothing, using the sinew as thread. The meat was roasted or boiled in hide pots. Bones provided marrow and nutritious fats before being stored until winter when they were made into tools.

The fate of the buffalo was sealed with the arrival of Europeans bringing horses and guns. At first the animals provided meat for voyageurs. Later they were hunted with repeating rifles to feed 'brigades' of ox-cart drivers and then railroad construction gangs. So-called adventurers took to shooting buffalo from the comfort of rail cars. Often only the tongue and hump, considered delicacies, were eaten. Skins were used for robes and coats or turned into leather.

But that was long ago. Now the only buffalo you will see are in zoos and park compounds.

peoples. Moreover, as with other lavishly appointed heritage sites in Alberta, admission is free.

It is a further 95km (59 miles) via Hwys 3 and 6 to **Waterton Lakes National Park**. This park is smaller, and just as beautiful, but not so well known as national parks to the north. In consequence it tends to be less crowded. Together with Glacier National Park in Montana it forms the Waterton-Glacier International Peace Park. Within the 528sq km (204sq miles) preserve are three Waterton Lakes, as well as valleys and mountains. There are 1,280km (900 miles) of back-country hiking trails, some of which are open to bicycles and horses. Shuttle buses take hikers from town to various trail-heads. Wildlife is so abundant that plants in the village have to be protected from grazing deer, and the fishing is superb. However, because the transition between Prairies and mountains is particularly abrupt here, the weather is changeable and rainstorms can suddenly occur. Hikers and campers should therefore bring suitable clothing and equipment. Hiking on one's own is not recommended because of resident bears.

Waterton Park village has stores and restaurants, churches, cinema, theatre, filling stations, bicycle and equipment rentals and other services. The park has an 18-hole golf course, riding stables, tennis courts and a swimming pool. Boat cruises on the Waterton Lakes cross the border into Montana. There are several hotels in the park. The full service campground on the town's outskirts is one of three within the park boundaries.

Leaving Waterton Lakes, those wanting to drive eastwards to Medicine Hat should take Hwy 5 to **Cardston**, a town founded by Mormons from Utah and named after a son-in-law of Brigham Young. From there, continue along Hwy 5 to **Lethbridge**. This city, (population 54,000) was originally called Coalbanks, and later renamed after a coal company president. Today the economy is based on oil and gas, grain and cattle, along with various crops produced by pivot irrigation — huge circular fields watered by a long rotating arm. A reconstruction of the original Fort Whoop-up is located south of the town. It is a further 165km (102 miles) from Lethbridge to Medicine Hat, via Hwy 3.

Calgary to Cypress Hills (400km/249 miles, 2 days)

This journey takes you eastwards to Saskatchewan's Cypress Hills and offers a diversion to the Dinosaur Provincial Park, which has many similarities with that in the Drumheller area.

Leaving Calgary follow the Trans-Canada Highway (Hwy 1) for about 140km (87 miles) to Basano, and then take Hwy 550 to **Dinosaur Provin-** **cial Park**. This 60sq km (23sq mile) preserve along the Red Deer River includes prairies and 'badlands' — those wild, barren expanses of steep-sided gullies and bluffs formed in clays and sedimentary rocks by 75 million years of erosion. The park, a World Heritage Site, protects one of the world's most extensive fossil beds, prized particularly for its dinosaur bones. Because of its unusual terrain the park also protects rare and endangered plant and animal species. The Tyrrell Museum of Palaeontol- ogy Field Station close to its entrance has an audio-visual presentation on the park and displays fossils of some thirty-five dinosaur species discovered on the site. Access to much of the park is restricted, and removing fossils is prohibited. Self-guided hikes and driving tours are suggested, while limited bus tours depart from the field station several times a day in summer. Along these trails displays illustrate the art of recovering dinosaur fossils, and full-sized dinosaur replicas are a delight to youngsters who love to climb on them. The park has a campground with full facilities.

Leave via Hwy 876 and drive about 30km (19 miles) to the Trans-Canada Highway. If overnight accommodation is needed turn west to nearby Brooks, or continue east for 100km (62 miles) to **Medicine Hat**. This city is said to be named after a battle between Cree and Blackfoot warriors in which the Cree medicine man lost his headdress in the river, a bad omen that led to his nation's defeat. Like so many Prairies communities, Medicine Hat had its origins in a tent town which sprang up around the newly constructed station when the railway arrived in 1883. A subterranean natural gas field prompted Rudyard Kipling to aptly describe it in 1907 as a place with 'all Hell for a basement'. The abundance of fuel attracted industry and now with a population of 40,000 Medicine Hat has a vigorous industrial economy. A huge underground river provides the city with cool water and irrigation for surrounding farmlands, allowing local greenhouses to supply flowers throughout western Canada. The Medicine Hat Exhibition and Stampede is a major event on the rodeo circuit which doubles the city's population over a three-day weekend in late July.

Leaving Medicine Hat continue east on the Trans-Canada Highway for 60km (37 miles) through a region of large wheat farms and cattle ranches to the Saskatchewan border. It is a further 40km (25 miles) to Hwy 21, which leads south to **Maple Creek**. This town (population 2,500) is in the heart of prime cattle ranching country. North of town a plaque commemorating the '76' Ranch recalls the huge spreads and cattle drives in the days before fences. This era is reinforced by the old-style storefronts on the town's main street, Pacific Avenue.

From Maple Creek via Hwy 21, **Cypress Hills Provincial Park** is 62km (39 miles) south, through rolling cattle-lands where cowboys can still be seen riding horses. The natural environment park which covers 184sq km (71sq miles) straddling the Saskatchewan/Alberta border encloses a portion of the Cypress Hills. (Early French explorers confused the local pines with a species in eastern Canada and erroneously called them *cyprès*.) This plateau was untouched by glaciation during the last Ice Age, leaving it with the highest elevation (up to 1,460m, 4,790ft) in Canada between the Rocky Mountains and Labrador. Steep conglomerate cliffs, affording superb views of the surrounding country, are an outstanding feature of the park.

The Cypress Hills are a well-watered oasis in the semi-arid prairies, a region of lakes and streams with animals and plants usually found in the Rocky Mountains to the west. Once a rich hunting ground for the Plains Indians, its moose, elk and deer remain abundant. Bird watchers come here to see some of the over 200 species of birds, including the endangered trumpeter swan.

Nature lovers will find the park great for hiking, horseback riding, cross-country skiing and primitive camping at any time of the year. The park also has a golf course, heated swimming pool, riding stable and other attractions, as well as a good resort.

Life-size dinosaur replicas in the Dinosaur Provincial Park, Alberta Badlands

The return to the USA of Chief Sitting Bull and his Sioux warriors after Custer's defeat at the Battle of Little Bighorn was negotiated at Fort Walsh

Fort Walsh National Historic Park adjoins the Cypress Hills Park. In 1875 a North West Mounted Police division under Inspector James Walsh built the fort to establish contact with the local Indians, both as a prelude to settlement and to suppress the whiskey trade. Police officers here negotiated the return to the United States of Chief Sitting Bull, and 4,000 Sioux warriors who had taken refuge in Canada following the Battle of the Little Bighorn against US General George A. Custer. The post was abandoned soon afterwards, but re-established in 1942 as a ranch for training police horses. Stones in the little cemetery tell much about the lives and deaths of the settlers, and of the mounties who gave their all to protect them. The nearby Farwell's and Solomon's trading posts recall the atmosphere of Whoop-up country. They have been reconstructed near the site of the Cypress Hills Massacre where American wolf hunters killed some twenty Assiniboine Indians, leading directly to Fort Walsh's establishment.

As well as accommodation in Cypress Hills Provincial Park's modern resort, there are also motels in Maple Creek. The park's campgrounds, suitable for RVs, are close to recreational facilities.

Cypress Hills to Regina (440km/273 miles, 2 days)

Retrace the road through Maple Creek to the Trans-Canada Highway (Hwy 1), turn east and continue 130 km (81 miles) to **Swift Current**. Once a transit point for fur traders, Swift Current became a North West Mounted Police post in 1874 and a significant railway depot in 1882. Today the city (population 15,000) is a trading centre for cattle and grain, a base for petroleum exploration, and Canada's only helium producer. Swift Current's Rodeo, one of Saskatchewan's largest, takes place at the end of June. The Old Tyme Fiddlers' Championships held here in late September attract entrants from across the Continent.

Although not on this itinerary, with time to spare you may like to visit the **Val Marie** region about 120km (75 miles) south of Swift Current via Hwy 4. This is part of the **Grasslands National Park**, now being assembled to preserve some 900sq km (348sq miles) of the few remaining undeveloped prairie grasslands. Self-guided eco-tours are available, and wilderness camping is permitted. Because the park is still being assembled and most of the land remains privately owned, it is wise to inquire of the reception centre in Val Marie for up-to-date information.

Moose Jaw, a further 175km (109 miles), may have been named after the shape of the bend in the river on which it is situated, or from an Indian word meaning 'warm breezes'. In any case it has a colourful history, most particularly during Prohibition when it was home to a band of bootleggers. The city (population 34,000) is Saskatchewan's third largest and now a major industrial, agricultural and distribution centre. Saskatchewan's excellent Western Development Museum has a branch here which traces the role of the railways, roads and aviation, as related to the development of the Prairies. The nearby Canadian Forces Base features the Saskatchewan Air Show in early July, the largest annual air show on the Prairies. Leaving Moose Jaw, it is a further 71 km (44 miles) to **Regina**. In 1882, the Canadian Pacific Railroad chose the location of this townsite beside Pile O' Bones (Wascana) Creek, so named after the refuse left behind by Indian buffalo hunters. That same year the capital of the North West Territories and the headquarters of the North West Mounted Police were moved to the settlement, which was then renamed Regina in honour of Queen Victoria. When Saskatchewan was made a province in 1905, Regina became its capital. Soon townspeople had planted so many trees that they transformed what was once a region of cheerless prairie into a city of shaded parks and streets.

Present day Regina (population 180,000) is a handsome city, a centre for government and education, agriculture and the petroleum and potash industries. Its Saskatchewan Centre for the Arts has one of the finest concert halls in North America; the symphony orchestra is one of Canada's oldest. The city has a thriving theatre and dance tradition. Dramatization of the *Trial of Louis Riel* has been presented every summer for over 25 years at the University of Regina's Shumiatcher Theatre. This is an emotion-charged re-enactment of Riel's trial following the North West Rebellion, in which he refused to plead insanity and was subsequently hanged.

Wascana Centre, a 930 ha (2,300 acres) park in the heart of the city, is the focal point for outdoors activities, such as hiking and bicycling along its tree-lined trails and sailing on the man-made lake. The park contains the handsome Legislative Building set in formal gardens, also the Saskatchewan Museum of Natural History in a handsome Manitoba Tyndall limestone building. Its galleries and dioramas depict two billion years of Saskatchewan's history, with emphasis on natural history and the story of the province's native peoples. The Diefenbaker Homestead, boyhood home of Canada's Prime Minister during 1957-63, is particularly interesting for its portrayal of Prairies life in the early part of this century.

On the 'must see' list of every visitor to Regina is the Royal Canadian Mounted Police Training Academy and Museum. Recent graduates conduct tours of the facility where all recruits to Canada's national police force receive their initial training. Included is the depot's little wooden chapel dating back to 1883, Regina's oldest building. The museum traces the history of this force from its formation as the North West Mounted Police in 1873 to preserve law and order in the North West Territories to the present day. Try to coincide a visit with the colourful Sergeant Major's parade held most weekdays at 12.30pm, or with the Sunset Retreat ceremony at 6.45pm on Tuesday evenings in summer.

Pile O'Bones Sunday at the end of July, and Buffalo Days Exhibition on the first weekend of August, are both exuberent celebrations of Prairies life. Canadian Western Agribition held in late November is Canada's largest agricultural show.

Regina has airline connections with other major Canadian cities, and by bus with Via Rail's trans-continental service through Saskatoon. The city has good hotels and motels, B & Bs, a hostel and YWCA residence. Two well-known downtown hotels and a full-service campground on the Trans-Canada Highway are listed in the Additional Information.

Regina to Winnipeg (580km/360 miles, 1 day)

The final drive in this itinerary follows the Trans-Canada Highway (Hwy 1), and some diversions are suggested for travellers with more than one day available for this section of their trip.

Leave Regina via Hwy 1 and drive to **Indian Head**, about 70 km (43 miles) to the east. This community (named after the appearance of a range of low hills to the southwest) is in the centre of Saskatchewan's prime wheat growing area and site of a Federal government experimental farm and tree nursery. Experimental farms such as this have been responsible for developing plant varieties suitable for Canada's climate, including the strains of wheat, rye, rapeseed and other crops seen during your drive. The tree nursery, established in 1902, has already donated over 400 million of the trees that are seen sheltering Prairies farm houses and buildings everywhere. It has an interpretive centre and picnic area.

Further along, at **Grenfell**, visitors with sufficient time should divert north via Hwys 47 and 247 which loop into the Qu'Appelle Valley before

Sergeant-major's parade at the Royal Canadian Mounted Police Academy, Regina

returning to the Trans-Canada Highway. This beautiful valley stretches from Lake Diefenbaker northwest of Regina to the Assiniboine River in Manitoba. The river valley with its sparkling lakes is holiday country for many prairie families, and a source of great interest to nature lovers because the area sustains such different types of vegetation. The north slope is covered with trees, while in summer the dry southern slope is a riot of grassland wildflowers. Birdlife includes white pelicans and blue herons, ducks and geese as well as half a dozen varieties of hawks. The picturesque Crooked Lake Provincial Park has a full-service campground. There is a golf course, with private resorts located nearby.

Another 50km (30 miles) brings you to Whitewood, and Hwy 9 leading to **Moose Mountain Provincial Park**. This is another holiday area which attracts Prairies families for some leisure time while crops ripen in the hot summer months. Although a large part of the park is home to herds of moose and elk, and a nesting place for many species of migrating birds, the recreational pursuits here include golf, tennis, horse riding, swimming and boating. The park has an interpretive center and a full service campground. There is a resort and restaurant, and more in neighbouring Kenosee Lake Village. Visitors staying at Moose Mountain will be interested in nearby the **Cannington Manor Provincial Historic Park**. It has an interpretive centre and several buildings recreating a pre-1896 farming settlement where English families brought their own upper-middle-class culture to the prairies, with such pastimes as cricket and fox-hunting, tea dances and a dramatic society.

Back on the Trans-Canada Highway, other communities founded by various immigrant groups around the end of the ninteenth century, will be encountered. Improbable as it seems now, **Whitewood** was once the venue for grand balls hosted by French counts who established country estates in the area. **Esterhazy**, to the northeast and site of the world's largest potash mine, was Saskatchewan's first Hungarian community. Forty Jewish families formed a successful agricultural settlement north of **Wapella**. Near **Moosemin** sturdy stone houses still in use are attributed to Scottish masons who worked with stones cleared from the land.

Approaching **Virden** in Manitoba, oil wells once again make you aware of Canada's petroleum resources. Here deposits are a mixture of oil and salt water, a reminder that this area was once part of a huge sea.

Brandon (population 36,000), Manitoba's second largest city, traces its beginnings to 1793 when the first Hudson's Bay Company post was established here. Settlers came from Ontario and the Atlantic provinces in the mid-nineteenth century, and the arrival of the Canadian Pacific Railway in 1881 made it an important distribution and administrative centre. Now its economy is based on regional administration, agriculture, food processing and petro-chemicals. Brandon's strong ties with the land result in a series of agricultural fairs and exhibitions, held in March, June and October. Visitors may be interested in the Commonwealth Air Training Plan Museum with its displays of World War II aircraft and air force memorabilia, located at the airport north of the city. Also, the Royal Regiment of Canadian Artillery Museum at Shilo's Canadian forces base 12km (7 miles) east of the city, displays artillery and military artifacts dating from the eighteenth century to the present day.

One hundred kilometres (62 miles) south of Brandon, reached via a very pleasant drive on Hwy 10, the **International Peace Garden** on the Manitoba/North Dakota border is mid-way between the Atlantic and Pacific Oceans. The 946 ha (2,338 acre) park commemorates the friendship between the two countries which share the world's longest unfortified border. It has truly beautiful formal gardens, a peace tower and floral clock, and in this lovely setting an International Music Camp attracts participants from many countries every June and July.

The 126km (78 mile) drive between Brandon and Portage la Prairie (see page 159) passes through the Carberry Sand Hills, scenic rolling countryside with ponds and spruce woods, and you can turn south on Hwy 5 to visit **Spruce Woods Provincial Heritage Park**. Here, surprisingly, are desert-like conditions supporting cactii and skittering lizards, all set in an area of agricultural land. The park has a reception centre and campgrounds, canoeing, and self-guiding hiking trails. It is a further 70km (43 miles) from Portage la Prairie to Winnipeg.

Additional information

Places to Visit

Battlefords, Sask
Fort Battleford National Historic Park
Hwy 4, Battleford
Open: mid-May to mid-October
☎ (306) 937-2621

Western Development Museum's Heritage Farm & Village
Hwys 16 & 40, North Battleford
Open: daily May to October
☎ (306) 445-8033

Batoche, Sask
Batoche National Historic Park
Open: daily, May to October
☎ (306) 423-6227

Brandon, Man
Commonwealth Air Training Plan Museum
Brandon Airport
Open: daily
☎ (204) 727-2444

Royal Regiment of Canadian Artillery Museum
Shilo, via Hwys 457 & 340
Open: weekdays all year, weekends June 1 to Labour Day
☎ (204) 765-3534

International Peace Garden
Open: daily
☎ (204) 534-2510

Calgary, Alta
Calgary Zoo, Botanical Gardens and Prehistoric Park
Memorial Dr & 12th St SE
Open: daily
☎ (403) 262-9300

Fort Calgary Interpretive Centre
750 9th Ave SE
Open: daily in summer, Wednesday to Sunday rest of year
☎ (403) 290-1875

Glenbow Museum
9th Ave and 1st St SE
Open: daily
☎ (403) 264-8300

Heritage Park Historical Village
Off Hwy 2, via Heritage Dr
Open: daily in summer, weekends only
part of year
☎ (403) 255-1182

Stampede Park
14th and Olympic Way
☎ (403) 261-0400
For Stampede (403) 261-0101
1-800-661-1260

Churchill, Man
Inuit Museum
La Vérendrye St
Open: Monday to Saturday in summer,
closed Mondays in winter
☎ (204) 675-2030

Cape Merry National Historic Site
Fort Prince of Wales National Historic Park
Parks Canada Reception Centre
Bayfront Plaza
Open: daily in summer, Tuesday to
Saturday rest of year
☎ (204) 675-8863

Cypress Hills, Sask
Fort Walsh National Historic Park
☎ (306) 662-3590

Drumheller, Alta
Tyrrell Museum of Palaeontology
Hwy 838, 6km west of Drumheller
Open: daily in summer, Tuesday to
Sunday, rest of year
☎ (403) 823-7707

Edmonton, Alta
Alberta Telephone Tower
10020 100th St
Open: daily
☎ (403) 493-3333

Fort Edmonton Park
Whitemud Dr & Fox Dr
Open: daily in summer, Sundays to
Thanksgiving
☎ (403) 428-2992

Provincial Museum of Alberta
12845 - 102 Ave
☎ (403) 427-1786

West Edmonton Mall
170 St & 87 Ave
☎ (403) 444-5200

Fort Macleod, Alta
Fort Macleod Museum
25th St & 3rd Ave
☎ (403) 553-4703

Head-Smashed-In Buffalo Jump
Hwy 785, 18km from Fort Macleod
Open: daily
☎ (403) 553-2731

Indian Head, Sask
*Prairie Farm Rehabilitation Administration
  Tree Nursery*
2km south
Open: weekdays
☎ (306) 695-2284

Moose Jaw, Sask
*Western Development Museum's History of
  Transportation*
50 Diefenbaker Dr,
close to Trans-Canada Hwy
Open: daily
☎ (306) 693-6556

Moose Mountain Park, Sask
Cannington Manor Provincial Historic Park
26km southeast of Kenosee Lake, via
grid roads
Open: mid-May to Labour Day
☎ (306) 787-2700

Regina, Sask
RCMP Training Academy & Museum
Dewdney Ave W
Open: daily
☎ (306) 780-5838

Saskatchewan Museum of Natural History
College Ave and Albert St
Open: daily
☎ (306) 787-2815

Saskatoon, Sask
Rt Hon John G. Diefenbaker Centre
University of Saskatchewan Campus
Open: daily
☎ (306) 966-8382

Mendel Art Gallery & Civic Conservatory
950 Spadina Cres E
Open: daily
☎ (306) 975-7610

Ukraina Museum
202 Ave M, South
Open: daily, Sundays by appointment in winter
☎ (306) 244-4212

Ukranian Museum of Canada
910 Spadina Cres E
Open: Tuesday to Sunday afternoons
☎ (306) 244-3800

Western Development Museum's Boomtown
2610 Lorne Ave
Open: daily
☎ (306) 931-1910

Wanuskewin Heritage Park
Hwy 11, 5km north
Open: daily
☎ (306) 931-6767

Steinbach, Man
Mennonite Heritage Village
Hwy 12, north of town
Open: daily May to September
☎ (204) 326-9661

Winnipeg, Man
Assiniboine Park
2799 Roblin Ave
Open: daily
☎ (204) 986-3130

The Forks National Historic Site
Open: daily, staff available May-September
☎ (204) 983-2007

Lower Fort Garry National Historic Site
Hwy 9, south of Selkirk
Open: daily mid-May to Labour Day, weekends in September
☎ (204) 482-6843

Manitoba Museum of Man and Nature
190 Rupert Ave
Open: daily mid-June to Labour Day, closed Mondays rest of year
☎ (204) 956-2830

Royal Canadian Mint
520 Lagimodiere Blvd
Open: weekdays
☎ (204) 257-3359

St Boniface Museum
494 ave Taché
Open: daily
☎ (204) 237-4500

Yorkton, Sask
Western Development Museum's Story of the People
2km west on Hwy 16
Open: daily mid-May to mid-October
☎ (306) 783-8361

St Mary's Ukranian Catholic Church
155 Catherine St
Open: daily in summer, otherwise by arrangement
☎ (306) 783-4594

National & Provincial Parks

Alberta
Dinosaur Provincial Park
Hwys 873 & 544 from Brooks
Open: daily late May to Labour Day, Wednesday to Sunday, rest of year
☎ (403) 378-4144

Waterton Lakes National Park
Waterton Park, Alta T0K 2MO
☎ (403) 859-2262

Manitoba
Bird's Hill Provincial Park
Hwy 59, 24km north of Winnipeg
☎ (204) 222-9151

Hecla Island Provincial Park
Via Hwy 8, beyond Riverton
☎ (204) 378-2945

Riding Mountain National Park
Wasagaming, Manitoba R0J 2H0
Open: all year, full services from mid-May to Labour Day
☎ (204) 848-2811

Spruce Woods Provincial Heritage Park
South of Trans-Canada Hwy, off Hwy 5
☎ (204) 827-2458

Whiteshell Provincial Park
Trans-Canada Hwy
Open: all year
☎ (204) 349-2201

Saskatchewan
Crooked Lake Provincial Park
On Hwy 247,
30 km north of Trans-Canada Hwy
Open: mid-May to Labour Day
☎ (306) 728-4491

Cypress Hills Provincial Park
Hwy 21 south of Maple Creek
☎ (306) 662-4411

Grasslands National Park
Reception centre: Hwy 4 & Centre St,
Val Marie
Open: weekdays
☎ (306) 298-2257

Moose Mountain Provincial Park
Hwy 9, 60km south of Whitewood
Open: daily
☎ (306) 577-2131

Prince Albert National Park
Waskesiu Lake, Sask S0J 2Y0
Open: daily
☎ (306) 663-5322

Accommodation, Campgrounds & Tour Organisers

Calgary, Alta
Delta Bow Valley Inn
209 4th Ave S.E.
☎ (403) 266-1980
1-800-268-1133

Sandman Hotel
888 7th Ave SW
☎ (403) 237-8626
1-800-663-6900

Calaway Park RV Campground
Jct Trans-Canada Hwy & Springbank Rd
☎ (403) 249-7372

West Calgary KOA Kampground
Trans-Canada Hwy, 2km west
☎ (403) 288-0411

Churchill, Man
Polar Motel
16 Franklin Street
☎ (204) 675-8878

Seaport Hotel
299 Kelsey Blvd
☎ (204) 675-8807

Churchill Wilderness Encounter (tours)
PO Box 9, Churchill, Man R0B 0E0
☎ (204) 675-2248

Churchill Nature Tours
PO Box 429, Erickson, Man R0J 0P0
☎ (204) 636-2968

Cypress Hills Park, Sask
Cypress Four Seasons Resort
Cypress Hills Park
☎ (306) 662-4477

Drumheller, Alta
Drumheller Inn
100 S Railway Ave
☎ (403) 823-8400
1-800-661-1460

Drumheller Travelodge
48 N Railway Ave
☎ (403) 823-3322
1-800-255-3050

Dinosaur Trail Campground
Hwy 838, 11km
☎ (403) 823-9333

Edmonton, Alta
Hotel Macdonald
10065 - 100th St
☎ (403) 424-5181
1-800-441-1414

Centre Suite Hotel
10222 - 102 St
☎ (403) 429-3900

Klondike Valley Campground
Hwy 2 at Elleslie Rd
☎ (403) 988-5067

Prince Albert National Park, Sask
Hawood Inn
Lakeview Dr, Waskesiu Lake
☎ (306) 663-5911

Waskesiu Lake Lodge
Lakeview Dr, Waskesiu Lake
☎ (306) 663-5975

Waskesiu-Beaver Glen Campground
1km from Waskesiu Townsite
☎ (306) 663-5322

Riding Mountain National Park, Man
Lee's Holiday Bungalows
Mooswa Dr, Wasagaming
☎ (204) 848-2511

Elkhorn Resort
Hwy 10, south of park gates
☎ (204) 848-2802

Wasagaming Campground
Wasagaming townsite
☎ (204) 848-2811

Regina, Sask
Delta Regina
1818 Victoria Ave
☎ (306) 569-1666
1-800-268-1133

Hotel Saskatchewan
2125 Victoria Ave
☎ (306) 522-7691
1-800-667-5828

Kings' Acres Campground
Trans-Canada Hwy, 1 km east
☎ (306) 522-1619

Saskatoon, Sask
Delta Bessborough Hotel
601 Spadina Cres E
☎ (306) 244-5521
1-800-268-1133

Sheraton Cavalier Hotel
612 Spadina Cres E
☎ (306) 652-6770
1-800-325-3535

Gordon Howe Campsite
Ave 'P' south of 11th St
☎ (306) 975-3328

Saskatoon KOA Kampground
Hwy 11, 3km south
☎ (306) 373-4554

Waterton Park, Alta
Prince of Wales Hotel
Waterton Park, close to entrance
☎ (403) 859-2231

Bayshore Inn
111 Waterton Ave
☎ (403) 859-2211

Waterton Park Townsite Campground
☎ (403) 859-2224

Winnipeg, Man
Fort Garry Hotel
222 Broadway Ave
☎ (204) 942-8251
1-800-665-8088

Delta Winnipeg
288 Portage Ave
☎ (204) 956-0410
1-800-268-1133

Tinkertown KOA Kampground
Murdoch Rd
close to junction Hwys 1 & 100 (Winnipeg Bypass)
☎ (204) 253-8168

Local Tourist Authorities

Calgary, Alta
Calgary Tourist and Convention Bureau
237, 8th Ave SE,
Calgary, Alta T2G 0K8
☎ (403) 263-8510

Edmonton, Alta
Edmonton Convention and Tourism Authority
9797 Jasper Ave,
Edmonton, Alta T5J 1N9
☎ (403) 422-5505

Winnipeg, Man
Winnipeg Convention and Visitors Bureau
375 York St,
Winnipeg, Man R3C 3J3
☎ (204) 943-1970

4
WESTERN CANADA

This chapter includes three separate itineraries which could, given sufficient time, be combined in a number of ways to see Western Canada. The first circular tour is from Calgary through the Rocky Mountains before driving to Vancouver Island and then returning to Alberta. This tour could equally start in Edmonton or Vancouver.

The second tour originates in Vancouver, travels up the coast and returns through the interior of British Columbia. The third itinerary is a short tour of the Yukon Territory which includes small sections of the US state of Alaska. It is possible to drive to the Yukon Territory from Vancouver (2,700km, 1,675 miles) or Edmonton (2,100km, 1,300 miles), but tourists usually fly to Whitehorse, or arrive by sea (via Alaska) and then rent a car or join a bus tour. It is assumed that this will be done, but a suggestion for those wishing to drive overland is included.

Alberta, described in the introduction to the Prairies (Chapter 3), has the peaks of the Rocky Mountains as its western boundary. This is one of Canada's most diverse regions where large mountain areas have been set aside as national parks, drawing visitors from around the world in all seasons. Here are world-class resorts with all the amenities implied by such a description, hostels and campgrounds, and a whole spectrum of facilities for all-year-round adventure, sports and leisure.

British Columbia lies between the Rocky Mountains and the Pacific Ocean, with Alaska and the Yukon to the north and the United States on the south. Enhanced by a long coastline, as well as snow-clad mountain ranges broken up by fertile valleys, rivers and lakes, British Columbia has the most varied scenery of all of Canada's provinces. With comfortable climates of coastal areas and valleys ensuring fairly mild vacations for up to nine months of the year, British Columbians have capitalized on their resources to build outdoors recreational opportunities. In consequence you will find just about everything from water sports to mountain climbing, and Alpine skiing. The province's highway system is excellent; numerous feeder airlines operate here, and as a bonus the government-owned ferry service takes its passengers through spectacular coastal scenery, often along routes followed by more costly cruise liners.

Well before arrival of the white man, the Pacific coastal region provided a hospitable home to aboriginal peoples. With food supply assured

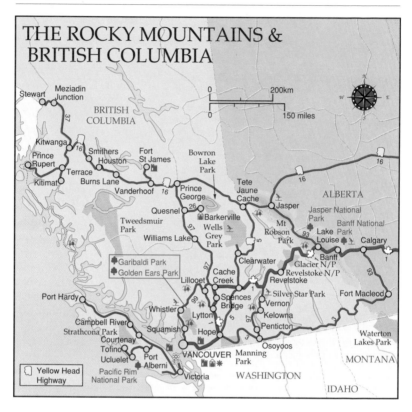

THE ROCKY MOUNTAINS & BRITISH COLUMBIA

through an abundance of game and fish, particularly salmon, they could devote time to developing a rich cultural heritage. For the modern traveller, this is interpreted in the many displays of totem poles and other native art in museums and public parks. Europeans arrived fairly recently. Spanish ships came from Mexico in the late 1700s and a Spanish settlement existed on Vancouver Island for a few years. James Cook visited the coast during one of his voyages of discovery; later George Vancouver claimed it for the British crown. But the forerunners of the permanent settlers travelled across the mountainous interior, driven first by an insatiable market for furs and then by the quest for gold. Next came the railroads bringing farmers and lumbermen. Now, all over the province historic sites record the story of these founding peoples.

In Canada's northwest corner Yukon Territory occupies nearly 5 percent of the country's landmass. Its population numbers about 23,000, of whom two-thirds live in the capital of Whitehorse. Like the Northwest Territories, it is a semi-autonomous region within the Canadian federal state.

The Yukon was home to native groups and a few fur traders until commercial quantities of gold were discovered in 1883. The find at Bonanza Creek resulted in the Yukon Gold Rush of 1897-8. World War II brought the Japanese occupation of the United States' Aleutian Islands, followed by the Americans' construction of the Alaska Highway through the territory from northern British Columbia to Alaska. This highway has now become an essential part of the territory's economy. There is still some gold-mining in the Yukon, but copper, zinc and lead have become more important.

The Rocky Mountains & The Pacific Coast

Calgary to Banff (130km/81 miles, 2 days)

Drive west from Calgary up the Bow River Valley via the Trans-Canada Highway (Hwy 1) to **Banff National Park**. This was Canada's first national park and remains its best known for reasons that are obvious. It is one of North America's greatest scenic areas and one of its most exhilarat-

Lake Minnewanka in Banff National Park

Canada's National Parks

Canada's National parks provide a welcome oasis for travellers, their purpose being to safeguard a unique beauty or natural region for posterity and to create recreational space. Almost all have campgrounds and picnic sites. Many provide comfortable and inexpensive cottage accommodation, some have luxurious resorts nestled in calendar-like scenery. Thirty-five national parks cover 180,000sq km (70,000sq miles). Every province and territory has at least one, and with the exception of those in the far north they can be reached via the Trans-Canada or other major highways.

The first link in the national park chain was forged back in 1885 when squabbles arose over ownership of newly discovered sulphur springs in the Rockies. Two years earlier three Canadian Pacific Railway workers found the springs when they lowered themselves into a cave. Soon entrepreneurs arrived to open small spa-hotels and sell the bottled water, as the sick and elderly flocked to sample the springs' curative powers. To preserve both the hot springs and a square mile around them, the Federal government created Rocky Mountain Park. As more scenic wonders were uncovered the park expanded to take them in, and now as Banff National Park it embraces 6,640sq km (2,564sq miles.)

Most national parks are open all year, with reduced facilities between October and May. Modern visitor centres present slide shows on park terrain and wildlife. Interpretive staff give out information, maps, descriptive brochures on self-guided tours and programmes for escorted walks and campground entertainments.

Sadly some of the best known parks have become over-developed in and around their townsite hubs, where summer crowds can distract from the region's natural beauty. But it is usually no more than a brief drive to trails and lakes leading to wilderness beaches, quiet coves, mountainous hideaways, and the unique environment that caused the park to be so designated.

ing tourist destinations. Towering peaks, glaciers, high meadows and waterfalls dominate the skyline. Below, sparkling rivers and lakes are imbedded in lush valleys. The park is home to elk, mule deer and bighorn sheep, coyote and black bear, all of which are highly visible. Moose, wolves, lynx, cougars and some grizzly bears inhabit forests and high meadows. There are not too many birds here, and although the rock flour produced by grinding glaciers turns the lakes a pretty emerald green, it also means that there are few fish.

The Trans-Canada Highway and Icefield Parkway are the park's major roads, opening up spectacular vistas and rendering large sections easily accessible to both pedestrians and motorists. More secluded regions are reached via the 1,100km (680 miles) of hiking trails radiating from Banff.

The park has a total of fourteen campgrounds and six hostels, including some in Banff and at Lake Louise.

Banff started as a settlement on the main Canadian Pacific Railway line and creation of the national park spurred tourism, causing the renowned château-like Banff Springs Hotel to be built in 1888. Since then, growth based on transportation and tourism has been continuous. The town soon established itself as a cultural centre with the founding in 1933 of the University of Alberta's Banff School of Fine Arts, predecessor of the prestigious Banff Centre.

Banff (population 4,500) is now a full-fledged resort town, which gets very crowded in summer. Its restaurants and commercial establishments are centred around the main street. Because of the influx of Japanese visitors many enterprises conduct business in that language as well as English. Banff has numerous companies organizing outdoors adventures. Trail-riding outfitters can equip you for a half day, a week or longer safaris, with or without a guide. Others lead mountaineering expeditions. White-water rafting and heli-hiking are popular. Golfers will enjoy the Banff Springs Hotel's course.

An information centre on Banff Avenue has details of local accommodation and attractions. Parks Canada's museum provides an excellent intoduction to the park and its wildlife. While in Banff take the gondola lift to the top of Sulphur Mountain for sensational alpine views. Also visit the Cave and Basin Centennial Centre, which explains the hot springs' discovery which led to the creation of the park. Its public pool, beautifully restored to celebrate the park's 100th birthday, uses warm waters (about 32 °C, 90 °F) from the springs. Upper Hot Springs swimming pool on Mountain Avenue has warmer waters (up to 42 °C, 108 °F). After a dip in this one you can relax even further with a massage.

Banff has numerous lodges, hotels and motels, as well as chalet rentals, B & Bs and hostels. There is more accommodation at Lake Louise and Canmore. The historic Banff Springs Hotel and the modern Inns of Banff Park are listed in the Additional Information. Advance bookings are advisable in summer. Campgrounds at Tunnel Mountain, about 3km (2 miles) from Banff, have full services for RVs. Two Jack Main campground, about 13km (8 miles) from Banff on Lake Minnewanka, suitable for RVs, is also very attractive. These campgrounds do not accept reservations.

Banff to Jasper (290km/180 miles, 2 days)

This majestic route, northwards through the Banff National Park and on to Jasper in the adjoining Jasper National Park, constantly unfolds vistas of snow-covered mountains, glaciers and waterfalls, lakes and rivers which drain away from the continental watershed. Well-engineered roads make for easy driving. Major sights are signposted, and there are countless lookouts where a pause to take in the scenery is well rewarded. Audio cassettes describing the route can be rented in Banff and returned in Jasper — but at times they annoyingly fill in with irrelevancies.

Leave Banff via the Trans-Canada Highway along the Bow River Valley and between many of the mountains that have already been seen from a distance, to Lake Louise, roughly 55km (34 miles) away. During this section of the drive, the different mountain characteristics will become apparent. Mount Rundle, overlooking Banff, is a dipping layered mountain. On one side it is a straight slope showing the layers of sedimentary rock thrust up from the earth's floor about 70 million years ago when these mountains were created. Mount Louis, to the right has formed into a sharp dogtooth. Castle Mountain, further on, is castelated with layers worn away to create steep cliffs and slopes.

Lake Louise is a turquoise jewel of a lake, framed by towering mountains and glistening icefields. Some say it is the most photographed spot in all of Canada. Chateau Lake Louise, one of the country's famous railway resorts, stands atop the huge moraine that dams the lake. The area also has more modest accommodation. The community of Lake Louise

Explore the Rocky Mountains by train — the rear observation coach at Jasper

Indian dancer at the Buffalo Nations National Festival, Banff

(population 350) is situated on the former site of Laggan railway station which housed 12,000 men during the construction of the line through the famous **Kicking Horse Pass** (elevation 1,624m, 5,328ft). This name comes from the occasion in 1858 when explorer and geologist Dr James Hector, who gave his name to a nearby lake and mountain, was kicked by a packhorse. The nearby **Great Divide**, reached via Hwy 1A, is on the continental watershed, where waters flow either north to the Arctic Ocean, east to the Atlantic, or west to the Pacific.

From Lake Louise, the Trans-Canada Highway continues on through Kicking Horse Pass to British Columbia, but this route branches north along the Icefield Parkway (Hwy 93). **Sunwapta Pass** marks the border between Banff and Jasper National Parks.

Quite different in character from Banff, **Jasper National Park** covers an area of 10,878sq km (4,170sq miles) of the Rocky Mountains' eastern slopes. Only 800sq km (310sq miles) are flat valley floors, the rest being mountains, high meadows and lakes. Bighorn sheep and mountain goats are so numerous as to be a nuisance. Elk, deer and black bear also inhabit the park, while moose and beaver can be seen in the marshy areas. Noteworthy among the birdlife are ptarmigans, golden eagles and ravens. The park has 1,000km (620 miles) of back-country hiking trails, ten campgrounds and five hostels. A very active interpretive program encompasses ranger-led walks, slide shows and topical presentations. Visitors staying in Jasper can take part in these activities at nearby Whistlers campground. There is also a park interpretive centre in the town.

About 5 km (three miles) north of the park gates the **Athabasca Glacier**, a tongue of the 389sq km (150sq mile) Columbia Icefield, reaches to within 2km (1¼ miles) of the highway. At its interpretive centre is a scale model of the icefield and an audio-visual presentation. In summer specially designed busses take visitors for tours on the glacier. The first public glacier tours used horses equipped with non-slip shoes. Even the tank-like vehicles of a few decades ago seemed very exciting, but now with a crowded parking lot and full-sized busses carrying passengers on a road cut through the glacier, there is no real sense of adventure.

A further 73km (45 miles) of driving through fantastic scenery leads to the Athabasca Falls, where the river is funnelled into a narrow gorge before plunging 22m (72ft) over the falls. Mount Edith Cavell in the distance was named after the British nurse executed by the Germans during World War I.

Jasper is close to the site of the North West Company post established in the early 1800s and named after the company's employee, Jasper Hawes. Modern development started in 1907 when the Jasper Park Reserve was established. The first railway arrived in 1911, and the forerunner to the present Jasper Park Lodge was built in 1915 as a tent community. A few years later the all-season road from Edmonton further increased the number of visitors. Today the town (population 3,300), which remains dependent on transportation and tourism, has avoided much of Banff's crowding and commercialism. Visitors will find restaurants and services to satisfy most needs. Several stores are stocked with native crafts, including magnificent soapstone carvings selling for thousands of dollars. Fishing, river-rafting, mountaineering and trail riding expeditions are easily arranged through hotels and agents in town. At Jasper's golf course the splendid scenery could prove distracting. In good weather, a rented bicycle is enjoyable transportation.

While here a ride in the tramway up Whistlers Mountain (named after resident marmots) to an observation station at the 2,285m (7,500ft) level is recommended. On a clear day the views of Jasper and its surrounding mountains are unmatched and hiking trails at this alpine level are all the more interesting for the plant-life encountered. Maligne Lake, 50km (31 miles) from Jasper, is an emerald-green body of water stretching 22km (14 miles) into the snow-covered peaks of the Front Range. This is a scene used often on postcards and calendars. When the weather is right, a boat ride on Maligne Lake is unforgettable.

Sixty kilometres (37 miles) north of the town Miette Hot Springs has the Rockies' hottest springs, cooled to a comfortable 40 °C (104 °F) and fed into large, rather utilitarian, outdoor pools. If you bring a picnic be prepared for uninvited guests by way of raggedy mountain goats.

Jasper is on Via Rail's trans-continental service. Bus connections are to the east and west, as well as to Banff and Calgary. The superb Jasper Park Lodge and a representative of the many less expensive places in the town are listed in the Additional Information. Wapiti and Whistlers, the park's campsites adjacent to Jasper, are suitable for RVs (they do not accept reservations). There is also a hostel at Whistlers.

Jasper to Kamloops (440km/273 miles, 1 day)

This journey is through some of the world's best mountain scenery, over the Continental Divide via the Yellowhead Pass, and down the North Thompson River Valley, stopping overnight in Kamloops then on to Vancouver. The road runs parallel to the route of Via Rail's transcontinental passenger service, a wonderful ride for train buffs. An alternative routing continues on Hwy 16 at Tête Jaune Cache to Prince George and connects with the second British Columbia itinerary (page 213).

Drive westwards from Jasper via Hwy 16, along the Miette River for 26km (16 miles) to the **Yellowhead Pass** (1,146m, 3,760ft). The pass lies between the Miette River, the waters of which eventually drain into the Arctic Ocean, and the Fraser River which flows into the Pacific. It provides the border between Alberta and British Columbia, and is the eastern limit of British Columbia's Mount Robson Provincial Park. On the right is Mount Robson, the highest peak in the Canadian Rockies (3,954m, 12,972ft). While the mountain is in sight for the entire 80km (50 mile) drive through the park, views from the west show the snow deposits to their best effect.

The Yellowhead Highway divides at **Tête Jaune Cache**, and the itinerary then follows the southward branch of Hwy 5. Both the town and the pass just crossed are named after a fair-haired Indian trapper and guide, who in the early 1800s stored his furs here. Between 1858 and 1862 the pass was used by prospectors during the Cariboo Gold Rush. One group, the Overlanders, comprised 200 men, women and children who struggled across the country from Quebec and Ontario in search of gold. Many perished. One woman gave birth to the first white child born in British Columbia's interior, and one Overlander found gold. Arrival of the railways in the early 1900s turned the pass into an important transportation route.

West of the valley lies the Premier Range with peaks named after Canadian Prime Ministers: Mackenzie King, Laurier, Abbott and so on. **Clearwater** is the main access point to **Wells Grey Provincial Park** where rafting and horseback expeditions can be arranged. The 5,153sq km (2,000sq mile) park offers camping, canoeing, hiking and terrific fishing, and is home to a wide variety of wildlife. Helmcken Falls (135m, 443ft) is one of a half-dozen spectacular waterfalls within its boundaries.

Kamloops, the recommended overnight stop, began as a fur-trading post in 1812 and matured into an outfitting post during the gold rush of the 1860s. Its location made Kamloops a natural trading and distribution centre with stern-wheeled steamboats plying the Thompson River until the Canadian Pacific Railway arrived in 1885. The present city (population 75,000) has a broad economic base, which includes lumbering, mining, ranching, and mixed farming. Tourism is important, with some 200 nearby lakes for good fishing and boating and a number of provincial parks and ski resorts in the vicinity. Local attractions include sternwheeler cruises to recall the gold-rush days. Walking tours designed to take in historic buildings are self-guided. The Kamloops Museum features displays of native culture and a reconstruction of the 1821 Hudson's Bay Company trading fort.

Of Kamloops' motels, the Additional Information lists two with good views over the city and valley. The campground listed is closest to town, but for its setting campers may prefer Lac Le Jeune Provincial Park. Suitable for RVs it is about 30km south, and close to the next part of the route to Vancouver.

Kamloops to Vancouver (360km/224 miles, 1 day)

This journey takes you through British Columbia's interior to the Fraser River Valley and Vancouver. Because the Trans-Canada Highway route is covered in the northwestern British Columbia itinerary, the suggestion is to drive along the Coquihalla Highway (Hwy 5), a new toll-road which joins the Trans-Canada Highway 200km (124 miles) south of Kamloops near Hope.

Hope, situated on the Fraser River and surrounded on three sides by the mountains of the Cascade Range, dates back to a Hudson's Bay Company post which was established here in 1848. It may owe its name to a hope that

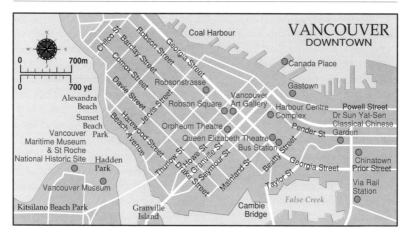

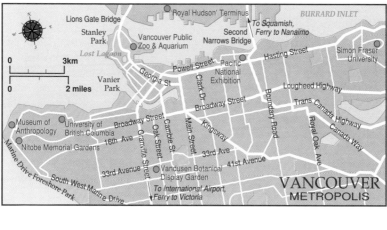

the pack trail from Fort Kamloops to Fort Langley would be on British (and not American) territory. The town was laid out in 1858 by Royal Engineers at a time when there was a rush for gold on the river's sandbars. Most visible feature is the huge rock slide which occured in 1965 when part of Johnson Peak collapsed and buried the highway under 45m (148ft) of rubble.

Continuing west along the Trans-Canada Highway, it is 36km (22 miles) from Hope to **Chilliwack**. This is the beginning of a 100km (60 miles) stretch of rich farmlands on the broad floodplain stretching along the Fraser River valley to the Pacific Ocean. Chilliwack is an agricultural centre and home to a large armed forces base. For a pleasant diversion visit Minter Gardens, where ten gardens presenting different floral themes have been created on a 10 ha (25 acres) site.

Given the time two or three days could be spent at **Harrison Hot Springs** reached by Hwys 9 and 7, or at the **Susquatch** or **Cultus Lake Provincial Parks** (see page 223).

Abbotsford (population 14,500) is a prosperous agricultural centre and scene of the annual Abbotsford International Airshow during the second weekend in August. **Fort Langley National Historic Park**, 6km (4 miles) north of the Trans-Canada Highway at Langley is a reconstruction of the Hudson's Bay Company trading post built on the south bank of the Fraser River in 1827 and moved to its present location in 1839. The post became a supply centre when gold was discovered in the area in 1858. On 19 November of that year the proclamation which declared the founding of British Columbia was read in the fort's Big House, the building used as the officers' quarters, guest rooms and community hall. The fort was abandoned in 1886. Parks Canada's reconstruction has costumed animators who demonstrate life here during the 1840s, as they go about their business as traders, carpenters, smiths, cooks and bakers.

It is a further 30km (19 miles) along the Trans-Canada Highway (Hwy 1) to downtown Vancouver.

Vancouver (2 days)

Located on the Burrard Inlet, with direct access to the Georgia Strait and the Pacific Ocean, **Vancouver** has a fine natural harbour for deep sea shipping while enjoying easy access to the interior along the Fraser River Valley. It was natural then that Vancouver grew rapidly to become one of the world's major seaports and Canada's third largest city. More than this, a balmy climate and the sheer beauty of its setting make the city a joy to both residents and visitors.

The Vancouver area was first settled by coastal Indians around 500BC. A Spanish naval vessel came here in 1791 and the following year Britain's Captain George Vancouver arrived offshore. Fur trader and explorer Simon Fraser travelled from the east in 1808 after descending the river which bears his name. However, little attention was paid to this peninsula until the 1860s when three Englishmen chose it for their brickyard. During the next decade several sawmills were established and a shanty town grew up. When the Canadian Pacific Railway moved its new Pacific terminus from Port Moody 20km (12 miles) westwards to this ramshackle settlement in 1886, it was incorporated as a city. The first train chugged in from the east in May of the following year, and the first trans-Pacific liner came into port in 1891. By 1900, Vancouver's population had risen to 100,000.

Present-day Vancouver (population of the city 415,000, of the metropolitan area 1.3 million) occupies most of the Burrard Peninsula between the Fraser River and the Burrard Inlet. In addition the municipalities of North Vancouver, New Westminster, Burnaby, Coquitlam, Richmond and Surrey have developed rapidly around the city. Although most of Vancouver's residents are of British or American stock, growing numbers of immigrants from Europe and Asia have introduced their own customs and traditions, transforming it into a truly cosmopolitan city. On the cultural scene Vancouver has a symphony orchestra and opera company, several theatre companies, excellent museums and art galleries.

The visually attractive downtown area situated on a small peninsula jutting into Burrard Inlet can happily be explored on foot, presenting as it does a delightful mixture of older buildings and new office towers on streets stretching down to the waterfront.

First-time visitors could well start with the Harbour Centre Complex on Hastings Street, with a film of Vancouver's colourful past and present, while an observation deck offers a fine view of the city and surroundings.

Canada Place, built as the Canadian Pavillion at Expo 86, dominates the waterfront. Looking for all the world like an enormous ocean liner with a roof of ten billowing sails, it houses a cruise ship docking facility, hotel, stores and the Vancouver Trade and Convention Centre.

Gastown to the east is named after 'Gassy Jack' Deighton, a garrulous saloon-owner in the early days of the sawmills. A pleasant upscale district now, it successfully blends late nineteenth-century buildings with modern structures. Further east is North America's second largest Chinatown (after San Francisco's). As the colourful focus of Vancouver's Chinese culture, it recalls times when Chinese fortune seekers came to join the nineteenth-century gold-rushes or to work as labourers building the railways. Many stayed on and imparted their own traditions to the city. While in Chinatown visit the Dr Sun Yat-Sen Classical Chinese Garden, modelled on private classical gardens dating from the Ming Dynasty.

Shoppers and browsers will enjoy downtown Vancouver. Robson Street has so many ethnic restaurants that several blocks are known as Robsonstrasse. Robson Square, a complex stretching from Nelson Street almost to Georgia Street, features gardens at ground level and a subterranean plaza with a skating rink, sidewalk cafés and an exhibition area. The impressive new structure with slanted glass roof on Robson Street's south side is the law courts building. The Old Court House, on the north side houses the Vancouver Art Gallery.

Reached by Robson or Georgia Streets, Stanley Park at the western end of the city is everything an urban dweller could want in a park. Within its 400 ha (1,000 acres) large wilderness areas are criss-crossed by walking trails. Stands of tall Douglas fir, cedar and hemlock trees are among its many botanical specimens. The flower gardens are a treat in early spring when most of the country is still buried in snow. The 8km (5 mile) seawall affords stunning views of the city and its harbour, and of ships lying at anchor in English Bay. From Prospect Point you can see the harbour and Lion's Gate Bridge with a backdrop of majestic mountains north of the city, and the collection of totem poles across from the city is a natural subject for photographers. Stanley Park also has a zoo with 570 animal species, including a collection of amusing king penguins and a hyperactive family of rare sea otters. The Vancouver Public Aquarium here contains 8,500 exhibits with whales and dolphins in pools designed for viewing from above and below the water's surface.

For a change of pace visit Granville Island, reached by Granville Bridge

or a brief boat ride across False Creek from the foot of Burrard Bridge. This
15 ha (37 acre) redevelopment has transformed one-time railway yards
and warehouses to a lively public market, art school, craft shops, theatres
and restaurants. The same mini-ferry service runs to the Vancouver
Maritime Museum in Vanier Park, overlooking English Bay. Exhibits here
illustrate the Pacific Coast's and Vancouver's maritime history. At the St
Roche National Historic Site is first the vessel to sail eastwards through
the elusive Northwest Passage. The *St Roche*, a Royal Canadian Mounted
Police supply boat commanded by Sgt Henry Larsen, set off from Vancouver in June 1940 and arrived in Halifax in October 1942 having spent two
winters trapped in the Arctic ice. The return voyage in 1944 took a mere
86 days. Close by in Vanier Park, the Vancouver Museum depicts city
history from fur-trading days to Victorian times. It also contains one of the

Vancouver's well-known steam-powered clock in Gastown

most comprehensive collections of West Coast Indian artifacts.

Because of the mild dampish climate, Vancouver's parks and gardens flourish and none more than the Vandusen Botanical Display Garden. Although a little further out from downtown it is well worth a visit for an impressive collection of ornamental plants, arranged to display their botanical relationships and geographical origins in more than thirty different gardens, lakes, waterfalls and sculptures. Queen Elizabeth Park, set on Vancouver's Little Mountain (150m, 492ft) is another enchanting park, beckoning with views of the city and harbour, and mountains to the north. Its centerpiece is a former quarry planted now as a pretty sunken garden.

Reached by the pleasant Northwest Marine Drive, the University of British Columbia's campus on Point Grey occupies 2,470 ha (6,100 acres).

Indian totem poles in Stanley Park, Vancouver

Its botanical gardens, which take up ten percent of the grounds, include plants native to British Columbia. The Nitobe Memorial Garden is one of the most accurate representations of a traditional Japanese garden to be found in North America. Also the university's Museum of Anthropology has impressive collections of Northwest coast Indian art, including huge war canoes and totem poles housed in an award-winning glass and concrete structure.

At the opposite end of the city Simon Fraser University's campus overlooks Burnaby Mountain Park, with exciting views of the Strait of Georgia, Fraser River delta and the distant mountains of Vancouver Island. Even more impressive is the panorama seen from the 1,192m (3,911ft) top of Grouse Mountain in North Vancouver. Reached by aerial tramway, the summit has restaurant facilities and entertainment, as well as walking trails and alpine meadows. In winter it provides Vancouverites with good skiing right on their doorstep.

Airline services connect Vancouver directly with many North American cities, South America, Australia and New Zealand, Asia and Europe. There are extensive long-distance bus connections and the city is the terminus for Via Rail's trans-continental service. Ferries connect with Victoria and various points on the British Columbia coast.

Drivers entering Vancouver from the east via the Trans-Canada Highway (Hwy 1) can best reach the downtown core from the Hastings Street exit. This is an easy city for drivers, but with a public transportation system that includes busses, SeaBus ferries and the SkyTrain rapid transit rail services, a car is not necessary.

The city has restaurants and night spots to suit all tastes. Among the numerous hotels and motels, B & Bs, university residences and hostels, the Additional Information lists the historic Hotel Vancouver, and the Westin Bayshore for its lovely views of the Burrard Inlet and Stanley Park. The three RV facilities are close to the city. However, at the time of writing there are no campgrounds suitable for tenting closer than Porteau Cove Park on Howe Sound, Golden Ears Park and those in the lower Fraser Valley (page 224).

Excursions from Vancouver

• *Squamish (130km/81 miles return)*
Leaving Vancouver by road via the Lion's Gate Bridge, join the Trans-Canada Highway (Hwy 1), and at Horseshoe Bay take Hwy 99 north. Cut in places through almost sheer cliffs this road, which is known as the 'Sea to Sky Highway', offers memorable views of Howe Sound's rugged coastline and surrounding mountains. An alternative is to make the same journey by rail or ship. The *Royal Hudson*, one of the few remaining steam locomotives in Canada, takes an excursion train along this route from its North Vancouver terminus to Squamish, a distance of 64km (40 miles). The cruise boat *Britannia* leaves from the foot of Denman Street in Vancouver for the same journey. Combination tickets are available for a train ride

in one direction and boat trip in the other.

In a picturesque alpine setting, overshadowed by snow-capped peaks, **Squamish** is a timber centre where huge log booms are assembled for towing to lumber mills to the south. Vacationers know it best as a gateway to the **Garibaldi Provincial Park**, a 1,958sq km (756sq mile) wilderness park encompassing mountain peaks, meadows, streams and lakes, and a series of unusual volcanic rock formations, the most prominent of which is Black Tusk.

• *Whistler (280km/174 miles return)*
This longer journey continues past Squamish along Hwy 99 to **Whistler** on the northwest side of Garibaldi Provincial Park. Whistler is a popular year-round European-style resort village with first-class accommodation, including the Chateau Whistler Resort. There are also lodges, condominiums and pensions as well as a full-service campground for RVs. Village amenities include swimming pools and health clubs, stores clustered around the village square, a movie theatre, and some thirty-five restaurants, bars and night clubs. As a ski resort it ranks with the best in North America. Whistler and Blackcomb Mountains have a total of 117 ski-runs up to 11km (7 miles) in length, while helicopters take experienced skiers further away to snowfields atop nearby glaciers. Summer visitors can still enjoy skiing, but most take advantage of the ski lifts for mountain hiking and bike riding, 1,220m (4,000ft) above the valley floor. There are golf courses as well as hiking and horseback riding trails, lake swimming and windsurfing.

All year the village features sporting events, special entertainment and festivals. Whistler can be reached by train, bus, or helicopter from Vancouver and direct by helicopter from Victoria. Because most facilities are within walking distance of the village, there is little need for a car once you are here.

Vancouver to Victoria (70km/43 miles, 2 days)

This journey is to Victoria via BC Ferries' service, a delightful 95-minute passage through wooded coastal islands. (The bus/ferry ride between downtown Vancouver and Victoria is so pleasurable, and inexpensive, that it is recommended as a day's outing from either city). If you are driving from downtown Vancouver, leave via Oak St (Hwy 99), then follow Hwy 17 to the Tsawwassen terminal. There are hourly sailings in summer. Leaving the ferry in Swartz Bay, take Hwy 17 to **Victoria**.

Like so many Canadian cities, Victoria's history started with the fur trade. The Hudson's Bay Company had established its Pacific Coast headquarters at Fort Vancouver, near the mouth of the Columbia River in present-day Washington state. In 1834, when it seemed likely that the mainland south of the 49th parallel was to become part of the United States, the company moved its headquarters to Vancouver island and named it Fort Victoria in honour of the Queen. A settlement around the fort had less than 1,000 inhabitants until the 1858 Fraser River gold rush on the mainland transformed it into a supply and transportation centre. Victoria was incorporated as a city in 1862, and three years later the nearby harbour at Esquimalt was made into a British naval base. In 1868 Victoria became capital of the newly amalgamated crown colonies of Vancouver Island and British Columbia and then, in 1871, capital of the new province of British Columbia.

Present-day Victoria (population 75,000, metropolitan area 250,000) does some lumber milling and shipbuilding, but its economy is based largely on government services and tourism. The equable climate makes Victoria a favourite with retired people, and has come to reflect the heritage of what used to be a largely British population. This is seen in the architecture and flower gardens, cricket pitches and lawn bowling greens. Also in the hotels and restaurants which serve afternoon tea, and shops selling British woollens and fine china. (Those familiar with Britain may find the connection dated and crassly commercial.) Beneath all this Victoria is her own city, with a full compliment of cultural attractions, good restaurants, interesting shops, galleries and museums.

Summer skiing at Whistler in British Columbia

Because the city is fairly small and hugs the harbour it is easy to tour on foot. Bastion Square, towards the west is all that is recognizable of the old Fort Victoria. Restored nineteenth-century buildings in the vicinity include the first Provincial Court House, now housing a maritime museum. Douglas Street is the major commercial centre, while Government Street is the main shopping venue with extensions along a number of side streets. In addition to stores stocking British china and woollens, you will come across traditional sweetshops, tobacconists and bookshops and other speciality stores. Most interesting for visitors are usually those specializing in Canadian arts and crafts, and in particular native artwork.

The harbour end of Government Street is dominated by two imposing buildings. The dignified grey stone structure set back in formal landscaping is the British Columbia Parliament Buildings. A gilded statue of Capt George Vancouver stands atop the dome, and in front a bronze statue of Queen Victoria looks to the harbour. At right angles to the parliament buildings stands The Empress Hotel, an important Victoria landmark built as a railway hotel in 1908. Recently restored it continues the best of its early British colonial traditions, including a restaurant featuring Indian curry and a substantial afternoon tea served in the lounge.

The Royal British Columbia Museum across from the parliament build- ings is one of Canada's best museums, a 'must' for anyone interested in the human and natural history of British Columbia. Admission tickets are valid for two days, so you do not have to take it all in on a single visit. Outstanding displays of Pacific Coast Indians show their way of life before the white man's arrival. Maritime galleries include presentations on Captains James Cook and George Vancouver. Other galleries depict the province's early days, the development of mining, logging, fishing and agriculture, and the province's present economy.

Within the museum grounds the Netherlands Centennial Carillon con- taining sixty-two bells was donated by British Columbians of Dutch origin. Close by is Thunderbird Park, with totem poles and other Indian carvings. Carvers are sometimes seen at work on replacements of totems which have become too weathered, or are commissioned by collectors. A short walk from Thunderbird Park along Douglas Street is Beacon Hill Park overlooking Juan de Fuca Strait. This 74 ha (183 acres) park is enhanced by lawns and flower gardens, an outdoor theatre and a cricket field. A plaque marks mile 0 of the Trans-Canada Highway — 7,821km (4,860 miles) from a similar marker in St John's, Newfoundland.

No visit to Victoria should omit Butchart Gardens, near Brentwood 22km (14 miles) north of the city. These gardens were started in 1904 by Jenny Butchart in a limestone quarry abandoned by her husband's cement company. During their world travels the Butcharts collected a mixture of rare and exotic shrubs, trees and plants. At first visitors were admitted free and even served afternoon tea. Now the gardens cover over 14 ha (35 acres) and are maintained by a permanent crew of thirty-five gardeners. The lovely rose garden, Italian and Japanese Gardens and the Ross Fountain with constantly changing water displays are memorable, and central to all is the grandest of sunken gardens. Plantings are arranged to ensure that there is always something to see, even in December when Japanese cherry trees, English daisies and wallflowers are among the specimens flourishing outdoors and the air in the greenhouses is heavy with scent from exotic blooms. At dusk in summer the gardens are illuminated by hundreds of hidden lights; July and August bring stage presentations and firework displays. Inclusive bus trips can be arranged from Victoria.

Victoria has numerous hotels, motels and B & Bs, as well as university residences and hostels. The KOA RV park is situated between the ferry terminal and the city. The public park west of the city accommodates campers as well as RVs.

There are direct airline connections with Seattle, Vancouver and elsewhere in Canada. In addition to the ferry and bus services mentioned, high-speed catamarans operate between Vancouver and Victoria. Fastest of all are the helicopters which connect with Vancouver and Whistler. Ferries sail to other British Columbia ports as well as to Washington state.

• *Excursion to Pacific Rim National Park (620km/385 miles return)*
This excursion from Victoria to Pacific Rim National Park on the west coast of Vancouver Island calls for an overnight stay in or near the park.

Leave Victoria via the Trans-Canada Highway (Hwy 1) and drive 120km (75 miles) to **Nanaimo**. The Hudson's Bay Company established a trading post here in 1849, and discovery of coal led the company to recruit miners in England and Scotland. The Bastion, a wooden blockhouse built to protect those miners is now a museum, while the Nanaimo Centennial Museum has exhibits illustrating more aspects of the city's early history. Coal was most important to the economy until deposits were exhausted and the city (present population 48,000) turned to wood products manufacture and fishing in the 1950s. The Nanaimo Bathtub Race is a much publicised event each July, when enthusiasts race motorized bathtubs and similarly outlandish craft for 55km (34 miles) across the Strait of Georgia to Vancouver. Nanaimo is also a terminal for BC Ferries to Vancouver.

Leaving Nanaimo, take Hwy 19 to Parksville and then Hwy 4 to **Port Alberni**. This community is at the head of the Alberni Inlet, named after the commander of the Spanish forces occupying the area in 1789-95. A sawmill was built here in 1860, founding the lumber industry which remains today. Mining and fishing are significant industries and Port Alberni (population 20,000) is British Columbia's third largest port. In summer a freighter from Port Alberni carries goods and passengers to ports in the area, including some within the Pacific Rim Park.

From Port Alberni it is 90km (56 miles) via Hwy 4, a winding stretch of mountain highway, to our destination which is the Long Beach section of **Pacific Rim National Park**. The park comprises three sections: the Long Beach area between Long Beach and Tofino, the Broken Island group of islands in Barkley Sound, and the West Coast Trail between Bamfield and Port Renfrew.

In all the 510sq km (197sq mile) park encompasses varied terrain, from snow-capped mountains and dense rainforests to rugged headlands and islands, river estuaries and 130km (81 miles) of shoreline with long sandy beaches. The park is home to considerable birdlife, ranging from forest-dwellers to shore-birds such as puffins, cormorants, geese, ducks and bald eagles. The forests are inhabited by bear and cougar, mink and martens. Seals and sea-lions laze on the beaches. In summer migrating grey whales feed off-shore.

In the most developed area of Long Beach leisure time favourites are hiking, swimming and surfing, and wandering on the broad beach to observe creatures in the tidal pools. An interpretation facility at the Wickaninnish Centre explains the park's features with lectures, slide shows and guided hikes, all aimed at teaching visitors about the region's human and natural history. Descriptive brochures of hiking trails along the shoreline and into the rain forest are also available.

South of the park entrance the fishing community of **Ucluelet** (population 1,500) is a centre of visitor accommodation, restaurants serving fresh seafood, boat rentals, charter fishing and whale-watching expeditions. **Tofino** (population 1,000) beyond the northern edge of the park is a fishing village with more accommodation. The Pacific Rim Whale Festival, held between mid-March and mid-April, celebrates the whales' migration between the Arctic and waters off Mexico's Baja California.

The Broken Group islands are reached only by boat across open water and this can be dangerous to small craft. The freighter service from Port Alberni to Gibraltar Island within the group brings campers, who explore the other islands by canoe and kayak. Sailing buffs enjoy the waters around the islands, while some fifty wrecks are popular with scuba divers.

The park's 77km (48 mile) West Coast Trail is a former footpath carved out of the wilderness so that shipwrecked sailors could reach safety. This rugged trail through coastal rainforest with stands of Sitka spruce and lush ravines, can be waterlogged in parts. It should only be attempted by experienced self-reliant hikers carrying up to a week's supplies. The northern trailhead is reached through Bamford, on 90km (56 miles) of gravel logging road, or freighter from Port Alberni. The southern end near Port Renfrew is 102km (63 miles) from Victoria via Hwy 14.

There are a number of motels and resorts in the Long Beach area. Advance reservations are essential in summer. The National Park campground at Green Point is suitable for RVs, but it is often full so that campers may have to use a commercial campground near the park gates. Because rainfall is heavy here, and the trails are often slippery, it is advisable to bring rainwear and waterproof footwear with good grip.

After visiting the park, a return to Victoria is suggested, or go straight to Vancouver via the ferry from Nanaimo to Horseshoe Bay.

Victoria to Osoyoos (440km/273 miles, 2 days)

This is a two-day itinerary to allow flexibility in taking the ferry from

Canada's Grand Old Railway Hotels

With completion of the trans-continental railway in 1885, Canadian Pacific Railway manager William Van Horne (he became president three years later) was well aware of Canada's tourism potential. His much quoted 'If we can't export the scenery, we'll import the tourists' was no idle promise. As one of Canada's greatest promoters, he attracted European vacationers with a guarantee of adventure, magnificent scenery, luxurious accommodation in his company's hotels and comfortable ship and train journeys to reach them.

In the next two decades these huge castle-style copper-roofed hotels became synonymous with the very best in Canada, assuring travellers of civilized facilities and service even in the wilderness. Soon the nation had competing railways whose builders erected similarly grand hotels along their routes. But by the 1950s travel patterns had changed, and most were in deep trouble. Hopelessly outdated amenities, threadbare furnishings and tiny rooms held no appeal for vacationers with the world as their playground.

Now the pattern has changed again, and with nostalgia in vogue these ponderous resorts are enjoying renewed success. Almost all have been beautifully restored and updated to meet the needs of the modern traveller. Resorts have excellent leisure facilities, and city hotels are conveniently located.

Most famous of the grand railway resorts is Banff Springs Hotel snuggled in the Rockies. Chateau Lake Louise overlooking a perfect mountain/lake view is a close second. Jasper Park Lodge has romantic log cabin accommodation around a central lodge. The legendary Château Frontenac is steeped in the history of Quebec City. Winnipeg's Fort Garry has its seventh floor converted to a plush European-style casino. Northern Ontario's Minaki Lodge offers unforgettable

Victoria to the mainland, and because you will be retracing the drive along the Fraser Valley as far as Hope. An overnight stay can be at any point in the valley that appealed when you travelled in the opposite direction.

The 250km (155 miles) of highway between Hope and Osoyoos passes through terrain that is mostly mountainous, but otherwise enormously varied. The drive starts in dense rain forest among majestic spruce trees, and ends at the northern tip of the North American continent's great central desert.

Leaving Victoria, retrace the road and ferry journey to Vancouver. Then join the Trans-Canada Highway (Hwy 1) to return through Haney, Abottsford and Chilliwack to Hope, spending the night in one of these communities. At Hope, take Hwy 3 (the Crowsnest Highway) and continue on for about 25km (16 miles) between mountain sides covered by dense rain forest to **Manning Provincial Park**.

fishing with guides and shore-cooked lunches. Chateau Whistler in British Columbia is newly built to resemble its green-roofed turn-of-the-century coun-terparts, while afternoon tea in Victoria's Empress Hotel is so popular that it starts at lunch time.

If you are not staying in any of these landmark resorts and hotels a visit when in the neighbourhood is recommended. Their capacious lounges with huge log-burning fire-places, plump sofas and regional crafts incorporated in the decor serve to typify a Canadian vacation in the grandiose style of the early years of the twentieth cen-tury.

The Palm Court of the Empress Hotel, Victoria

This park, which covers 660sq km (255sq miles), contains three distinct vegetation zones. The western end has the typical damp, dense forest of British Columbia's coastal regions. Noteworthy in this section are Rhodo-dendron Flats where thousands of these shrubs grow wild, presenting masses of blooms in early summer. After climbing through the Allison Pass (1,352m, 4,435ft), the road enters a transitional zone of aspen, juniper, pine and red cedar. Later, the route follows the Similkameen River into a section of dry, sagebrush country so typical of the province's central valleys. The park has four campgrounds and a number of hiking trails, including two to the scenic Lightning Lake and Three Brothers Mountain. Summer travellers will come upon alpine meadows shaded in pastels by lupins, yellow snow lillies, Indian paintbrush and other wildflowers. A diversion along the road between the park headquarters and Blackwall Peak can be rewarding for these carpets of flowers alone. Park wildlife

🦌 includes mule deer and black bear and grey-crowned rosy finches which nest in rock crevices within the snowfields and glaciers. The community of **Manning Park** at the preserve's eastern end has a resort and facilities
🏂 for fishing, canoeing and horseback riding as well as winter skiing.

About 25km north of the park gates the road passes **Copper Mountain**, with ruins of a coppermine which was largest in the British Commonwealth until the ore was exhausted. There is a very productive copper mine close by. Granite Creek, near **Princeton**, was a community of 2,000 people during an 1890s gold rush. This town used to be called Vermillion or Red Earth Forks for the mineral ores so apparent, and was renamed after the Prince of Wales visited Canada in 1860. Further along **Hedley** produced gold and silver, copper and arsenic until its mines closed in the 1950s. Now, lumbering, agriculture and tourism have become the region's major economic base.

Continuing west, the highway passes through rolling hills covered with sagebush and cactus, where small groups of thoroughbred cattle browse on the scant vegetation. This is the northern tip of the American Great Basin Desert extending south through the United States and into Mexico.

Osoyoos, the destination of this trip, lies on a sandspit which almost bisects Lake Osoyoos just north of the border with the United States. Its name is derived from the local Indian's expression meaning 'where two lakes meet'. Hudson's Bay Company supply trains passed through this region between 1812 and 1848, and gold prospectors later helped open the area. A few years after, a cattle and horse ranch was established here. In 1919 an irrigation canal brought water for agriculture and now the town, (population 3,000), is the centre of flourishing orchards and vineyards. The lake's warm waters attract tourists,while the townspeople capitalize on the area's similarity with parts of Spain by adopting a Spanish theme.

Restaurants, resorts and campgrounds are located in the town and beside the lake. Two resort motels are listed in the Additional Information, while Haynes Point Provincial Park, on the lake, has full RV facilities.

Osoyoos to Vernon (180km/112 miles, 1 day)

This drive is up the Okanagan Valley, one of Canada's most favoured regions because of its beautiful scenery and sunny climate. This area's prosperity followed the introduction of large-scale irrigation which transformed the valley into Canada's fruit basket. Lakes are excellent for fishing and watersports. There are good public beaches and picnic
🏂 grounds. Winter brings good ski conditions, while in spring you can actually ski the mountains in the morning and play golf in the valley in the same afternoon.

Vernon has been selected for an overnight stop because of varied accommodation in the nearby provincial park, and to shorten the following day's journey. There is also plenty of accommodation at Kelowna and elsewhere in the valley, as well as at the provincial parks and commercial campgrounds.

> ## Pacific Salmon
> Salmon fishing in British Columbia is the finest to be had anywhere. The five species of Pacific salmon: sockeye, pink, coho, chinook and chum, leave the sea to swim inland often for hundreds of kilometres to spawn and then die. Their offspring remain inland for about two years before swimming downstream to the ocean, where they remain for two to five years. Upon reaching maturity, they migrate inland and start the entire process again.

Leaving Osoyoos Hwy 97 passes through a region of orchards, market-gardens and vineyards in this lush oasis created by irrigation of the surrounding desert. (Those who have already seen the Okanagan, or who are in a hurry, could continue along Hwy 3, crossing the Rockies via the Crowsnest Pass.)

Penticton, about 60km (37 miles) to the north lies between Lake Skaha and the lower end of Lake Okanagan. The town is derived from *Pen-tak-tin*, a very apt Indian expression meaning 'a place to stay forever'. The early European history of this area and the valley to the north revolves around the fur trade. By 1813 the North West Company (which later merged with the Hudson's Bay Company) had established a route between the Columbia and Fraser Rivers. Until 1848 their Brigade Trail ran along the west side of Lake Okanagan, then north to Fort Kamloops. The first orchards appeared in the Penticton area in 1890. Irrigation systems were started in 1905, and ten years later the Kettle Valley Railway connected the town with Hope and the Crowsnest Pass. Today the city (population 22,000) has a mixed ecomony based on agriculture, mining, manufacturing and tourism.

Summerland, on the highway, is a prosperous community of 7,500 surrounded by orchards and vineyards. This was site of the valley's first commercial orchards and still depends on fruit cultivation as its main industry. Here, as elsewhere along the highway, stands offer local fruit fresh from the tree. **Peachland** (population 3,500) is a fruit-growing and logging community which has been able to add a molybdenum and copper mine to its already prosperous economy. An agricultural research station on the highway just south of town has a pleasant picnic ground surrounded by spacious lawns and exotic flower gardens.

Driving along the lake, keep an eye out for Ogopogo, Okanagan's answer to the Loch Ness monster and equally elusive. Indian legend has this creature living in a cave near Kelowna. It is said to measure between 9 and 22m (30-72ft) long, with the head of a horse — or perhaps a sheep — or even one at each end of its body. Recent sightings of Ogopogo were of a two-headed creature rising from Lake Okanagan.

Entering **Kelowna** from the south, Lake Okanagan is crossed by a long floating bridge. Oblate priests built a mission here in 1859 and planted the valley's first fruit trees. The townsite was laid out in 1892, and its name derived from an Indian word meaning 'grizzly bear'. Today Kelowna (population 60,000) is the valley's largest community. It ships one third of all apples harvested in Canada, as well as peaches, pears, plums, apricots and cherries. It also supports a number of fruit and vegetable packing and processing plants. The wineries in the area include Canada's largest. The city has a well-known theatre company, a symphony orchestra, art gallery, museum and college.

Kelowna welcomes tourists with a good beach and a pretty harbour. It holds regattas and festivals throughout the summer, a wine festival at harvest time, and a number of winter sporting events. The city is connected by direct airline services with Calgary and Vancouver, and vacation accommodation is plentiful. Lake Okanagan Resort, beautifully sited

An Okanagan farmer comes to market in Vernon

Beware of Bears

They look like cute, cuddly balls of black fur bounding across the road ahead of your car, but remember that almost every cub has a very big mother and she is probably close by. Bears encountered in national and provincial parks are wild. They should not be fed or lured closer to your car. Park naturalists will tell you that bears are after your food rather than you. In consequence campers are advised to stow food in their cars at night, or at least 8ft up in a tree. You cannot be too careful. In Glacier National Park bears smashed open our wooden box containing nothing but dishes, but which presumably smelled of food.

Park visitors are given pamphlets explaining how they can protect themselves from bears should they have a face-to-face meeting. For example, when a bear approaches you on a walking trail — unlikely but not impossible — climb a tree. If you cannot do that be quiet and still. What you **do not** do is offer it your lunch so that you can get a close-up with your camera or camcorder.

In attempting to lure a bear to your car with food you may be signing its death warrant. Even 'nuisance' bears who scrounge round town-sites and campgrounds are banished to wilderness areas far from home. So, accept the cautions, for your own safety and that of the bears.

on the lake, has its own golf course, tennis courts, horseback riding and marina. Lunch on the patio drenched in sunshine can be heaven.

History buffs will enjoy the reconstructed Father Pandosy Mission, founded by the Oblate fathers and the first place in the valley where fruit and vine crops were grown. Also, try to include Gray Monk Cellars north of the city, or one of the other estate wineries. Many are operated by migrants who brought their own vines and vintner skills from Europe.

Vernon was a camp on the fur trade route and site of a mission settlement in the 1840s. Several large cattle ranches were established here in the 1890s and fruit farming started in the early 1900s. Vernon (population 20,000) is still a major centre for most of the valley's vegetable crops. **Silver Star Provincial Park** offers year-round recreational activities as well as a variety of resort accommodations. Cedar Springs, on the road leading to the park, has pools fed by hot mineral springs. To get a feel of ranching in the valley visit the O'Keefe Historic Ranch, a living museum north of the city on Hwy 97. In 1867 Cornelius O'Keefe and his partner Thomas Greenhow decided that there was more money to be made from feeding miners than digging for gold, and so they drove cattle overland from Oregon to the northern end of Lake Okanagan. For the next 40 years their property grew from an initial 65 ha (160 acres) to an empire of 6,000 ha (15,000 acres); it included a village complete with post office and the area's oldest Roman Catholic church.

Vernon has good motels and resorts, as well as the resort hotels in Silver Star Provincial Park where there are also RV facilities. The campground listed is close to town, and is one of several in the area.

Vernon to Calgary (560km/348 miles, 1 day)

This drive to Calgary, through the mountainous interior of British Columbia, then the Rocky Mountains, and returning to the Prairies, completes the circular itinerary.

Leave Vernon via Hwy 97 and branch eastward on Hwy 97A north of Swan Lake to pass through Armstrong and Enderby. Continue along the Shuswap River and Mara Lake to join the Trans-Canada Highway (Hwy 1) east of Sicamous. This region is well-known for its watersports, and for its trout and salmon fishing in particular. Every October and especially every fourth year (1994, 1998, 2002, etc), the nearby Adams River turns crimson, as up to two million sockeye salmon return after a journey of 500km (310 miles) from the Pacific Ocean to spawn and die.

Continuing along the Trans-Canada Highway, which runs parallel the Eagle River, to reach **Craigellachie**. This point, named by the railway builders after a high rock in Scotland, is the scene of Canada's most famous photograph. It was here that the symbolic 'last spike' was driven on 7 November 1885 to mark completion of the Canadian Pacific Railway, the nation's first transcontinental railway.

Revelstoke (population 5,500) was founded as a railway construction settlement, and named after the British banker who funded the company. North of the town the 175m (575ft) high Revelstoke Dam which generates hydro-electric power has a visitor centre. The town is on the edge of **Mount Revelstoke National Park**, 260sq km (100sq miles) of mountains, meadows and valleys on the western edge of the Selkirk Range. Summit Road rises through 26km (16 miles) to the top of Mount Revelstoke (1,938m, 6,358ft) passing through various vegetation zones as the eleva-

tion rises. There are hiking trails but no campgrounds in this park.
Glacier National Park straddles a section of the Selkirk Mountains, an
ancient range formed millions of years before the Rockies. The 1,350sq km
(521sq mile) park encompasses over 400 glaciers. Heavy snowfalls on the
steep mountain sides often result in avalanches, the consequences of
which are the long light green streaks where vegetation is regenerating
after a slide. There are snow sheds (perhaps half a kilometre long) which
protect the road on its most vulnerable sections, and the sites for army
howitzers used to dislodge dangerous accumulations of snow. **Rogers
Pass** (1,320m, 4,330ft), one of Canada's most beautiful stretches of mountain road, is in the middle of the park. There are camping and hiking trails,
some of which lead to the glaciers. An information centre near Rogers Pass
features descriptive displays on the local environment, including of
course the glaciers and avalanches. Bears can be a particular nuisance
here, so be sure to follow the park rangers' instructions.

Leaving Glacier Park, the road descends into the Rocky Mountain
Trench and the Columbia River valley. The town of **Golden** (population
3,600) at the confluence of the Columbia and Kicking Horse Rivers is an
outfitting centre for expeditions into the region's national parks.

Yoho National Park occupies 1,313sq km (507sq miles) of the Rocky
Mountains' western slopes, providing scenic hiking and horseback riding, canoeing and camping. The park headquarters in the village of **Field**
has an information centre. Close by is the Burgess Shale Deposit, a
UNESCO World Heritage Site because of its fossils of some 120 species of
marine animals dating to the Cambrian period 530 million years ago. Just
east of Field, and visible from a viewpoint on the highway, are the
entrances to the Canadian Pacific Railway's famous spiral tunnels, constructed to avoid a very steep gradient in the line.

It is approximately 16km (10 miles) from Field to Kicking Horse Pass,
the boundary between British Columbia and Alberta. Calgary is about
190km (118 miles) from the pass via the Trans-Canada Highway.

Northwest British Columbia

Vancouver to Prince Rupert (580km/360 miles, 2 days)

This two-day journey takes you by road and ferry from Vancouver to Port
Hardy near the northern tip of Vancouver Island, and then for a 15-hour
ferry ride to Prince Rupert on British Columbia's northwest coast. If you
are taking a vehicle, during summer especially, it is essential to pre-book
the ferry passage as well as overnight accommodation in Port Hardy and
Prince Rupert. Although this trip is part of a longer itinerary, it could also
serve as an exciting excursion from Vancouver or Victoria. Cabins are
available and some passengers sleep on board while the ship is docked at
Prince Rupert, then return with the ship next day.

Because delays can occur with the ferry services from Vancouver to

Vancouver Island, telephone BC Ferries for the suggested route. Shortest is via the Horseshoe Bay (West Vancouver) terminus to Nanaimo. Ferries leave Horseshoe Bay every two hours from 7am for the 1½ hour sailing. From Nanaimo it is a six or seven hours' drive to Port Hardy, so it is best to get a fairly early start.

Arriving in Nanaimo, follow Hwy 19 north towards **Courtenay**, named after a British admiral who surveyed this coast in the 1840s. Abundance of game and berries brought Commox Indians to the area before the first European visitors, Spanish navigators, arrived in 1791. Ten years later the Hudson's Bay Company established a store here, and then migrants came from Britain and other parts of Canada from the 1860s onward. Present-day Courtenay (population 9,000) is a prosperous logging, fishing and agricultural centre with good skiing and sailing among its recreational opportunities.

Campbell River was already inhabited by Kwakiutl Indians when Vancouver surveyed the coastline in the early 1790s. By 1900 loggers had settled in the area. Now Campbell River (population 16,000) remains a wood-products centre as well as an important salmon-fishing port. Charter boat captains here are so confident that they offer money-back guarantees of a catch, while the town's Tyee Club awards membership to anyone who lands a salmon weighing more than 30lb. In July the annual Salmon Festival features fishing competitions and war-canoe races. Campbell River is an attractive town with waterfront parkland, a good stop for a restaurant or picnic lunch. A refuel here is recommended as there are no more service stations until Port Hardy.

Visitors with sufficient time may enjoy a diversion from Campbell River to one or two of British Columbia's provincial parks, reached via Hwy 28. It is a short drive to **Elk Falls Provincial Park** where the Campbell River drops 27m (89ft) into a deep rocky canyon. The park has picnic sites and camping and the salmon fishing here is legendary. About 50km (31 miles) further inland the 2,120sq km (820sq miles) **Strathcona Provincial Park** offers a complete range of outdoors activities. In the centre of the park is Vancouver Island's highest peak, Golden Hinde (2,200m, 7,218ft) and Della Falls (440m, 1,444ft) which is among the world's highest waterfalls. The park houses wolverine, wolf, cougar and the island's last elk herd. There are virgin stands of Douglas fir here, including one 1,000-year-old giant which has reached a height of 93m (305ft).

Port Hardy (named after the captain of Nelson's HMS *Victory*) is a further 230km (143 miles) from Campbell River. The economy of this community (population 5,000) is based on copper mining, lumbering and fishing. As terminus for the ferry to Prince Rupert this is an overnight stop, for which accommodation suggestions are listed in the Additional Information.

Queen of the North leaves Port Hardy at 7.30am for her 441km (274 mile) voyage up the Inside Passage. Most spectacular of all is the 70km (45 mile) Grenville Passage where the narrowest section is only 550m (1,800ft) wide. The Inside Passage is one of the world's most scenic natural water-ways with a constantly changing panorama of deep fjords and island passages, with densely wooded mountains sweeping down into the sea. You can expect to meet luxury cruise liners which leave southern oceans to ply this route in summer, also resident dolphins and perhaps cruising pods of killer whales.

Arrival in Prince Rupert is at 10.30pm, so accommodation here should have been booked in advance. Named after the first governor of the Hudson's Bay Company, **Prince Rupert** was designated in the early 1900s as the terminus of the Grand Trunk Pacific Railway, and intended to rival Canadian Pacific's Vancouver as a major trans-Pacific port. The railway arrived but the expected boom never materialized. It did become an important fishing centre, and World War II brought shipbuilding and work connected with construction of the Alaska Highway (see page 226). Present-day Prince Rupert (population 16,000) is an important transpor-

Sailing up the Inside Passage — one of the world's most scenic natural waterways

tation centre, terminus of both the Canadian National Railway and the Yellowhead Highway. Its huge natural harbour has a busy deep-sea port, and a sizable fleet fishing primarily for halibut. BC Ferries connect with the Queen Charlotte Islands, while Alaska Ferries provides access to the Yukon through Skagway. Via Rail operates passenger services to Prince George, Jasper and points east.

Kaien Island, where Prince Rupert is located, was once a meeting place for the Tsimshian and Haida peoples. Now city parks preserve totem poles and other relics of this heritage. The Museum of Northern British Columbia contains displays on native culture over 10,000 years, as well as developments since the arrival of the first fur traders and pioneers.

Prince Rupert to Hazelton (300km/186 miles, 1 day)

This journey, via Highway 16 (the Yellowhead Highway), is along the scenic Skeena River Valley, called by local Indians 'The River of Mists'. First, check your fuel because there is none available between here and Terrace, 160km (100 miles) away. Although the first section is a broad valley, you never lose sight of 2,000m (6,000ft) high snow-capped mountains in the distance on either side of the highway.

Port Edward, about 15km (9 miles) south of Prince Rupert, is a major commercial fishing community and centre for boating and sport fishing. Its North Pacific Cannery Village Fishing Museum is a restoration of one of some 200 remote cannery complexes which dotted this coast around the turn of the century. This is an authentic living museum, presenting the main cannery and reduction plant as well as parts of the village that used to house 400 people.

Terrace is named after the natural terraces which form the nearby river banks. The community (population 11,000) is a major forest products and recreational centre. Snowfall in the mountains to the north is the greatest in North America, providing excellent skiing in spectacular scenery. About 20km (12 miles) south, Mount Layton Hot Springs Resort has waterslides and a pool filled with hot mineral springs water. With pleasant accommodation, Terrace is a good overnight stop for those who had a late start. **Kitimat**, about 40km (25 miles) southwest via Hwy 37, is the site of one of the world's largest aluminum smelters. Fuelled by the area's abundant hydro-electric power, it converts alumina from Australia. The Kitimat River, parallel to the highway, has good salmon and trout fishing.

A few kilometres east of Terrace at **Kitselas** the valley narrows as the Skeena surges through steep-sided rocky canyons. Particularly impressive are the Seven Sisters, a series of snow-covered peaks to the east.

At **Kitwanga**, Hwy 37 leads 730km (453 miles) north to Upper Laird, YT, on the Alaska Highway. The drive to the Yukon on this partly gravelled road is beyond the scope of this itinerary. However, a 440km (273 mile) return excursion along the paved section as far as Meziadin Junction and then to Stewart via Hwy 37A is recommended if you can spare an extra day.

Stewart is at the head of the 150km-long Portland Canal, a fjord forming part of the border between British Columbia and Alaska. The town owes its origins to gold discoveries in 1898, and while lumbering is very important, gold and silver are still mined here. Tourists come for the scenery and the wildlife. Surrounded by towering mountains which rise directly from the ocean, the fjord offers magnificent scenery. Approaching Stewart, some twenty glaciers are visible along the mountain peaks at one time. Local tours into the mountains include a long stretch of road skirting the stunning Salmon Glacier. At Fish Creek, bald eagles and baby bears compete with humans for the salmon catch. Freshwater fishing for Dolly Varden and steelhead (a variety of rainbow trout renowned for its fighting qualities) is superb, as is the saltwater quest for chinook salmon.

Hazelton, our destination, was originally a Gitksan Indian village, occupied for centuries and known as *Git-an-maks* or 'the place where people fish by torchlight'. Living in this mild climate, its people prospered on the fishing and hunting. Spare time was devoted to carving the red cedar into totems and other meaningful objects, and to colourful ceremonies with song and dance. European settlers arrived in 1872, naming the village after the many hazelnut trees growing in the rich soil. Soon, the Gitksan started to earn money for the European trade goods they came to depend on. Next, missionaries and government officials tore down their totems, and banned their 'pagan' ceremonies and dances.

Concern over loss of the Gitksan heritage led, in 1970, to the development of **'Ksan Village**. Traditional cedar-plank methods were used to build tribal longhouses, a carving school, workshop, museum, craftshop and reception centre. Native carvers produced totems and the other artifacts that can be seen on the site. In summer, there are escorted tours daily and traditional song and dance are presented on Friday evenings.

Two small motels in nearby New Hazelton are listed in the Additional Information. It is well to make reservations in advance. Full service camping is available at 'Ksan Village or Seeley Lake Provincial Park.

Hazelton to Prince George (580km/360 miles, 1 day)

This part of the route starts by following the Bulkley River, continuing on Hwy 16 across the interior of British Columbia. Within the Moricetown Indian Reserve, and visible from the highway, the river narrows into a 15m (50ft) wide canyon before plunging over a 60m (200ft) drop. During the summer and autumn salmon runs, teams of residents can be seen gaffing these very large fish as they fight their way upstream. Some of the salmon are cleaned right there and sold to those who have means of cooking their own dinner. In a tent by the highway, smoked salmon is for sale at a remarkably low price.

Smithers, at the base of the 2,560m (8,400ft) Hudson's Bay Mountain, is a year-round skiing centre. Some of the seventeen ski trails have a vertical drop of over 500m (1,640ft). This is also a centre for mountain climbing, trail riding, rockhounding and fishing for salmon and steelhead. **Houston**

Welcome to Barkerville in the Gold Rush Era

The fight between town busybody Mrs Bowron and Fanny Bendixon 'late of the fashionable parlours of Paris, London and San Francisco' is getting physical. Earlier slurs and name-calling were largely ignored, but when Mrs B tore down the poster advertising Madame B's dancing girls she got herself slugged with a purse. The butcher leaves his business to watch, a prospector tries to intervene, and a little boy takes advantage of the growing crowd to sell a few extra copies of his *Cariboo Sentinel*. Sensing that the people are against her Mrs Bowron goes off to fetch her policeman husband, muttering darkly about a lawsuit. Unperturbed, Mme Bendixon dusts herself off and continues with our tour. From her we learn of the disastrous fire in 1868 that burned 116 buildings and left only one unscathed. With rolling eyes and an exaggerated French accent she explains how one of her girls had been ironing a dress when assaulted by a drunken miner. In the resulting struggle a stove was overturned, and in less than two hours the town was destroyed. Reconstruction began the next day.

Welcome to Barkerville, one of Canada's liveliest and most enjoyable historic recreations, where visitors are treated to a day in the life of the Cariboo Gold Rush. The tours are especially entertaining, as actors portray real characters of the time. Mme Bendixon, for example, is promoting her upcoming dance and the bell-dance competition, in which anyone who can swing his partner so high her feet touch the ceiling is awarded a prize. Mrs Bowron has already told how these teenage girls were sold by their fathers in Europe, and are now virtual slaves until they can repay their passage to North America. She also had sharp words about the evils of drink and loose morals, and about Dr Bell who doesn't wash his hands before attending a to wound, 'because he is a gentleman and gentlemen do not carry disease ....'

There is a miner's improbable story about his successful fight with a grizzly bear. Local dressmaker Mrs Neate offers tips on good manners and deportment, as well as sewing. Judge Begbie delights in recalling gory details of hangings. And it is a very earnest Rev James Maynard who escorts visitors along the original Cariboo road to the cemetery. On the way he tells matter-of-factly that he preached in a saloon at first, and when his appeal for funds met with little response he had personally to

claims to have one of the most beautiful settings in British Columbia. **Burns Lake** is a recreational centre, very popular with rockhounders and fishermen.

Approximately 65km (40 miles) north of Vanderhoof via Hwy 27, **Fort St James** dates from 1806 when the North West Company's Simon Fraser established a trading post here. When this company merged with the Hudson's Bay Company in 1821, it became the headquarters of the vast New Caledonia district between the Rocky and Coast Mountain ranges.

build a one-room home for his family of six (soon to be seven) and a church. At each graveside he has a poignant story to tell, of the terrible accidents and the fights, the heroics, the disease, fortunes won — and as quickly lost — in Barkerville.

Try to allow several hours and preferably longer for a visit. Have lunch in one of the restaurants, attend a bawdy musical comedy in the Theatre Royal or a class in the schoolroom and join some of the tours. They all contribute to an unforgettable day in British Columbia.

Mrs Bowron and the butcher are just two of Barkerville's colourful characters

A Roman Catholic mission was built in 1843. Services continue to be held in Our Lady of Good Hope Church, which was built in 1870 and is now one of the province's oldest churches. Gold was found nearby in 1869, and mercury in the 1940s. Today's town (population 2,000) is an important air transportation centre which links the highway and railway to the south with otherwise isolated lumbering and mining communities. Fort St James National Historic Park has original buildings from the 1880s, and reconstructions of others to reflect this period when the fur trade started to decline. The modern reception centre has exhibits and audio-visual presentations on the fort's long history.

Prince George, 162km (100 miles) east of Fort St James, also traces its beginnings to trading company explorers. Alexander Mackenzie came here in 1793, followed by Simon Fraser in 1806. Fort George, a trading post named after King George III, was established a year later. The Overlanders (see page 194) passed by on their way to the gold fields in 1862, but settlement was negligible until construction of the Grand Trunk Railway (now the CNR) started early in the twentieth century. Real growth got underway with expansion of the forest products industry after World War II. Now Prince George (population 70,000) is British Columbia's third largest city, the major administration and transportation centre for the northern part of the province, and site of several sawmills and pulpmills.

The Fort George Regional Museum in Fort George Park presents the area's natural and human history and the development of its transportation and lumber industries. Preserved historic buildings within the adjacent stockade include a schoolhouse, while its railway station is served by an operating narrow-gauge steam train.

Visitors here will find a number of art galleries and craft shops stocked with interesting souvenirs of their visit to British Columbia's interior. Mountains, lakes and rivers in the surrounding area provide rugged outdoors experiences, including superb fishing and skiing. Two of Prince George's hotels as well as an RV campground fairly close to the town are listed in the Additional Information.

Prince George to Quesnel via Barkerville (280km/174 miles, 1 day)

Leave the Yellowhead Highway (Hwy 16) which continues on to Jasper, and turn south along the so-called Gold Rush Trail, Hwy 97. There is an excursion to the restored gold rush town of Barkerville before a return to the highway and an overnight stop in Quesnel.

Following Hwy 97 south, the drive is through the gentle hills of British Columbia's vast central plateau, passing through ranching country dotted with small settlements. While most communities in western Canada's interior owe their existence to fur trade routes or railway construction, it was gold more than anything that brought settlers to this region.

Over millions of years glaciers ground away at veins of gold in the Cariboo Mountains. Rain washed the heavy nuggets, flakes and dust into the sand and gravel beds of creeks and rivers flowing from the mountains. Indians started trading the gold at Hudson's Bay Company posts. The company in turn sold it in San Francisco, and stories about gold in British Columbia's interior spread. By 1858 the Cariboo Gold Rush was on, bringing miners prospectors and adventurers — first from California, followed by more from as far away as Europe, Australia and China.

By 1860 gold yields convinced the colonial government to build roads, initially from Lillooet at the head of a series of lakes, and then from Yale, the head of navigation on the Fraser River, to Barkerville. Royal Engineers surveyed the 650km (404 mile) long route and blasted the most difficult sections through solid rock. Most of what remained was built by private contractors. The Cariboo Road (now replaced by the modern Cariboo Highway) was completed in 1864. When the gold was exhausted after less than 20 years, most miners drifted away from the Cariboo. Others stayed to become ranchers, farmers and lumbermen.

Just north of Quesnel turn east on Hwy 26 for a scenic 90km (56 mile) drive along the Cariboo Highway into the mountains. Cottonwood House Provincial Park contains Cottonwood House, erected in 1864 and furnished in period style. This nineteenth-century equivalent of a motel is the last remaining roadhouse built for travellers on the Cariboo Road. **Wells**, named after a prospector who discovered gold-bearing quartz nearby, is a reminder of a mine which operated between 1933 and 1956.

Barkerville Historic Park contains about seventy-five buildings, re- stored or reconstructed to their 1870s style when Barkerville was capital of the Cariboo. The town was named after Billy Barker, an English canal worker turned California gold miner who arrived here in 1861. With six companions, Barker staked a claim in an area already abandoned by others as being unproductive. Mindless of old-timers' jibes, they sank a shaft into the gravel. Eight days later and 16m (52ft) down, they struck pay dirt with $1,000-worth of gold in a 30cm (1ft) layer.

Other miners rushed to stake claims nearby and the buildings which sprang up around the workings became the settlement named after Barker. Over four years Barker's shaft was to yield $600,000 at a time when gold sold for $16 per ounce. Barker married a widow who helped him spend his money as fast as he earned it and then left him. He died a pauper in Victoria nearly 30 years later.

In all the Cariboo produced $50 million in gold. At the height of its boom Barkerville had nearly 10,000 inhabitants. As well as miners (who, when lucky, wintered in Victoria or San Francisco), there were builders, merchants, bankers, saloon keepers, entertainers, gamblers and preachers — all the characters movies have led us to expect of a wild frontier town. Catering to them were hotels and bunk houses, saloons, dance halls, a church, even a race course — and a cemetery. Chinese miners living in their own separate community sent earnings home to the families they dreamed of rejoining one day. And in the days before the mounties arrived, colourful Judge Baillie Begbie enforced law and order.

The town reception centre explains mining techniques, community life in the Cariboo and the impact of gold discoveries on British Columbia. Reconstructed buildings include hotels, stores, assay office, etc. Actors, given the roles of the town's prominent — if not always entirely respect- able — citizens, play out their lives and conflicts. St Saviour's Anglican Church is an unusual wooden structure where regular services are held. Restaurant menus include sour-dough bread and stew and tasty Chinese food. Visitors are invited to try their hand at panning for gold. Some even find a few grains.

A return to Hwy 97 and a night spent at Quesnel is recommended. Campers may prefer to stay here at the Barkerville Provincial Park, where there are tenting and RV facilities.

The river and lake on which **Quesnel** is situated were named by Simon Fraser after a companion in his famous 1808 expedition. Settlement started in 1860, when it became a transit point for miners who had taken passage up the Fraser River and disembarked here for their trek into the Cariboo Mountains. An interesting riverside walk leads past a series of exhibits explaining the area's history. Today Quesnel (population 8,000) is a centre for forest products, mining and ranching. Sportsmen come for the fabulous hunting and fishing; other visitors enjoy a stay at one of the local dude ranches or one of the city's hotels. Ten Mile Lake Provincial Park, on Hwy 97, has a suitable campground.

Quesnel to Harrison Hot Springs (540km/336 miles, 2 days)

This section of the itinerary starts with a fairly long and very scenic drive down stretches of the Thompson and Fraser River valleys. It is followed by a suggested two-night stay at a resort community which has roots in the gold-rush era north of the lower Fraser River Valley. An alternative route is to Whistler — an excursion from Vancouver described on page 201, along a less travelled road through remarkable mountain scenery.

Leaving Quesnel continue south along the old Cariboo Road, now Hwy 97. **Soda Creek** at the head of a canyon of the same name, was a place where marine engines and boilers were brought overland and assembled into stern-wheeled paddle-boats. They were used to ferry miners and supplies along the navigable stretch of river between here and Quesnel.

Williams Lake (population 10,000) is the centre of the cattle ranching country of the Cariboo and Chilcotin plateaux. Cattlemen, with a ready market for beef among the Cariboo miners, first settled here in the 1860s, and it is still open range country where cowboys work on horseback. The Williams Lake Stampede, held each July, attracts entrants from Canada and the United States and is regarded as British Columbia's best annual rodeo. Now the highway turns east to **150 Mile House**, a stagecoach stop in Cariboo Road days, and named after the distance from Lillooet. At **Cache Creek**, another town which began as a stagecoach stop, follow the old Cariboo Road by branching southwards onto the Trans-Canada Highway (Hwy 1). Hwy 97 continues on to Kamloops and then down the Okanagan Valley.

The Trans-Canada Highway enters the Thompson River valley close to **Ashcroft**, running between bare granite slopes eroded by constant weathering, with the Canadian National Railway on one bank and Canadian Pacific's main line on the other. The Steelhead Inn in the little town of **Spences Bridge**, is said to be the oldest in British Columbia. It has been imaginatively restored as a comfortable B & B and restaurant, with tables indoors and on a deck overlooking the river.

Lytton, another staging post and supply centre for the gold-fields, stands at the fork where the clear waters of the Thompson River meet the muddy Fraser. This village was named after Sir Edward Bulwer-Lytton, the nineteenth-century British writer and politician. Today Lytton (population 430) is a village of pleasant tree-lined streets and claims to be one of the warmest and dryest spots in Canada. There is good fishing and white-water rafting on the local rivers, so not surprisingly it has several resorts.

Jackass Mountain to the south, named after the mules employed in hauling loads up this steep slope, affords fine views of the river. In this region the road and railways run through a series of tunnels, driven through bluffs that once forced travellers to cling to perilous ledges overhanging the river below. Nobody seems to know why the two lines cross the canyon by massive bridges here to exchange sides.

At **Hell's Gate** the river rushes through a canyon only 36m (118ft) wide, but 180m (590ft) deep. This name was given by early pioneers to the swirling, racing waters at this point. When the gap was made even narrower by rock slides during construction of the railway, it became an impossible challenge for the two million migrating salmon who pass this way each year. In consequence concrete 'ladders' were built to re-open the passage. An airtram takes visitors into the canyon where a footbridge spans the rushing waters. A restaurant and toilets are located at the base, as well as a visitor centre where the salmon's life cycle is explained.

Yale was the site of a fur-trading post built in 1848. Ten years after that it became a boomtown of 2,000 people when gold was found in its river–bed gravel. Later it was the southern terminus of the Cariboo Road, and then an important railway construction link. When the line was completed in 1885 Yale was left to become a virtual ghost town. Plaques record Yale's past history, while the 1859 Anglican church of St John the Divine here is the oldest church in British Columbia standing on its original site.

Just north of **Hope**, leave the Trans-Canada Highway and take Hwy 9 west for about 30km (18 miles) to **Harrison Hot Springs**. This resort village (population 600) lies in a beautiful setting at the foot of Harrison Lake. The 64km (40 mile) long lake was part of the goldfields route until the Yale-Lytton section of the Cariboo Road was built. Legend has it that in 1859 three prospectors canoeing along the lakeshore were overturned, and instead of freezing found themselves in waters fed by hot mineral springs. A spa grew up around the springs which are now channelled into a large municipal swimming pool, and spa facilities in the Harrison Hot Springs Hotel. The lakeside village has a wide beach trimmed by pleasant walks and flower gardens. There are a number of nice stores, restaurants and various inns, motels and the excellent Hot Springs Hotel. Nearby **Susquatch Provincial Park** has extensive facilities for camping (including RVs), hiking, swimming and fishing. It is named after the ape-like creature twice the size of man believed to inhabit area mountains. Although such creatures have been reported on dozens of occasions, sightings are generally viewed with scepticism. **Cultus Lake Provincial Park**, set in the Cascade Mountains 10km south of Chilliwack, also has camping, hiking, swimming, boating and fishing. The Cultus Lake Indian festival held here in June brings participants from British Columbia and Washington State.

- *Alternative Route: Lytton to Whistler (170km/106 miles)*
This route follows the original section of the Cariboo Road (now Hwy 12) northwest from Lytton and up the Fraser River Valley to Lillooet, a distance of 64km (40 miles). The road is fairly narrow, and while its curves and rock outcrops may prove daunting to RV drivers the memorable valley views make the drive more than worthwhile. This is sagebrush country where ranching is a major occupation, and irrigation has brought cultivation. Large sections of the valley are covered with the dark plastic arbours erected to shade ginseng, a lucrative medicinal crop with a ready market in the Orient.

Lillooet is a village (population 1,800) in an area with a large Indian population. During the 1850s gold rush, it was a major staging post for miners travelling to the interior, and the terminus of the Cariboo Road until the section through the Fraser Canyon was built. Lillooet is a 'pull out' point for river rafting trips down the Fraser.

Soon after leaving Lillooet via Hwy 99, Seton Lake is reached, with gorgeous views of the mountains reflected in the lake's deep blue-green waters. Shortly afterwards, the road along Lake Duffey's south shore gives picture-postcard views of the Joffre Glacier, alpine meadows and lakes. Without a doubt it is one of the most majestic segments of highway in the whole of Canada.

It is about 50km (30 miles) from Lake Duffey, with one short stretch of gravelled road along the Lillooet River, to the agricultural community of **Pemberton**. As you approach the Garibaldi Park and **Whistler** the Coast Mountain scenery becomes increasingly beautiful, and will surely tempt you to stay for one or two days or longer.

Harrison Hot Springs to Vancouver (130km/81 miles, 1 day)

This short return to Vancouver takes Hwy 7 through agricultural valley lands between the north bank of the Fraser River and the Coast Mountains.

Leaving Harrison Hot Springs, drive south to Agassiz and turn west on Hwy 7 parallel to the Fraser River. **Mission** is named after St Mary's Indian Mission founded here by Oblate Fathers in 1860. The site soon became a popular stop for travellers. Large-scale development occurred when the Canadian Pacific Railway arrived in 1885, and then a bridge was built across the Fraser River. With a population of around 20,000, Mission's economy is based on lumbering, dairying and fruit and vegetable farming. Westminster Abbey, a Benedictine monastic complex with its 51m (167ft) high bell tower, is open to visitors in the afternoons.

Maple Ridge is gateway to **Golden Ears Provincial Park**, a 556sq km (215 sq mile) area dominated by the snow-covered twin peaks of Golden Ears Mountain to the east of Pitt Lake. The park has 60km (37 miles) of hiking trails as well as camping, boating and swimming facilities. It is popular with Vancouverites, and could serve as a base for campers while they explore the city. Visitors from the Netherlands may be interested in the Pitt Polder east of the Pitt River, since Dutch immigrants drained the marshes here in the 1940s, turning them into prosperous dairy farms.

Immediately past Maple Ridge, the road becomes a multi-lane controlled access highway leading to the Trans-Canada Highway and then to Vancouver, a distance of about 40km (25 miles).

The Yukon

Whitehorse (2 days)

Many travellers arrive at Whitehorse in the Yukon by air from Vancouver or Edmonton as part of a comprehensive package tour or with the intention of renting a car or RV once they get here. Others come by bus or train from Skagway, Alaska, having travelled by cruise ship from various west coast ports, or aboard one of the Alaska State ferries which sail from Prince Rupert and the US port of Bellingham, WA.

Whitehorse can also be reached overland from British Columbia and Alberta. If you are driving first consult the provincial tourism authorities regarding driving practices, special equipment and supplies for the trip. RV rental companies may charge a premium for driving to the Yukon.

Yukon's first non-native visitors were Russian. They came after Vitus Bering, a Dane serving in the Russian navy, explored the coast in 1741. His written accounts led to the fur trade in what became Russian America (Alyeska). Sir John Franklin, searching for the North West Passage, mapped the Yukon's Arctic coastline in 1825. Within a few decades American whalers were coming to the area. By the mid-1800s the Hudson's Bay Company had established a number of trading posts in the interior and on the Pacific coastline of what is now Alaska. Anglican and Roman Catholic Missionaries arrived in the 1860s.

Russia sold Alaska to the USA in 1867. This was followed by a dispute between Britain and the United States over ownership of the head of the Lynn Canal, where Skagway is located. It was awarded to the USA after years of negotiations, suddenly rendered urgent by the discoveries of gold in the Klondike region of what was then the Northwest Territories.

On 17 August 1896 prospector George Washington Carmack and two Indian companions, Skookum Jim and Tagish Charlie, discovered a rich streak of gold in Bonanza Creek which runs into the Klondike River, a tributary of the Yukon. As soon as the news got out, thousands of gold-seekers from southern Canada and the United States headed north. Within two years, the Yukon's population reached 40,000 and the Canadian government gave it the status of a separate political entity. The North West Mounted Police had jurisdiction over the goldfields. In the absence of any other administration they also acted as magistrates, postmasters and welfare officers.

During this period the goldfields were served by stern-wheeled paddle

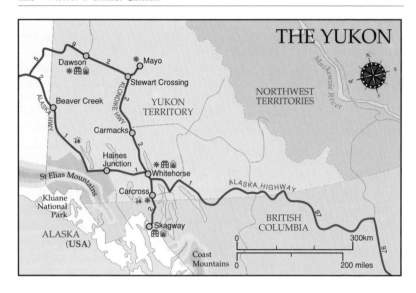

boats travelling down the Yukon River from Whitehorse. The White Pass and Yukon Railway which opened in 1900 connected Whitehorse with Skagway. In doing so it replaced the grim pack trails and mountain passes between the ocean and the Yukon River.

Life among the miners has been immortalized in the works of Jack London and other writers. Robert Service, who was a bank clerk here in gold rush times, wrote such poems as *The Shooting of Dan McGrew*, the *Cremation of Sam McGee* and his collected *Songs of a Sourdough*.

Gold worth ninety-five million dollars was extracted between 1896 and 1903, when the easily mined deposits gave out. The boom ended and by 1918 the Yukon's population had shrunk to a tenth of its earlier size. Large hydraulic dredges kept some gold mines profitable until the 1960s, by which time silver, lead and zinc mines had become more important.

Construction of the Alaska Highway in 1942-3 brought 30,000 American soldiers and contractors to the Yukon. While most left after the road was completed, the transportation link that they built brought prosperity and increased population. Today the Yukon's economy is based on mining, government administration and tourism. Some 24,000 people live here, 15,000 of them in Whitehorse.

Visitors come for the fabulous scenery and great outdoors, and in mid-summer for the never-ending daylight due to its high latitude. Yukon is one of the world's last great wildlife preserves, home of black and grizzly bears, wolves, wolverine, moose, caribou, Dall sheep and mountain goats, ducks, geese and grouse. Strict regulations require hunters to be accompanied by a licensed guide. Fish — Dolly Varden, grayling and pike — mature slowly in these cold waters, which means that the biggest catches are found in remote lakes and rivers best known by the guides, and usually reached by float plane. Visitors can readily locate outfitters in

SS Klondike II, *the last of the sternwheelers to sail on the Yukon River*

The annual dog-sled race at Whitehorse in the Yukon

Whitehorse who provide the guides, gear, accommodation and licences required for any kind of wilderness excursion. Fortunately for the wild-life, guides are equally happy to lead photographic safaris.

The search for history in the area is a simple matter of starting with a tour of **Whitehorse**, after calling in at the information centre on Steele Street for brochures and a map for a self-guided walking tour. Exhibits in the MacBride Museum relate to wildlife, Indian culture, the gold rush era and the highway construction project. The Government Administration building has more historic documents and photographs, and a collection of local art. SS *Klondike II* on the Yukon riverbank was one of the last sternwheelers to ply the river between Whitehorse and Dawson. She is preserved in a National Historic Site where, in a reception centre, the role of stern-wheeled riverboats in Yukon's history is explained.

A day trip to **Skagway**, Alaska, will help to relive the gold rush experience. It also goes through the Coast Mountains and some of the Yukon's most dramatic scenery. (Non-Canadians require a US visitor's visa.)

The 360km (224 mile) return trip can be made by car, tour bus or train, but note that part of the road is closed in winter. From the historical viewpoint, this journey is best described as starting in Skagway. This is where the stampeders landed after sailing north from Victoria or San Francisco, and this is where they stayed while preparing for the overland journey. Around 1900 Skagway's population was 15,000. Most famous of its citizens was the notorious outlaw and con-man 'Soapy' Smith who cheated many a greenhorn. In true frontier fashion Soapy was eventually challenged by an outraged citizen and both men died in the shoot-out.

Skagway is now a respectable little town of 800 people. Broadway, the main street with its wooden sidewalks and false-fronted buildings recall-ing the brash and bawdy gold rush era, is part of the Klondike Gold Rush National Historic Park. In summer months the US parks service operates an interpretive centre, from where walking tours are available.

A 53km (33 mile) hiking trail following the miners' route from Skagway and over the Chilkoot Pass (1,062m, 3,484ft) is maintained jointly by the United States and Canadian parks services. A difficult trip still, it is recommended only for the experienced and well-equipped, or you can cheat and take a helicopter from Skagway over the pass. In gold rush days the Canadian border was strictly controlled by the NWMP, who admitted miners only if they had enough equipment and supplies to last for a year. It was not a journey for the faint-hearted. Each man's load weighed about 800kg (1,760lb). His 'ton' had to be broken into perhaps thirty or forty packs for carrying up steps hacked out of the ice and rock to the pass summit, and then down the other side.

The terrain encountered as you rise to the pass is enormously varied. Vistas along the beautiful Skagway Valley include lush coastal vegetation and cascading waterfalls. All too soon this gives way to a landscape that is desolate and forbidding, with clumps of snow even in mid-summer, pools of icy water, swamps and lichen-covered rocks. From lookouts on the international border close to the point where weary miners paused to rest, you can enjoy the magnificent scenery of the interior as viewed from the Chilkoot Pass. To the east is White Pass (879m, 2,884ft), also called the Dead Horse Trail for the number of horses who died of exhaustion before reaching the summit. The mounties closed White Pass as being too dangerous. Railway engineers used the route though, and the line was built in record time by miners down on their luck. The scenery viewed from this section of the tracks is even more compelling than from the road.

The Klondike Hwy skirts Tutshi Lake, Windy Arm and Tagish Lake past quite incredible and uncommonly varied vistas. Mountain sides plunge down into brilliant blue lakes, and meadows are literally sprinkled with wildflowers. There is even a miniature desert. Nowadays tourists admire it all, but the miners viewed it quite differently. After struggling through the mountains they reached Bennett Lake to the west of the highway, where they stayed long enough to cut down trees and build boats to transport their goods down the Yukon River. Hikers following the Chilkoot Trail will come across remnants of this tent town and of the saw-mills that sprang up here 100 years ago.

Prospectors used to float past **Carcross** where the road meets the old trail. This is the settlement from where George Carmack's party set off on the prospecting trip which ended in Bonanza Creek. The Caribou Hotel here is regarded as the Yukon's oldest. Close by is a reception centre with a sternwheeler, stagecoach and locomotive on display to illustrate transportation in the Yukon's early days. Tour bus passengers usually stop at the Riverboat Warehouse for a miners' stew lunch and a vaudeville show.

Miles Canyon above Whitehorse was the miners' final challenge before reaching the White Horse rapids and the river boats. Here the mighty Yukon River ran through a narrow passage of rushing waters and dangerous whirlpools. Miners had to transport their gear around the waters and many a man died when his boat was dashed against the canyon walls. Although a power dam has tamed the river now, cruises aboard MV *Schwatka* retrace the route, accompanied by an interesting commentary on its earlier hazards.

Locals seem to keep going throughout the daylight hours in this Land of the Midnight Sun, but it is suggested that a Miles Canyon cruise is left until next day, which could also include a trip to Takhini Hot Springs, about 16km (10 miles) from town off the Klondike Hwy. Here pools fed by the natural hot springs are maintained at 36°C (97°F). A park offers camping and picnic facilities, while serving as base for hikes and horseback rides into the surrounding mountains.

Panning for gold is fun here, since gold might actually be found in the gravel. If this proves unsuccessful, jewellery made of local nuggets is for sale in the uniformly high quality crafts stores. Of the visitor entertainment available in Whitehorse the Frantic Follies — a vaudeville tradition featuring dancing girls, Robert Service verse, frontier humour and lots of audience participation — is recommended.

Whitehorse has very good inns, motels and campgrounds as well as B & Bs and a hostel. The RV park is downtown. Robert Service Campground, beside the river and handy to the city, permits tenting.

Whitehorse to Dawson City (540km/336 miles, 1 day))

This trip is north from Whitehorse along the Klondike Hwy (Hwy 2) which in places runs parallel to the Yukon River. Outdoors enthusiasts often take to their canoes here and follow the prospectors' trail down the Yukon, from the head of the Chilkoot Pass on Bennett Lake to the Klondike, a distance of 980km (609 miles). As the early stampeders discovered, there are innumerable places to camp on the riverbanks and sandbars.

Campers may want to use one of the ten Yukon Government parks on the Klondike Highway. All have RV facilities and are inexpensive. At **Montague** are the remains of a roadhouse, an earlier version of the government's campground principle established to accommodate travellers at 20 mile (32km) intervals.

The trail over the Chilkoot Pass — a route taken by miners during the Klondike Gold rush — is only recommended for the experienced hiker

Carmacks, 175km (109 miles) from Whitehorse, is named after George Washington Carmack, who started here as a fur trader, then found coal on the site before going on to fame and fortune in the Klondike. It was an important stop on the overland trail between Whitehorse and Dawson, and a refuelling point for riverboats. Five Finger Rapids, to the north, consist of limestone rocks which split the Yukon into five streams. These rapids claimed the lives of many an unwary stampeder in his makeshift boat. Riverboats had to be winched with cables through the narrow passage which remains a hazard to navigation even now.

Stewart Crossing stands at the junction of the highway and the Silver Trail (Hwy 11) leading to Mayo, 53km (33 miles) to the northeast. In the early 1900s this was a shipping point where gold and silver and other mineral ores mined in nearby Elsa were loaded onto sternwheelers. Their journey took them down the Stewart River to the Yukon, then to Whitehorse for shipment to the coast by rail. A visitor kiosk in Stewart Landing provides information for those interested in travelling the Silver Trail.

About 40km (25 miles) southeast of Dawson, is the beginning of the Dempster Highway. This is Canada's most northerly road, running 740km (460 miles) through the Richardson and Ogilvy mountain ranges to **Inuvik,** NWT, on the Mackenzie River delta.

Dawson City stands on the east bank of the Yukon at the mouth of the Klondike River. In August 1896 prospector Joseph Ladue anticipated a stampede following the gold discoveries and so staked out the townsite, named after the then Director of the Geographical Survey of Canada.

Dawson grew quickly as the transhipment centre for men and equipment heading for the goldfields. In 1899, with a population of 30,000, it was Canada's largest settlement west of Winnipeg. Mostly a rough and tumble town of tents and log cabins, it also had stately homes and large government buildings complete with running water, electricity and telephones.

The decline was slow at first, but speeded up once the easily mined gold was exhausted and prospectors drifted off to try their luck elsewhere. There was some expansion after World War I, but never on a large scale. The Alaska Highway enabled Whitehorse to overtake Dawson as the territory's commercial centre. The capital was moved there in 1951 and the last gold mining operation on the Klondike closed down in 1966. But Dawson was not destined to become a ghost town. These days, with its restored buildings and a population of 800, it welcomes a lot of visitors for a taste of the gold rush era.

Parks Canada operates a number of facilities collectively known as the Klondike National Historic Sites. The visitor centre on Dawson's Front Street has interpretive programs and audio-visual presentations, as well as conducted tours. The old post office, the sternwheeler *Keno,* and Harrington's Store Exhibit offer insights into the period. The Dawson City Museum tells about regional history. In Robert Service's refurbished cabin, a ghost reads his verses, and there is also an exhibit on Jack London, whose *Call of the Wild* was based on his Yukon experience.

❋   There is even a chance to live it up, Yukon style, in the Palace Grand Theatre. A faithful reconstruction of the flamboyant original built in 1899, it features nightly entertainment reminiscent of the era, complete with can-can girls and garishly costumed *chanteuses*. Diamond Tooth Gertie's Gambling Hall was until recently Canada's only legal casino. It offers roulette, poker, blackjack and crown and anchor games, as well as Gay Nineties floor shows every night.

At Bonanza Creek (called Rabbit Creek until the discoveries), 12km (7 miles) south of the town on Bonanza Creek Road, a cairn marks Discovery
❋   Claim while a series of signs tells the story of gold mining along the creek. Would-be prospectors can still try their hand at panning for gold here. *Dredge #4*, a mammoth wooden mining machine which operated on the creek for years, is open to visitors.

Also out of town is Midnight Dome visited at midnight in summer for a panoramic view of the city, the mighty Yukon and the mining creeks. The name is a reminder that Dawson, only 256km (159 miles) south of the Arctic Circle, has almost continuous sunlight at that time of year.

Summer brings great festivals and events to Dawson. Best known is the four-day Discovery Days weekend when Yukon citizens commemorate George Carmack's discovery of gold on 17 August 1896 with parades, dances, gold-panning contests and canoe races. The town has a number of inns and motels, as well as some B & Bs. Advance reservations are essential. There is a commercial RV campground in Dawson and highway campgrounds each side of the town.

Dawson to Whitehorse via Kluane National Park (940km/584 miles, 3 days)

The first section of this drive is along a gravelled highway accessible only in summer, which loops into the state of Alaska and then terminates back in the Yukon. United States and Canadian customs services operate at this crossing between 9am and 9pm and travellers cannot cross when the border posts are closed. Non-Canadians require passports and visa for entry into the USA.

Since accommodation is fairly limited on the Alaska Highway three motels at various points are listed in the Additional Information. As is usual in this region, they also provide RV facilities. Campers have an alternative in the government roadside campgrounds. Beaver Creek and Haines Junction would be appropriate overnight stops on this three-day itinerary. A drive to the United States border along the Alaska Hwy in the reverse direction can also serve as an overnight excursion from Whitehorse.

Leaving Dawson, cross the Yukon river by free ferry to the Top of the World Highway. This road goes through 108km (67 miles) of mountains and valleys to the United States border and the community of **Boundary**.

At this point it becomes the Taylor Hwy, leading south for 120km (75 miles) to Tetlin Junction, on the Alaska Highway. It is about 180km (112 miles) to the Canadian border and **Beaver Creek**. This village (population 100) is Canada's most westerly community. The Nutzotin Mountains, and other landmarks with Russian names in the United States' Wrangell St Elias National Park to the west, are a reminder of the area's early European roots. Mile 1202 on the Alaska Hwy is the point where, in August 1942, construction crews working northwards through Canada connected with crews who had brought the road from Alaska.

About 40km (25 miles) south of Beaver Creek, the highway starts to form the boundary of the Kluane Game Sanctuary and **Kluane National** **Park**. Majestic mountains visible in the distance (named by the Danish/ Russian explorer Vitus Bering) include Mt St Elias, and Mt Logan which at 6,050m (19,850ft) is Canada's highest peak and the second highest on the continent. Dominating the park is the world's largest collection of non-polar glaciers and icefields, but there are also tundra, alpine meadows, boreal forests and lush valleys. The park is renowned as having the most diverse collection of wildlife in any national park. Wolves, wild sheep and goats, moose and caribou and one of the world's largest populations of grizzly bears live here. Also, golden eagles and 170 other species of birds, as well as trout, grayling, pike and kokanee salmon.

The Kluane National Park originated with the construction of the Alaska Highway. Established in 1972, it incorporates land set aside for a game reserve. Now covering 22,000 square km (8,500 square miles) the park has been declared a UNESCO World Heritage Site.

Although there are camping, fishing and picnic facilities at Kathleen Lake in the south, this is primarily a wilderness park. Back-packing, cross-country skiing and fishing are popular pursuits. There are no formal roads in the interior and only 250km (155 miles) of hiking trails. The mountains, some of which have never been scaled, attract climbers from all over the world.

Destruction Bay on the shores of Kluane Lake is so named because the camp here was destroyed in a windstorm during the 1940s. The community has accommodation and other services; outfitters provide equipment and guides for expeditions into the park. South of here, the 1,810km (1,128 mile) lookout has superb views of the Donjek River Valley, surrounding Icefield Ranges and the St Elias Mountains.

Haines Junction (population 600) stands at the foot of the Kluane Range. The park headquarters are located here and a visitor centre features award-winning interpretive programmes. More are presented at the Kathleen Lake campground. This community has various types of accommodation, service stations, stores, bank and other services. It is 160km (100 miles) from Haines Junction to Whitehorse via the Alaska Hwy.

Additional Information

Paces to Visit

Banff National Park, Alta
Cave and Basin Centennial Centre
Cave Ave
Open: Centennial centre daily, pool
open mid-June to Labour Day
☎ (403) 762-4900

Parks Canada Museum
93 Banff Ave
Open: daily
☎ (403) 762-3324

Sulphur Mountain Gondola Lift
Mountain Ave, adjacent to Upper Hot
Springs Pool
☎ (403)762-2523

Upper Hot Springs Pool
Mountain Ave, 3 km from town
Open: daily
☎ (403) 762-2966

Barkerville, BC
Barkerville Historic Town
☎ (604) 994-3332

Chilliwack, BC
Minter Gardens
Trans-Canada Hwy and Hwy 9
Open: daily April to October
☎ (604) 794-7191

Dawson City, YT
Klondike National Historic Sites
Box 390, Dawson YT, Y0B 1G0
Open: daily June 1st to mid-September
☎ (403) 993-5462

Dawson City Museum
5th Ave
Open: daily May to September
☎ (403) 993-5291

Fort St James, BC
Fort St James National Historic Park
Open: daily May to October
☎ (604) 996-7191

Hell's Gate Canyon, BC
Hell's Gate Airtram
Trans-Canada Hwy at Hell's Gate
Open: daily April to mid-October
☎ (604) 867-9277

Exploring the glaciers in Kluane National Park

Jasper National Park, Alta
Columbia Icefield Tours
Open: daily late May to late September
☎ (403) 762-3332

Jasper Tramway
6km south of Jasper via Hwy 93 and
Whistler Mountain Road
Open: daily March to October
☎ (403) 852-3092

Miette Hot Springs
Hwy 16, 60km north of Jasper
Open: daily, late May to Labour Day
☎ (403) 852-6176

Kamloops, BC
Kamloops Museum and Archives
207 Seymore St
Open: daily
☎ (604) 828-3576

Kelowna, BC
Father Pandosy Mission
Benvoulen Rd, off Hwy 97
Open: daily in summer
☎ (604) 860-8369

Gray Monk Cellars
Camp Road, 23km north via Hwy 97,
west of Winfield
Open: daily
☎ (604) 766-3168

Langley, BC
Fort Langley National Historic Park
6km north of Trans-Canada Hwy
Open: daily
☎ (604) 888-4424

Mission, BC
Westminster Abbey
Hwy 7 north of Mission
Open: daily
☎ (604) 826-8975

Nanaimo, BC
Nanaimo Centennial Museum
100 Cameron St
Open: daily, closed Monday September-May
☎ (604) 753-1821

New Hazelton, BC
'Ksan Indian Village
6km north of Hwy 16 at New Hazelton
Open: daily mid-May to mid-October,
closed Tuesday and Wednesday rest of year
☎ (604) 842-5544

Port Edward, BC
North Pacific Cannery Village Fishing Museum
1889 Skeena Dr
Open: daily mid-May to mid-September
☎ (604) 628-3538

Prince George, BC
Fort George Regional Museum
20th Ave and Gorse St
Open: daily mid-May to mid-September, closed Monday rest of year
☎ (604) 562-1612

Prince Rupert, BC
Museum of Northern British Columbia
1st Ave and McBride St
Open: daily mid-May to Labour Day,
closed Sunday rest of year
☎ (604) 624-3207

Vancouver, BC
Dr Sun Yat-Sen Chinese Garden
578 Carrall St
Open: daily
☎ (604) 689-7133

Grouse Mountain Tramway
6400 Nancy Green Way,
North Vancouver
Open: daily
☎ (604) 984-0661

Royal Hudson Train to Squamish
Daily in August, Wednesday to Sunday,
May to July and September
☎ (604) 687-9558
1-800-663-1500

UBC Botanical Gardens
6408 Southwest Marine Drive
Open: daily
☎ (604) 228-4804

UBC Museum of Anthropology
6393 Northwest Marine Drive
Open: Tuesday to Sunday
☎ (604) 228-5087

Vancouver Art Gallery
750 Hornby St
Open: daily mid-May to Labour Day,
closed Tuesday rest of year
☎ (604) 682-4668

Vancouver Public Aquarium
Stanley Park
Open: daily
☎ (604) 682-1118

Vancouver Maritime Museum
1905 Ogden Ave
Open: daily
☎ (604) 737-2211

Vancouver Museum
1100 Chestnut St
Open: daily mid-May to Labour Day,
closed Tuesday rest of year
☎ (604) 736-4431

Vandusen Botanical Display Garden
5251 Oak Street
Open: daily ☎ (604) 266-7194

Vernon, BC
O'Keefe Historic Ranch
Hwy 97 12km north of Vernon
Open: daily Easter to mid-October
☎ (604) 542-7868

Victoria, BC
Butchart Gardens
Off Hwy 17, 22km north
Open: daily
☎ (604) 652-4422

Royal British Columbia Museum
675 Belleville St
Open: daily
☎ (604) 387-3701

Whitehorse, YT
MacBride Museum
1st Ave & Wood St
Open: daily mid-May to mid-September
☎ (403) 667-2709

SS Klondike II National Historic Site
2nd Ave and Alaska Hwy south access
road
Open: daily mid-May to mid-September
☎ (403) 667-4511

Takhini Hot Springs
Takhini Hot Springs Road, 10 km from
Km 198, Klondike Hwy
Open: daily

*Yukon Government Administration
  Building*
2071 2nd Ave
Open: Monday to Friday, closed Tuesday in winter ☎ (403) 667-5811

National & Provincial Parks

Alberta
Banff National Park
Box 900, Banff, Alta T0L 0C0
☎ (403) 762-3324

Jasper National Park
PO Box 10, Jasper, Alta T0E 1E0
☎ (403) 852-6161

British Columbia
Barkerville Provincial Park
At Barkerville
☎ (604) 565-6270

Cultus Lake Provincial Park
11 km south of Trans-Canada Hwy
(Hwy 1) at Chilliwack
☎ (604) 858-7161

Elk Falls Provincial Park
6km inland, off Hwy 19
☎ (604) 248-3931

Glacier and Mt Revelstoke National Parks
PO Box 350, Revelstoke, BC V0E 2S0
☎ (604) 837-5155

Golden Ears Provincial Park
10km north of Hwy 7 at Maple Ridge
☎ (604) 929-1291

Haynes Point Provincial Park
Hwy 97 South (2km south of Osoyoos)
☎ (604) 494-0321

Lac Le Jeune Provincial Park
29km south of Kamloops off Hwy 5
☎ (604) 828-4494

Manning Provincial Park
Hwy 3, east of Hope
☎ (604) 858-7161

Pacific Rim National Park
PO Box 280, Ucluelet, BC V0R 3A0
Open: all year, interpretive centre open
mid-March to mid-October
☎ (604) 726-7721

Porteau Cove Provincial Park
Hwy 99 on Howe Sound (35km north of
Vancouver)
☎ (604) 898-3678

Seeley Lake Provincial Park
Hwy 16, south of South Hazelton
☎ (604) 847-7322

Silver Star Provincial Park
10km north of Vernon
☎ (604) 494-0321

Strathcona Provincial Park
Via Hwy 28
☎ (604) 248-3931

Susquatch Provincial Park
6km north of Harrison Hot Springs
☎ (604) 858-7161

Ten Mile Lake Provincial Park
Hwy 97, ten km north of Quesnel
☎ (604) 398-4414

Thetis Lake Park (Victoria)
1938 Trans-Canada Hwy
(10km west of city)
☎ (604) 478-3845

Wells Grey Provincial Park
40km north of Clearwater
☎ (604) 828-4494

Yoho National Park
PO Box 99, Field, BC V0A 1G0
☎ (604) 343-6324

Yukon Territory
Kluane National Park
Haines Junction, YT, Y0B 1L0
☎ (403) 634-2251

Accommodation & Campgrounds

Banff, Alta
Banff Springs Hotel
Spray Ave, Banff
☎ (403) 762-2211
1-800-441-1414

Inns of Banff Park
600 Banff Ave
☎ (403) 762-4581
1-800-661-1272

Beaver Creek, YT
Westmark Inn Beaver Creek
Mile 1202 Alaska Hwy (1,934km)
☎ (403) 862-7501

Dawson City, YT
Eldorado Hotel
3rd Ave and Princess St
☎ (403) 993-5451

Westmark Inn Dawson
5th Ave & Harper St
☎ (403) 993-5542

Gold Rush Campground
5th Ave and York St,
☎ (403) 993-5247

Destruction Bay, YT
Talbot Arm Motel
Destruction Bay
☎ (403) 841-4461

Harrison Hot Springs, BC
Harrison Hot Springs Hotel
100 Esplanade Ave,
Harrison Hot Springs
☎ (604) 796-2244

Harrison Village Motel
280 Esplanade Ave
☎ (604) 796-2616

Haines Junction, YT
Mountain View Motor Inn
Haines Junction
☎ (403) 634-2646

Kathleen Lake Campground
Kluane National Park
27km south on Hwy 3
☎ (403) 634-2251

Jasper, Alta
Jasper Park Lodge
5km north via Hwy 16 and Maligne Rd
☎ (403) 852-3301 / 1-800-441-1414

Lobstick Lodge
94 Geikie St
☎ (403) 852-4431

Kamloops, BC
Hospitality Inn
500 W Columbia St
☎ (604) 374-4164

Panorama Inn
610 W Columbia St
☎ (604) 374-1515

Kamloops RV & Mobile Home Park
1-4395 E Trans-Canada Hwy (10km east)
☎ (604) 573-3255

Kelowna, BC
Lake Okanagan Resort
2751 Westside Road, Kelowna
☎ (604) 769-3511

Lake Louise, Alta
Chateau Lake Louise
Beside Lake Louise
☎ (403) 522-3511
1-800-441-1414

New Hazelton, BC
28 Inn Motel
4545 Yellowhead Hwy
☎ (604) 842-6006

Robbers Roost Lodge
Yellowhead Hwy
☎ (604) 842-6916

'Ksan Campground
'Ksan Village (Hazelton)
☎ (604) 842-5940

Osoyoos, BC
Bella Villa Resort Motel
6904 64th Av
☎ (604) 495-6751

Safari Beach Resort
1609 89th St
☎ (604) 495-7217

Pacific Rim National Park, BC
Thornton Motel
Peninsula Rd at Bay St, Ucluelet
☎ (604) 726-7725

Pacific Sands Beach Resort
1421 Pacific Rim Hwy, Tofino
☎ (604) 725-3322

Green Point Campground
Pacific Rim National Park
20km north of Ucluelet on Hwy 4
☎ (604) 726-7721

Port Hardy, BC
Pioneer Inn
4965 Byng Rd
☎ (604) 949-7271

North Shore Inn
7370 Market St
☎ (604) 949-8500

Wildwoods Campsite
Forestry Road, south of ferry terminal
☎ (604) 949-6753

Prince George, BC
Coast Inn of the North
770 Brunswick St
☎ (604) 563-0121

Holiday Inn Prince George
444 George St
☎ (604) 563-0055
1-800-HOLIDAY

KOA Prince George Kampground
Kinball Rd (Hwy 16, 5km west of Hwy 97)
☎ (604) 964-7272

Prince Rupert, BC
Crest Motor Hotel
222 First Ave W
☎ (604) 624-6771
1-800-663-8150

Highliner Inn
815 First Ave W
☎ (604) 624-9060

Park Avenue (Municipal) Campground
1750 Park Ave
(1km east of ferry terminals)
☎ (604) 624-5861

Quesnel, BC
Cariboo Hotel
254 Front St
☎ (604) 992-2333
1-800-665-3200

Good Knight Inn
176 Davie St
☎ (604) 992-2187

Spences Bridge, BC
Steelhead Inn
☎ (604) 458-2394

Terrace, BC
Inn of the West
4620 Lakelse Ave
☎ (604) 638-8141

Vanvouver, BC
The Westin Bayshore
1601 Georgia St W
☎ (604) 682-3377
1-800-228-3000

Hotel Vancouver
900 Georgia St West
☎ (604) 684-3131
1-800-441-1414

Anmore Camplands Inc
3230 Sunnyside Rd, Port Moody
☎ (604) 469-2311

Burnaby Cariboo RV Park

8765 Cariboo Place
near Trans-Canada Hwy Cariboo exit
☎ (604) 420-1722

Capilano RV Park
295 Tomahawk Ave, North Vancouver
☎ (604) 987-4722

Vernon, BC
Swiss Hotel Silver Lode Inn
Silver Star Mountain Road, Vernon
☎ (604) 549-5105

Vernon Travelodge
3000 28th Ave
☎ (604) 545-2161

Silver Star RV & Trailer Park
Stickle Road,
1km north of Vernon on Swan Lake
☎ (604) 542-2808

Victoria, BC
The Empress Hotel
721 Government St
☎ (604) 384-8111
1-800-441-1414

The Bedford
1140 Government Street
☎ (604) 384-6835

KOA Victoria East
3000 KOA Road, Saanichton
☎ (604) 652-3232

Whistler, BC
Chateau Whistler Resort
4599 Chateau Blvd
☎ (604) 938-8000
1-800-441-1414

Whitehorse, YT
Westmark Whitehorse
201 Wood St
☎ (403) 668-4700

Gold Rush Inn
411 Main St
☎ (403) 668-4500

Sourdough City RV Park
2nd Ave
☎ (403) 668-7938

Robert Service Campground
South Access Road
☎ (403) 668-8325

Ferry Services

Tsawwassen (Vancouver) to Swartz Bay (Victoria)
Summer sailings hourly on the hour, starting at 7am, crossing time 95 minutes. There can be line-ups in peak periods.

Horseshoe Bay (West Vancouver) and Nanaimo
Sailings every two hours from 7am, crossing time 95 mins

Tsawwassen (Vancouver) to Nanaimo
Eight sailings daily, starting at 8am

Port Hardy to Prince Rupert
Sailings every other day late May to September, twice weekly in May, weekly the rest of year
One way fare for car, driver and passenger approx $325
☎ Vancouver (604)-669-1211
Victoria (604) 386-3431

Local Tourist Authorities

Banff, Alta
Banff Information Bureau
224, Banff Ave
Banff, Alta T0L 0C0
☎ (403) 762-1550

Jasper, Alta
Jasper Information Centre
500, Connaught Dr
Jasper, Alta T0E 1E0
☎ (403) 852-6161

Vancouver, BC
Vancouver InfoCentre
1055 Dunsmuir St
write to:
Pavilion Plaza
Four Bentall Centre, PO Box 49296,
1055 Dunsmuir St
Vancouver BC, V7X 1L3
☎ (604) 683-2000

Victoria, BC
Travel Victoria
812 Wharf St
Victoria BC, V8W 1T3
☎ (604) 382-2127

CANADA FACT FILE

Accommodation

Tourism material available from every province and territory contains lists of suitable accommodation, campgrounds and restaurants. The Canadian and American Automobile Associations jointly operate an inspection and rating system of between one and five diamonds, and listed establishments display the organizations' distinctive logos.

Cities have hotels in all price ranges. Canadian chains include Delta, Four Seasons and Canadian Pacific hotels and resorts. The major international groups include Sheraton, Hilton, Ramada, Best Western and Holiday Inn. Hotel prices are similar to those in the United States, and possibly a little lower than in Western Europe.

The Journey's End motel chain has more modest accommodation in most cities east of the Rocky Mountains. They provide fairly new and consistently spacious rooms, accommodating up to four persons. There are, of course, numerous smaller chains and individually-managed motels.

Hotels and campgrounds are mentioned throughout the itineraries, to ensure that visitors have a bed for the night. In most cases the authors are personally familiar with these places. Where they are not, listed hotels belong to chains we are confident in recommending.

Especially during the holiday season, telephone reservations are advised. Most establishments will hold a room until 6pm, but they will almost certainly require a major credit card number.

Bed and breakfast lodgings, available throughout Canada, are listed in provincial tourist guides. Some farms welcome paying guests. Dude ranches, fishing and hunting camps can offer a unique Canadian experience.

Many colleges and universities offer accommodation during the summer months. Elderhostel Canada operates in about 250 locations in Canada, serving people 60 years old and over. Address: 308 Wellington Street, Kingston, Ontario, K7K 7A7, ☎ (613) 530-2222.

The Canadian Hostelling Association operates hostels in every province. There is no age limit for guests. Many have private rooms and family accommodation. Address: 1600 James Naismith Drive, Suite 608, Gloucester, Ontario, K1B 5N4, ☎ (613) 748-5638.

Canada has approximately 3,000 campgrounds, some of the best located in national, provincial and municipal parks where sites can be hedged with tall trees and velvety deer come visiting at dawn. Facilities range from paved sites with electricity, water and sewage hook-ups suitable for large recreational vehicles to unserviced wilderness sites. The predominant chain of commercial campgrounds, KOA Kampgrounds, provides RV operators with predictably clean sites, full services and facilities.

Climate & Clothing

On a first visit, summer is recommended as the best time to enjoy Canada. Southern sections of the central and prairie provinces can be very hot and humid in July and August, but air-conditioning is virtually universal in commercial buildings. May and June are usually very attractive in these regions, although warm clothes will be required at night and biting insects such as mosquitoes and black flies can be a nuisance. Insect repellant and cover-up clothing helps.

During summer, coastal regions enjoy a mild maritime climate similar to that of Western Europe. September is perhaps the best month for mild days and cool nights and colourful autumn foliage. On the minus side, many tourist facilities are reduced to skeleton staffs or closed for the season after the first weekend in September (Labour Day). Temperatures can be very low between December and late April all over the country, except in the southern and coastal areas of British Columbia. Heavy outdoor clothing is necessary at this time of the year. It is, of course, the season for ice skating, skiing and other winter sports.

Canadians lean towards informality in clothing. Visitors from Europe and the United States will be comfortable with the leisure clothes they would wear at home. In the cities, hotels and more formal restaurants usually expect men to wear jackets and ties in the evening, and women to be appropriately attired.

Crime

Generally speaking it is safe to walk the streets at night. However, Canada does have its share of crime particularly in the larger cities, and visitors should take the same precautions against theft, pickpockets, etc., as they would at home. Handguns are prohibited. Buying or selling illicit drugs is severely dealt with by the courts.

Currency, Banking & Credit Cards

Canada's currency is dollars and cents. Coins consist of copper-coloured cents, silver-coloured 5, 10, 25 and 50 cent denominations and gold-coloured dollars. Bills in two, 10, 20, 50, 100 and 1,000 dollar denominations are all the same size but different colours. United States currency is widely accepted at the prevailing exchange rate. Canadian banks are large national corporations, with branches in most communities. Hours of operation are, at the minimum, 10am to

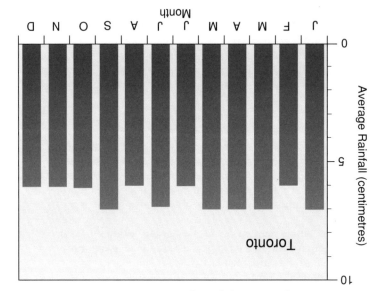

Average monthly precipitation

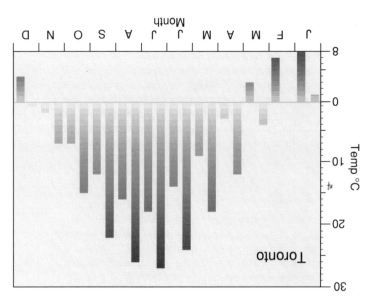

Maximum and minimum daily temperatures

Maximum and minimum daily temperatures

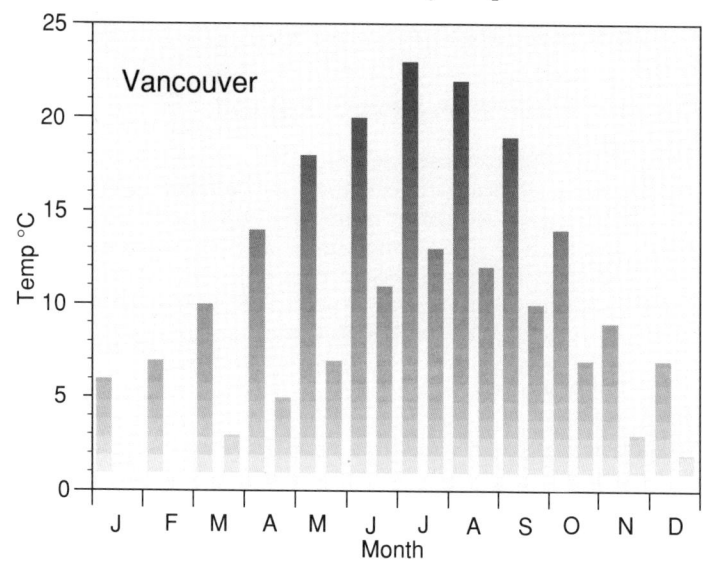

Vancouver

Average monthly rainfall

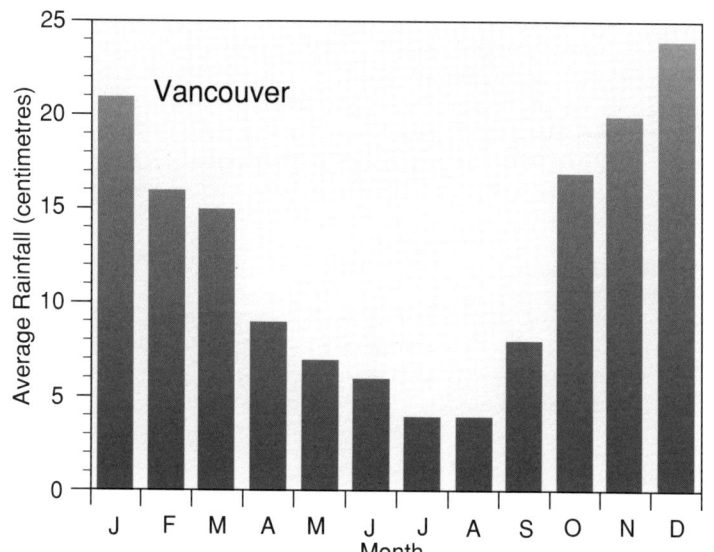

Vancouver

3pm on weekdays, but much longer in urban centres. Banks are closed on legal holidays, when exchange bureaus in cities, airports and at border crossings are usually open.

Major credit cards: American Express, MasterCard and Visa, are widely accepted as are American Express, Thomas Cook and Visa travellers cheques. Those issued by Barclays Bank, Citibank and other international banks may be accepted less frequently.

Customs, Immigration & Health Regulations

Visitors from overseas will find Canada's entry requirements simple and for the most part its Customs and Immigration officials courteous. Citizens or permanent residents of the United States do not need passports or visas. Visitors from all other countries require a valid passport; citizens of Great Britain and many other British Commonwealth and European countries do not need a visa. Prospective visitors who are in doubt should clarify their status with their travel agent or a Canadian consulate before departure.

Non-Canadian visitors going from Canada to the United States (even just to look at Niagara Falls from the American side) will require a visa obtained through a United States consulate before leaving home.

Personal effects for use during your stay are allowed without restriction. Duty-free limits for adults are 40oz (despite Canada's adoption of metric measurement) of spirits or wine, or forty-eight 12oz bottles of beer, and 200 cigarettes or 50 cigars or 2.2lb of tobacco.

Plants, fruit and vegetables must be declared to Customs on arrival and may be subject to inspection and possible confiscation. Regulations on the importation of plants, pets and firearms can be obtained from Canadian consulates.

There are no health restrictions to visitors from most Western countries. Since visitors are not covered by government-operated medical insurance plans you are strongly advised to purchase health and accident insurance before leaving home.

Disabled Visitors

Shopping centres, public buildings, national parks and most large hotels and restaurants attempt to accommodate the physically disabled. Anyone who anticipates serious problems should consult tourist information offices before setting out.

Driving

Canada accepts most other countries' current driving licences. Accident liability insurance is required. Rental cars are available at airports and in most urban centres from the international chains: Hertz, Avis, Budget and Dollar, as well as Tilden and other Canadian companies. Driving is on the right of the road. Highways are excellent and well-maintained. Some lesser-used roads have a gravel surface. Speed limits, posted and fairly strictly enforced, are usually 100km/hour on major highways, less on secondary roads or in urban areas. In most provinces, highway interchanges are numbered sequentially from the beginning, but in Ontario, Quebec and New Brunswick they are numbered for the closest kilometre from the start. Highways are called Routes in Quebec and New Brunswick, and the term 'route' indicates smaller roads in some other provinces. In our itineraries, we have followed the local convention as shown on road maps, etc.

Seatbelts must be worn by drivers and front-seat passengers, and by rear-seat passengers in some provinces. Babies and young children must be secured by approved seats. Radar detectors are forbidden. In later model cars, headlights turn on automatically when the ignition is switched on. Drivers of older cars are encouraged to use headlights during daylight as well as at night.

There are numerous well-equipped automobile service stations (gas stations). On major highways they often have restaurants or fast-food establishments attached. Currently, fuel is approximately 60-70¢ per litre depending on grade. Highway signs frequently show the distance to the next service station. In remote areas, be sure to refuel when you can. In case of breakdown, lift the hood as sign of a problem, then stay with the vehicle to wait for a police or highways department patrol. Truck-drivers will often stop and help or radio for assistance.

Electricity

Canada operates on 110volt, 60 cycle current, and uses US-type plugs and sockets. Transformers and adaptors are necessary to use 240volt appliances.

Emergencies

Dial 911, without charge to telephone police, fire or ambulance services.

Food & Drink

Restaurant food is similar to that in the United States and Great Britain, but there are some national and regional specialities. Heritage fare, handed down from the time before refrigeration and modern stoves, tends towards meat (especially pork), fish and vegetables, baked goods, and a wide selection of preserves and chutneys. Quebec also offers visitors a mixture of French cuisine and 'habitant' dishes. Corn and bean soups are part of the Aboriginal heritage.

The coastal regions are justifiably renowned for fresh seafoods such as salmon, crab and lobster, as well as cod, halibut, Arctic char and most other cold-water fish. Their rich chowders are a meal in themselves. Newfoundland has its own specialities such as cod tongues and seal flipper pie.

In the prairies superb grain-fed beef is often served in very large portions.

The country's foreign-born population has introduced interesting ethnic restaurants. In the larger cities it is possible to find cuisines familiar to visitors from Argentina to New Zealand as well as most European and Asian countries. All of this in addition to the international hamburger and pizza chains and home grown varieties of 'fast food' outlets.

Holidays

Legal holidays common to all parts of Canada are:

New Year's Day
Good Friday
Victoria Day — 24 May or Monday preceding it
Canada Day — 1 July
Labour Day — first Monday in September
Thanksgiving Day — second Monday in October
Christmas Day

In addition, Easter Monday, the first Monday in August, Remembrance Day (11 November) and Boxing Day are holidays in various provinces. St John the Baptist Day (24 June) is observed in Quebec.

Language

Canada has two official languages, English and French. French is the sole official language of Quebec (an indication of the country's linguistic politics). There are substantial French-speaking communities outside Quebec, particularly in New Brunswick, Ontario, and Manitoba. Also a large English-speaking population in Quebec, particularly around Montreal. French-speaking Canadians are often bilingual, most anglophone are not.

Visitors may assume English is spoken everywhere in Canada, except in parts of Quebec which do not cater for many tourists. French speaking visitors will be warmly received in Quebec. Others will find a small dictionary and phrase book useful, if only because many signs are in French only.

Canadian-spoken English is often somewhat mid-Atlantic. There are distinct dialects, particularly in Newfoundland, but also in the Maritimes and Ontario's Ottawa Valley. Spelling is somewhere between British and American usage.

Maps & Brochures

These are freely available by writing to the provincial tourism information offices listed in this Fact File. Some information is available from Canadian embassies and high commission offices abroad. In

246

Canada, tourism bureaus are located in most cities and on major highways close to provincial and US border points. Usually hotels and motels have a selection of local information.

National & Provincial Parks

Currently a daily permit to use a vehicle in the more developed national parks costs $5, while an annual vehicle permit is $30. Camping charges for fully serviced campsites vary up to $20 a day, but wilderness camping is usually complimentary. Admission to less developed parks may be free.

A permit is required to fish in park waters. Valid for any national park, this can be bought at a visitor centre, warden's office or campground. Hunting is not permitted and most national parks prohibit firearms.

If you plan on wilderness hiking or canoeing, it is wise to pick up a topographic map that shows secondary paths, creeks and rivers. Drive with caution, especially at dawn or dusk when wildlife can be on the roads, and do heed bear precautions received at the park entrance.

In addition to the national system, provinces, territories and municipalities operate parks and recreation areas, often with overnight camping, motel and resort accommodation. User fees are comparable with those in national parks. Provincial fishing permits are required in these parks, and in fact anywhere else within individual provinces.

Newspapers & Magazines

Local newspapers, as well as the *Globe and Mail* and *The Financial Post* are available across the country. Major international magazines are sold everywhere, as are *Maclean's*, *Chatelaine* and smaller Canadian magazines. The Smithbooks chain sells British newspapers. Lichtman's of Toronto is an example of booksellers stocked with a wide selection of international newspapers.

Radio & Television

The Canadian Broadcasting Corporation (CBC) provides AM and FM radio and television services in both official languages across the country. CTV is an independent national television network; various cities have their own independent TV stations. Private radio stations are numerous and American services can be received in most communities. Drivers will find small highway signs listing the frequency of radio stations within reception distance. Some provinces list radio stations and frequencies on their road maps.

Recreational Vehicles (RV)

Throughout these itineraries campgrounds which provide full RV services are included. Rentals are available across Canada, but it is essential to make reservations for summer months well in advance. To ensure receiving a reliable vehicle insist that it is no more than two years old.

Go Vacations, is an RV rental company, 129 Carlingview Drive, Rexdale, Ontario M9W 5E7, ☎ (416) 793-8763, near Toronto's Pearson International Airport. It also has branches in Montreal, Winnipeg, Edmonton, Calgary and Vancouver, and permits final drop-off in these cities for about $250 extra. Canada Campers Inc, 2720 Barlow Trail N.E., Calgary, Alberta T1Y 1A1, ☎ (403) 250-3209, has branches in Vancouver, Whitehorse and Toronto. It also permits drop-off in its other locations at an extra charge.

Naturally, cost differs with vehicle size, but a new unit which will comfortably house four adults for three weeks and cover 4,000km (2,500 miles), would cost about $5,000, for rental, insurance, fuel, campground charges and taxes. Many companies do not permit drop-off in another city, so you may be better off to follow one of the circular itineraries. Provincial tourism offices will supply addresses of other RV rental companies.

Shopping

Canada has an enormous range of retail shops. Typically stores are open from 10am to 6pm, six days a week, but most downtown shopping districts are open until about 9.30pm from Monday to Friday. Sunday shopping laws vary depending on the province, though shops are generally open on Sundays in tourist areas.

Sales taxes are levied on most items by the Federal Government (the Goods and Services Tax is currently 7 per cent) and also by each Provincial Government except Alberta (from 8 per cent to 12 per cent compounded on top of Federal tax). Yukon and Northwest Territories do not have additional taxes. Sales taxes are usually added to the advertised price at the cash register, so be prepared to pay at least 15 per cent more than the price shown.

Clothing sizes follow the American system rather than the Imperial or Continental systems.

Canada has adopted the metric system, but some remnants of the old Imperial system are still used informally, particularly in food stores. One kilometre = 0.6 miles. One litre = 0.2 Imperial gallons or 0.26 US gallons. One kilogram = 2.2 pounds.

Sports & Outdoor Events

The major spectator sports are baseball, (Canadian) football, and ice hockey (described simply as 'hockey'). Most visitors will want to

248

attend at least one of these sports events. Soccer, cricket and other sports have their adherents. Golf and tennis are popular. Canoeing and hiking, often combined with fishing are common weekend and vacation activities in summer, while snowmobiling, skating and both Nordic and Alpine skiing are popular in winter.

Telephones

The telephone system is the same as in the United States. Numbers consist of a three-digit area code (omitted in local calls) followed by the seven-digit dialing number. When calling long distance dial 1 first. If you require operator assistance as when using a telephone company credit card or calling collect, dial 0 first. Detailed instructions are in the front of all telephone directories. Cost of a local call (unlimited length) from a call box is currently 25¢. Toll-free numbers are prefixed by 1-800. Their use may be limited to certain sections of the country.

Time & Time Zones

The 24-hour clock is used on air, train and bus schedules.

Canada stretches over six time zones. Newfoundland is 3½ hours behind Greenwich Mean Time. The Maritime provinces are on Atlantic Standard Time, which is four hours behind GMT. Quebec and most of Ontario are on Eastern Standard Time. Manitoba is on Central Standard Time, Saskatchewan and Alberta are on Mountain Standard Time, and British Columbia and Yukon Territory are on Pacific Standard Time.

Daylight saving time is in effect from the last Sunday in October, when the clock is put back one hour, to the last Sunday in April. Saskatchewan, northeast British Columbia, and some communities bordering the USA do not use daylight saving time.

Tipping

Service charges are not usually added to the bill, except in resorts. In most hotels, tipping is optional. Gratuities of 10 per cent to 15 per cent before taxes are customary for good service in restaurants, hairdressers, taxis, etc. Porters, bellmen, etc, customarily receive a dollar per bag, the room-maid a dollar or two per night.

Toilets

Public toilets are invariably called restrooms or washrooms. There are very few on-street facilities, but numerous restrooms in shopping centres, department stores, restaurants and service stations. Many are suitable for use by the physically impaired and some provide facilities for changing babies. Usually they are clean, and almost always free.

Tourism & Tourist Information Offices

Canadian tourism, concerned with attracting visitors and anticipating their needs and expectations, earns over $20,000 million annually. This represents more than 4.5 per cent of Gross National Product and is a major source of foreign exchange. Some 100,000 businesses employing 600,000 people are involved in the industry; services include 300,000 hotel and motel rooms, and approximately 40,000 restaurants. Tourists from the United States account for the largest volume of visitors, followed, in order, by the United Kingdom, Germany, Japan and France.

Provinces operate tourism information centres at most major entry points from the United States and other provinces. Cities and towns usually have tourist offices and many have reservation services. Tourist information can be obtained from the following sources (toll-free numbers can be used in Canada and the United States):

Newfoundland
Department of Tourism and Culture,
PO Box 8730,
St John's,
Newfoundland, A1B 4K2
☎ (709) 729-2830
or 1-800-563-6353

Northwest Territories
NWT Tourism,
PO Box 1320,
Yellowknife, NWT X1A 2L9
☎ (403) 873-7200
or 1-800-661-0788

Nova Scotia
Nova Scotia Tourism,
Suite 515,
1800 Argyle St,
Halifax,
Nova Scotia, B3J 3N8
☎ (902) 425-5781
or 1-800-565-0000 (in Canada),
1-800-341-6096(from US)

Ontario
Ontario Travel,
Queen's Park,
Toronto,
Ontario, M7A 2R9
☎ (416) 314-0944
or 1-800-ONTARIO

New Brunswick
Tourism New Brunswick,
PO Box 6000,
Fredericton,
New Brunswick, E3B 5H1
☎ (506) 453-3984
or 1-800-561-0123

Manitoba
Travel Manitoba,
155 Carlton St,
Winnipeg,
Manitoba, R3C 3H8
☎ (204) 945-3777
or 1-800-665-0040

British Columbia
Tourism British Columbia,
1117 Wharf St,
Victoria, BC, V8W 2Z2
☎ (604) 685-0032
or 1-800-663-6000

Alberta
Travel Alberta,
10155 102nd St,
Edmonton,
Alberta, T5J 4L6
☎ (403) 427-4321
or 1-800-661-8888

Trans-Canada Highway

The itineraries in this book include long stretches of the Trans-Canada Highway which links many of Canada's major population centres. This road between St John's, Nfld and Victoria, BC is 7,821 km (4,860 miles) long and the longest national highway in the world. The route incorporates provincial highways, their numbers shown within the characteristic green logo marking the highway. There are alternative sections in some parts of the country.

Some tourist information is available from Canadian Consulates, but for specific and useful information it is better to contact the provincial tourist offices in Canada. The major Canadian Consulates (contact the Tourism Section) are:

Australia
Consulate General of Canada
5th Level, Quay West
111 Harrington Street
Sydney NSW 2000
☎ (2) 364-3000

Ireland
Canadian Embassy
65 St Stephen's Green,
Dublin 2
☎ (1) 781 988

New Zealand
Canadian High Commission
61 Molesworth Street
Thornton
PO Box 12049
Wellington
☎ (4) 473 9577

UK
Canadian High Commission
Canada House
Trafalgar Square
London SW1Y 5BJ
☎ 071 258 6600

USA
Canadian Consulate General
1251 Avenue of the Americas
16th Floor
New York
NY 10020-1175
☎ (212) 596-1600

Canadian Consulate General
300 S Grand Ave, Suite 1000
Los Angeles
CA 90071
☎ (213) 687-7432

Prince Edward Island
Visitor Services,
PO Box 940,
Charlottetown, C1A 7M5
☎ (902) 368-4444
or 1-800-565-0267

Quebec
Tourisme Quebec,
PO Box 20,000,
Quebec City,
Quebec, G1K 7X2
☎ (514) 873-2015
or 1-800-363-7777

Saskatchewan
Tourism Saskatchewan,
1919 Saskatchewan Drive,
Regina,
Saskatchewan, S4P 3V7
☎ (306) 787 - 2300
or 1-800-667-7191

Yukon
Tourism Yukon,
PO Box 2703,
Whitehorse,
Yukon Y1A 2C6
☎ (403) 667-5340

Transportation

Major international airlines, in addition to the national carriers, Air Canada and Canadian Airlines International, operate services into Toronto, Montreal and Vancouver, with more limited services to some other cities. There are also numerous connections with United States points and within Canada.

Busses of the Greyhound Line, Gray Coach and Voyageur as well as many local lines connect with United States points and all parts of the country. Their telephone numbers are listed in tourist literature and telephone company yellow pages. Greyhound Line sells 15- and 30-day passes for unlimited travel, available only from travel agents outside North America.

As well as passenger services across Canada, Via Rail goes to New York, Chicago and Seattle. Travel passes, group, seniors' and youth fares, and reduced car-rental rates are available. Reservations may be made through travel agents. Or telephone Via Rail direct, ☎ (416) 366-8411 or toll free, 1-800-561-3952 in Atlantic provinces, 1-800-361-5390 in Quebec, 1-800-361-1235 in Southern Ontario, and 1-800-561-8630 elsewhere in Canada.

Major ferry services operate along the coast of British Columbia, on the Atlantic coast between the mainland and Prince Edward Island and Newfoundland, and between Nova Scotia and Maine. There are also numerous services across lakes and rivers.

Water

Tap water is perfectly safe to drink. Imported and Canadian bottled water is available everywhere. Often preferred for its taste, it is not necessarily more pure. In campsites and picnic areas, etc, there are usually warning notices where untreated water is intended only for washing.

INDEX